AF753752

FUNDAMENTALS OF ACCOUNTING

Awassa Souad

Toronto Academic Press

Fundamentals of Accounting

Awassa Souad

Toronto Academic Press
224 Shoreacres Road
Burlington, ON L7L 2H2
Canada
www.tap-books.com
Email: orders@arclereducation.com

© 2024 Toronto Academic Press

ISBN: 978-1-77469-754-2

This book contains information obtained from highly regarded resources. Reprinted material sources are indicated and copyright remains with the original owners. Copyright for images and other graphics remains with the original owners as indicated. A Wide variety of references are listed. Reasonable efforts have been made to publish reliable data. Authors or Editors or Publishers are not responsible for the accuracy of the information in the published chapters or consequences of their use. The publisher assumes no responsibility for any damage or grievance to the persons or property arising out of the use of any materials, instructions, methods or thoughts in the book. The authors or editors and the publisher have attempted to trace the copyright holders of all material reproduced in this publication and apologize to copyright holders if permission has not been obtained. If any copyright holder has not been acknowledged, please write to us so we may rectify.

Notice: Registered trademark of products or corporate names are used only for explanation and identification without intent of infringement.

Toronto Academic Press publishes wide variety of books and eBooks. For more information about Toronto Academic Press and its products, visit our website at www.tap-books.com.

ABOUT THE AUTHOR

Awassa Souad is an accomplished economist with over ten years of experience in the field. She holds a Master's degree in Economics from the Faculté des sciences économiques et de gestion Tunis Manar, where she gained a deep understanding of economic theory and analysis. Throughout her career, Awassa has worked with a variety of clients, including government agencies, non-profit organizations, and private sector companies. She has a proven track record of developing effective economic policies and strategies that help her clients achieve their goals. Awassa is well-versed in a wide range of economic models and methodologies. She has particular expertise in the areas of microeconomics, macroeconomics, and econometrics. She has also conducted extensive research in the field of development economics, focusing on issues related to poverty reduction and economic growth. In addition to her technical skills, Awassa is a strong communicator and collaborator. She enjoys working with others to develop solutions that are both effective and feasible. She is also committed to staying up-to-date with the latest trends and developments in the field of economics, and is always looking for ways to improve her skills and knowledge. Overall, Awassa's expertise, experience, and commitment to excellence make her a valuable asset to any organization or project in need of sound economic analysis and advice.

Contents

List of Figures

List of Tables

List of Abbreviations

AICPA	American Institute of Certified Public Accountants
AS	Accounting Standards
ASB	Accounting Standards Board
ASs	Accounting Standards
CIMA	Chartered Institute of Management Accountants
COSO	Committee of Sponsoring Organizations
CPA	Certified Public Accountants
EOM	End of the Month
FOB	Free on Board
GAAP	Generally Accepted Accounting Principles
IASB	International Accounting Standards Board
ICAI	Institute of Chartered Accountants of India
IFRSs	International Financial Reporting Standards
IT	Information Technology
JIT	Just-in-Time
SEC	Securities and Exchange Commission
WDV	Written Down Value

PREFACE

Accounting is the method of recording a business's financial transactions. It includes summarizing, analyzing, and reporting these activities to oversight authorities, authorities, and national tax entities. The financial statements used in accounting summarize a company's operations, economic status, and cash flows throughout a specific accounting period. Accounting is among the essential corporate functions. It may be managed by bookkeeping, an accountant in a small business, or a vast financial department with dozens of staff in more prominent organizations. The reports created by various accounting streams, such as costing systems and financial reporting, are crucial for assisting management in making well-informed business choices.

The discussion in this book starts with the basic concepts of accounting, followed by the accounting process and adjustment of accounts. Moreover, concepts of accounting depreciation and reconciliation, along with financial statements, are described in detail in this book. Furthermore, Accounting for Merchandising Operations is also explained in detail to emphasize the practical applications of accounting in businesses. Cash flow is another critical accounting concept described in depth in this book to let the readers know the working of cash in the economic and accounting market. Essentials of cost and management accounting are crucially important to understand accounting as a whole fully; therefore, this book defines these concepts well. Finally, concepts of fraud and internal control in accounting, along with the prospects of accounting, are given in the book.

This book comprises of eight-chapter; the first chapter discusses the basics of accounting along with its scope, nature, and objectives. The second chapter deals with the accounting process followed by organizations and various businesses to run their accounting model. Moreover, the adjustment of accounts is also described in this chapter.

The third chapter is about the ideas of deprecation and reconciliation, which is in practice in various businesses, organizations, and banking sectors. The fourth chapter is about the practical implications of accounting in the real business world, and it deals with the accounting used for merchandising operations.

The fifth chapter is about the cash flow in the accounting procedure. Moreover, the foreign currency flow mechanism is also presented in this chapter. The sixth chapter deals with the essentials of cost and management accounting, which is an integral part of accounting.

The seventh chapter deals with the fraud and internal control systems used in accounting. Finally, the eighth chapter is about the prospects of accounting for businesses and organizations.

This book has been written specifically for students and scholars to meet their needs in terms of knowledge and to provide them with a broad understanding of accounting. We aim for this book to be a resource for academics in many subjects since we believe it will provide clarity and insight for its readers.

—Author

CHAPTER 1

BASICS OF ACCOUNTING

UNIT INTRODUCTION

Every profit or nonprofit organization needs a reliable accountability system. A business accounting system offers this accountability by tracking all operations generating cash inflows from sales revenue and cash outflows from operating activities. The accounting system provides the financial data required to assess the efficacy of past and current activities. In particular, the accounting system stores the data necessary to generate reports displaying the state of the corporate entity's financial assets, creditor obligations, and ownership equity. In the past, most of the work necessary to operate a successful accounting system consisted of laborious, irritating, and time-consuming manual labor. An individual effort was required to continuously record transactions, add, subtract, analyze, and verify for faults in such systems (Muniroh & Yuliati, 2021).

The fast development of computer technology has enhanced operational speed, storage systems, and dependability while reducing costs significantly. Affordable microcomputers and accounting computer programs have improved to the point that the computer program can swiftly offer posting, computations, error checks, and financial statements.

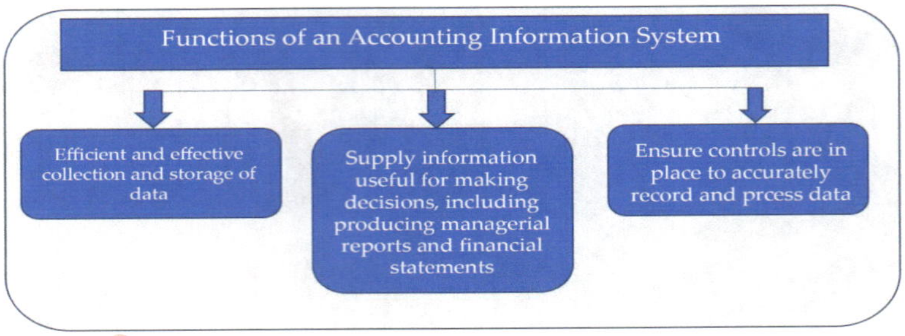

Figure 1.1. Schematic of the functions of an Accounting Information System (Source: Tally Solutions, Creative Commons License).

Financial accounting entails the monitoring and analysis of financial transactions to aid in the formulation of corporate decisions. Management accounting is focused on giving executives accountability for overseeing and regulating activities within business-specific secret communications. Internal knowledge is the foundation for planning different short- or lengthy actions to be taken and determining which action to pursue (Makar et al., 2013). The implementation of the chosen plan of action is described in detail.

The accounting terminology provided by the American Institute of Certified Public Accountants (AICPA) is apparent. According to this definition, accounting is

"The art of recording, classifying, and summarizing in a significant way and regards to money, transactions as well as events that are, at minimum in part, of a financial nature and evaluating the outcomes thereof."

The term accounting highlights the following characteristics (Rayburn, 1986):

- Accounting is an art. Accounting is considered an art since it assists in determining the economic outcomes, that is, operational profit and financial position, by analyzing and interpreting financial information, which needs specialized knowledge, expertise, and discretion.

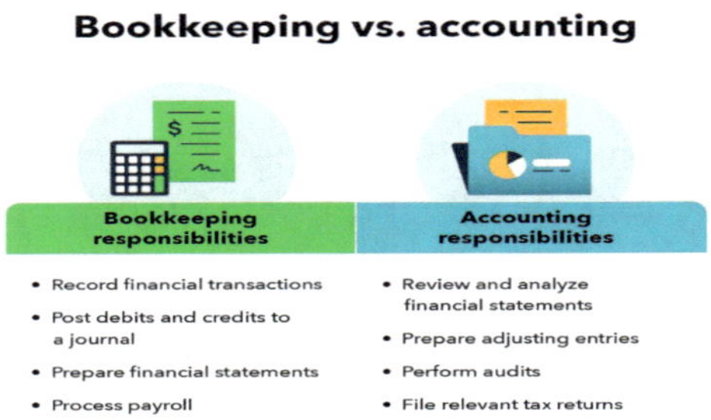

Figure 1.2. Diagram representing the difference between Bookkeeping and Accounting (Source: Quickbooks, Creative Commons License).

- It entails documenting, categorizing, and summing up. Recording entails systematically noting activities and occurrences in account books as soon as they occur. Classifying is the practice of gathering together transactions or items of a similar kind in one location. This is accomplished by opening accounts in a book known as a ledger. The production of summaries and declarations from the classified material (ledger) that are intelligible and beneficial to leadership and other interested individuals is summarization. This includes the production of final accounting, including a statement of profits and losses and a balance sheet.
- It documents transactions in monetary terms. All transactions are logged using a standard unit of measurement, capital, that enhances the comprehension of the status of the business.
- It solely documents transactions and occurrences that have a financial nature. If an occurrence has no economic implications, this would not be quantified concerning money and will not be registered.
- It is the skill of assessing the outcomes of activities to assess the enterprise's financial status, progress, and the job it is doing.

Accounting consists of the following steps (Rapp, 2010)*:*

- Identified and documented are the activities of a firm that are of minimum a partial financial nature.
- The recording is carried out in a manner that recognizes the various transaction categories and kinds.
- The resulting data are presented so that company owners and other relevant individuals can view the cumulative consequences of all transactions. The reports produced by the reviewing procedure are referred to as financial statements. They will display the company's loss or profit over time and the total capital the business utilizes. Management uses such financial data to make company choices.

Branches of Accounting

- There are three primary types or divisions of accounting:
  - Managerial accounting
  - Financial accounting
  - Standard costing
- Financial Accounting entails recordkeeping for the creation of trial balances, profit and loss statements, and balance sheets.
- Cost accounting is the method of recording and reporting costs. It is a method for systematically calculating the unit cost of an item or activity. The significant purposes of cost accounting include determining the price of a product and assisting management with cost control.

- Management accounting mainly focuses on the supply of data relevant to managers for decision-making, enhancing the organization's effectiveness, and maximizing profitability (Laughlin, 1981).

Learning Objectives

After studying this chapter, readers will be able to:

- Explain the need for accounting
- Understand the objectives of accounting
- Understand the basics of accounting
- Define the terms in accounting
- Discuss the conceptual framework of accounting
- Understand the accounting conventions
- Define accounting equation and balance sheet
- Explain the profit and loss account for noncorporate and corporate entities

Key Terms

- Accounting Equation
- Balance Sheet
- Credit
- Current Asset
- Current Liabilities
- Accounting Policies
- Accounting Standards
- Accounting Conventions

1.1. NEED OF ACCOUNTING

Accounting is closely related to private lives as it pertains to each business. Whenever people anticipate what they will do with cash, they all consciously or unconsciously produce accounting-related ideas. People must determine how much money would be spent and how much would be saved. By use of this action, a budget is made (Maskell & Kennedy, 2007). People are acquainted with this commonly accepted idea that money should be spent with caution.

The same applies to businesses. A firm must be aware of the internal and external financial resources and their consequences. Due to the diversity between management and ownership, accounting is necessary for a firm to give information essential for making solid economic decisions (Kavanagh & Drennan, 2008). Accounting also referred to as "The Language of Business," is necessary for a business organization to determine its position.

Figure 1.3. Illustration of the need for Accounting (Source: Lorginee Nagapa Chetty, Creative Commons License).

It is of the utmost importance to establish a foundation for budget planning, as well as dealing with the measure of economic operations and communicating financial information for decision-making. Accounting also aims to safeguard a firm's assets and share the outcomes of the income statement with all parties, such as stockholders, creditors, and investors, while adhering to regulatory obligations (Hopwood, 2009).

Accounting is among the fields that are expanding at a higher rate in the current period. It is dynamic and satisfies the expanding demands of trade, business, and industry. It is crucial to note that the advent of the industrial age and technical improvements have resulted in the expansion of company opportunities and a change in the accounting field, which is now recognized as a managerial planning tool and regulating processes. Therefore, it is accurate to assert that no economic growth could be conducted efficiently in the modern day without accounting.

The following are the primary accounting features (Hopwood, 2009):

- *Keeping Systematic Records:* Accounting is performed to establish a methodical financial transaction record.
- *Protecting and Controlling Business Properties*: Accounting ensures that none of the firm's assets or materials are used or disposed of in a way that is not allowed by maintaining accurate records. Accounting will provide information regarding money owed to different parties and numerous people. The company can ensure that all funds owed to it are collected promptly and that no payments are paid in error.
- *Determining the Operational Profit/Loss:* Accounting assists in determining the results of actions during a specific period, often a year, that is, how much loss or profit has been generated. This is done by keeping accurate records of a period's income and spending and comparing the payment to its associated costs.
- *Ascertaining the Financial Position of the Business:* A balance sheet is generated to determine the company's financial condition after a specific period. It shows the amounts of an organization's assets and obligations.
- *Facilitating Rational Decision Making*: Accounting aids the gathering, evaluating, and reporting of data at the appropriate time and to the appropriate management hierarchy to aid logical decision-making.

KEYWORD

Economic growth can be defined as the increase or improvement in the inflation-adjusted market value of the goods and services produced by an economy in a financial year.

1.2. SCOPE OF ACCOUNTING

Accounting has a vast scope and field of application. Its application is not limited to the corporate world but rather permeates all sectors of society and all disciplines (Parker, 1993). Today, all social institutions and professional endeavors must engage in financial transactions regardless of whether they generate a profit. Consequently, there is a requirement for documenting and analyzing such transactions as they happen and determining their net effect at the end of a specific period. In addition, this includes the necessity for interpreting and disseminating this data to the appropriate parties. Only accounting may support resolving these issues (Tillema, 2005).

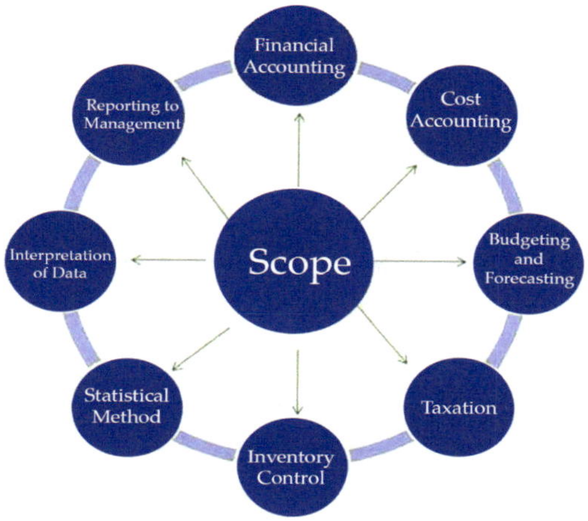

Figure 1.4. Schematic showing scope of accounting (Source: QS Study, Creative Commons License).

1.3. NATURE OF ACCOUNTING

Accounting systematically records financial activities and presents pertinent data to the appropriate individuals.

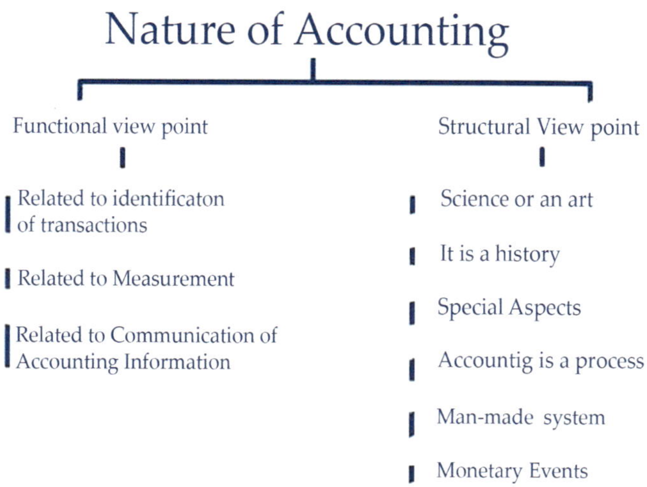

Figure 1.5. Illustration of the nature of accounting (Source: Sanjoy, Creative Commons License).

The fundamental aspects of accountancy are as follows (Maines & Wahlen, 2006).

1.3.1. Accounting as a Procedure

A procedure is a method for accomplishing a specific task following its objectives or goals. Accounting is a method because it fulfills the extraordinary responsibilities of gathering, processing, and disseminating financial data. It takes specific procedures, such as data gathering and recording, categorization summary, completion, and presentation.

1.3.2. Accounting as an Art

The process of documenting, categorizing, analyzing, and concluding financial information. The term "art" relates to how something is performed. Behavioral knowledge involving creativity and expertise can assist us in achieving specific goals.

KEYWORD

Behavioural knowledge, causal beliefs and self-efficacy as predictors of special educators' emotional reactions to challenging behaviours.

Accounting is frequently referred to as the business language since it is how a firm interacts with the external world. For this language to be comprehensible and generally known, it must adhere to scientifically determined, standardized norms (Kamla et al., 2006). These requirements are known as accounting standards.

Accounting principles are "the collection of ideas usually associated with accounting research and practice, acting as a justification of existing methods and a guideline for the choice of standards or methods where options are available." Accounting principles are, in a nutshell, recommendations that define standards for effective accounting techniques and processes in evaluating a business's financial condition and performance over time. Such principles could be divided into accounting ideas and norms (Broadbent, 1998).

1.4. BENEFITS OF ACCOUNTING

Listed below are the benefits of accounting (Rebele & Pierre, 2019).

1.4.1. Maintenance of Business Records

There is no reason to rely on recollection because all money transfers are systematically recorded in the account books. It has become difficult to recall the business transactions that have increased in size and intricacy.

1.4.2. Preparation of Financial Statements

The recording of events simplifies the creation of financial statements, including the trade and profits and losses account and the income statement.

1.4.3. Comparing of Outcomes

Accounting information, when reported correctly, can be utilized to contrast the outcomes of one year to that of prior years, allowing for an analysis of significant modifications.

1.4.4. Decision Making

Accounting information aids managers in making decisions by facilitating the preparation of budgets and the execution of tasks across divisions.

KEYWORD

A budget is a spending plan based on income and expenses.

1.4.5. Evidence in Legal Matters

Accounting information that has been adequately documented can be used as testimony in a court of law.

1.4.6. Gives Information to Stakeholders

Interested parties, such as investors, creditors, managers, workers, consumers, and the government, can obtain financial data about the organization.

1.4.7. Contributes to Tax Matters

Taxes on income and sales tax offices rely on the business's accounting records for tax matters.

1.4.8. Business Valuation

Financial accounting may be used to evaluate the business's worth whenever a company is to be purchased.

1.5. BASICS OF ACCOUNTING

Accounting is an ancient science whose purpose is to maintain data on various transactions. Accounting is considered necessary for keeping records of all payments, receipts, expenses, and revenue (Košovská et al., 2020).

In general terms, accounting can be classified into three types (Gray, 2013):

- *Financial Accounting* strives to determine the revenue or loss of an accountancy year in addition to the position of assets and obligations via the systematic monitoring of numerous transactions.
- *Cost Accounting:* assists the business in determining the price of production/services provided by the company and gives vital data for making decisions and reducing costs.
- *Management Accounting:* assists management in conducting business operations more efficiently (Bacheva, 2019).
- *Financial accounting* seeks to determine the outcomes of a given accounting period regarding profits or losses, investments, and obligations. To achieve this, it is necessary to document transactions methodically. Financial accounting is described as the "art and science of identifying, evaluating, and documenting business transactions in a structured manner to generate a report at the end of the year to figure out the outcomes of the relevant accounting year."

KEYWORD

A cost is the value of money that has been used up to produce something or deliver a service, and hence is not available for use anymore.

The following definitions are provided:

- *A transaction is an action:* a business deal is any activity that establishes a legal connection. For instance, the sale and purchase of commodities, the hiring, and pay of a worker, the repayment of various expenses, the inventory of goods, etc. (Bacheva, 2019).
- *Classification of Transactions*: Before documenting any transaction, it is necessary to classify it. A transaction may be categorized as either a cash transaction or a credit transaction. Likewise, transactions involving the receipt of income and the payment of expenses can be separated.
- *Transaction Recording*: Transaction recording is the foundation of financial accounting. Accounting terminology documents a transaction as an item (Benston, 1997).

There are established guidelines for monitoring various transactions in accounting books.

- *Cost Accounting:* This form of accounting aims to quantify a company's manufacturing costs by evaluating the production costs of every production stage and fixed expenses like loss of capital equipment. Cost accounting will then check and validate findings to outputs or actual outcomes to assist corporate management in monitoring financial results. Cost accounting is frequently utilized within a firm to help decision-making, whereas outside investors usually regard financial accounting. Financial accounting is a depiction of economic and cost achievement that incorporates the assets and responsibilities of a company. Cost accounting is beneficial as a management tool for planning and establishing cost control initiatives, which could also increase the firm's future means of gaining (Matušek & Hornyák 2019).
- *Accounting for Management*: Accounting for management uses technical knowledge and expertise to create and present accounting information to aid management in formulating strategies and controlling and planning the organizational framework.

Did you get it?

The first accounting entries were discovered within the more than 7,000-year-old remains of ancient Babylon, Assyria, and Sumeria.

The primary objective of management accounting is to give info to the leadership team at all management units for specific goals (Országhová & Horváthová, 2015):

- Trying to formulate the policies – strategic planning
- Managing the organization's actions – corporate planning
- Controlling the organization's operations
- Determination – long-term as well as tactical
- Evaluation of both operational and strategic effectiveness

An accounting report provides managers with information for planning, controlling, and organizing corporate activities. A cost accounting system serves the following functions (Kučera, 2019):

- To offer product costing information to be utilized in financial accounts.
- To supply data for planning, managing, and arranging.

Accounting, the word of business, is utilized to convey financial and other data about different commercial and non-business units to people, organizations, governments, etc. For instance, whenever a business seeks a line of credit, it must provide information about its operations, including its functional outcomes (profit or loss) and its financial condition (assets and liabilities) (Ulrychová, 2016). Similarly, economic data is necessary for shareholders or potential investors to assess managerial performance. Numerous regulations mandate that detailed financial data be provided to government agencies, including income tax, sales tax, business law boards, and others. Accounting is a field of study that compiles reports and analyzes financial data regarding the operations of various companies. Thus, basic accounting aims to convey an organization's performance (Drábeková, 2014).

Remember

Accounting records are the original documents, ledgers, and journal entries for your business.

1.5.1. Users of Accounting Information

Accounting is of primary importance to the proprietors and the managers. However, other persons, such as creditors, prospective employees, etc., are also interested in the accounting information.

- *Owners/Shareholders*: The main goal of accounting is to give owners the data they require for their company (Maksimović & Boroja, 2016).
- *Managers:* The managerial and ownership duties are separated into major firms and business groups. Since they must answer to the investors, the executives of this type of corporation are more interested in the accounting data.
- *Prospective Investors:* People thinking about investing in a company will want to hear about its economic condition and success. They get this data from the company's accounting records.
- *Banks, Creditors, and Other Lending Institutions*: Banks, creditor firms, and other lending institutions want assurances that they will be paid timely payments. They can judge this condition with the aid of the income statement. Accounting statements significantly affect how banks and other financial institutions evaluate loan applications.
- *Government:* Based on tax, labor, and corporate rules, the government is concerned about the financial reports of business enterprises.
- *Employees:* Since the magnitude of the profit determines how much they can expect to be paid in bonus payments and salary increases, employees are fascinated by financial figures.

- *Regulatory Agencies:* Several government agencies and departments, including the Company Law Board, the Registrar of Companies, and the Tax Authorities, among others, utilize financial statements to evaluate how well numerous companies are complying with regulatory laws as well as to determine their tax liability (Kohanova, 2012).
- *Researchers:* Research academics utilize accounting data in their studies of company operations and concept in addition to accounting.
- *Customers:* Customers might also be interested in the multinational corporation in the long or short term and want to understand how profitable, liquid, and solvent it is.

KEYWORD

Prudence is the ability to govern and discipline oneself by the use of reason.

1.5.2. Features of Accounting Information

Accounting information has several different features, including the following (Klůfa, 2016):

- *Relevance*: By assisting users in constantly evaluating the events, relevant information might impact their financial decisions. Accounting data aspects must be considered in helping creditors, investors, and other users assess past and future occurrences. It either verifies or disproves earlier assumptions. The form and substance of data have an impact on its usefulness.
- *Reliability:* Reliability is related to faith in accounting data in the idea that the information should accurately reflect what it is intended to provide. The information must be devoid of substantive bias and mistakes. Faithful portrayal, substance above form, lack of bias, prudence, and thoroughness are the main characteristics of reliability.
- *Comparability:* Accounting data for an enterprise is beneficial if it can be compared to data from an identical enterprise at different times and data from similar firms simultaneously. As a result, the data should be presented consistently throughout time and across organizations to enable users to draw meaningful comparisons (Pechočiak, 2020).
- *Understanding:* Material should be simple to comprehend for users who would be anticipated to have adequate knowledge of business, economics, and accounting, as well as the desire to investigate the data with fair thoroughness.

- *Timeliness:* The more promptly people are informed or given information, the more probable it will impact their choices. As a result, accounting data should be provided without interruption at the right time to enable a fast decision.
- *Cost-benefit Analysis:* For financial statements to be helpful for most users, they should not be expensive or time-consuming to prepare. The importance of cost-benefit analysis is highlighted, and the value of the data should typically outweigh the expense of delivering it.
- *Verifiability:* Verifiability assures that the records are accurate and that they can be verified by someone other than accounting (Boháčková & brožová, 2012).
- *Financial reporting:* should be clear of prejudice and not benefit one party over another. This is what is meant by the term "neutrality." Particularly for the exterior recipients of accounting information, neutrality is essential.
- *Completeness:* Completeness refers to the accounting reports' disclosure of all relevant information required by creditors, shareholders, and other consumers to evaluate the organization's financial standing and operating results.

KEYWORD

Profit is the difference between revenue that an economic entity has received from its outputs and total costs of its inputs.

1.5.3. Role of Accountant

The following is a summary of an accountant's duties:

- *Maintenance of Books of Accounts:* To determine the gross profit or loss for the accounting cycle as well as the economic standing as of a specific date, an accountant's primary responsibility is to give his skills for keeping meticulous accounting records (Collins et al., 2011).
- *Statutory Audit:* Each limited company must hire a chartered accountant as their auditor, who is obligated by law to notify every year if the income reports are ready in generally accepted accounting concepts, relevant laws, and accounting rules, as well as whether they provided a true and accurate representation of the company's finances and loss and profit.
- *Internal Audit*: Large companies hire their employees to perform internal audits related to statutory audits to ensure that transactions have been recorded, categorized, and summed up in line with established financial accounting

and that management orders are carried out across the board.

- *Budgeting:* Prior preparation of business activities is referred to as budget planning. When the actual activities during a specific period are finished, the action plans are contrasted with the real ones to determine any differences (Ascani et al., 2021).
- Before any tax authorities resolve the tax burden following the current law, he also helps to lower the tax burden through wise tax preparation.
- *Investigation:* Accountants are frequently asked to conduct investigations to determine the company's financial standing for the benefit of relevant parties.
- *Management Advisory Service:* An accountant is primarily in charge of internal monitoring to leadership for long-term budgeting, monitoring, and decision-making. He offers management advisory services in organizational information systems, cost management, and technique assessment.
- *Other Activities:* In addition to their numerous other responsibilities, accountants carry out tasks like share registration, liquidator, cost accountant, etc.

KEYWORD

A transaction that includes an exchange of services or goods for a certain amount of money is known as a sale.

1.6. ACCOUNTING TERMS

Every discipline has a few key foundational concepts, and accounting is no exception.

1.6.1. Business Items for Trading and Non-Trading

One must have contacted numerous companies. It might have been noted that many goods businesses are concerned about buying to sell later. Additionally, it might have mentioned many other things the company uses but are not intended for sale (Duffie & Lando, 2001).

For instance, a stationery store has many different things, such as books, pens, pencils, scales, notebooks, charts, gum bottles, etc. The merchant buys such things intending to sell them. The stationery store also sells fans, air conditioners, generators, furniture, etc. The businessman buys such things for his use, not for resale. Based on the instances above, everything in a commercial issue can be divided into two groups: trade and non-trading.

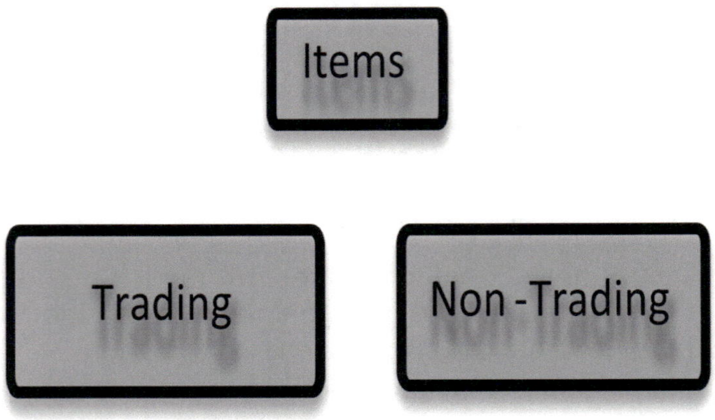

Figure 1.6. Schematic diagram representing trading and non-trading business elements (Source: Jaipur National University, Creative Commons License).

1.6.2. Trading

Trading is the buying and selling of goods and services. Trading things are any products or items that a businessperson buys to resell them and make a profit. Books, pens, pencils, and other stationery products are all trade goods in the stationery store, which is a commercial activity (Yu, 2005).

1.6.3. Non-Trading Items

Items that a business organization buys to utilize internally are non-trading goods. They are not intended for sale. Furniture, fans, generators, and other products are non-tradeable in the stationery store. Other company units have trading and non-trading things, just like the stationery store.

1.7. CONCEPTUAL FRAMEWORK

The following concepts are employed in the conceptual model (Ronen & Sorter, 1989):

Federal and provincial tax laws require reliable financial records following Generally Accepted Accounting Principles (GAAP). In addition, the Generally Accepted Accounting Principles (GAAP) provide a summary of the basic foundations for good accounting practice (GAAP).

- *Accounting Entity Concept (Business Entity Concept):* A company is distinct from its operator. It has responsibilities and rights different from those of its owner.

For instance, the firm is responsible for filing its tax returns and paying its bills. The proprietor must submit a separate personal income tax return from the business report. The assets and property owned by a business must be registered independently from the owner's private property.

- *Going-concern Presumption:* Whenever a business is founded, it is assumed to endure or keep operating for an extended period. It does not intend to declare bankruptcy or disband quickly. It appears to be able to fulfill its obligations to supply services or products to its consumers or clients. Even after a transfer of ownership, the business typically remains in operation (Tsiligiris & Bowyer, 2021).
- *Period Principle:* Even though it is assumed that a company will keep operations for a longer length of time (Going-Concern Assumption), this should disclose commonly and at periodic intervals on its condition and modifications for a variety of reasons, like the annual report to owners, revenue declarations for tax reasons and regular business choices, etc. This fluctuating requirement for reporting necessitates periodic measurements of many business components (monthly, quarterly or yearly). Thus, for assets, it is essential to understand how long they are projected to last to determine their worth at different times.
- *Monetary Principle:* For a company to reflect on its advancement and progress, we must be capable of quantifying the assets and activities it possesses (Heath, 1988). It has been determined that cash will be utilized to deliver this data – Canadian dollars, Japanese yen, etc.

Consequently, all resources are denominated in dollars on the balance sheet, while earnings and costs are recorded in dollars on the financial statements. This concept also implies that the currency is constant, having the same value as it did twenty years ago and so as it is going to twenty years from now. Obviously, with deflation, this is no longer true; yet, a better method has not been discovered for presenting business information. That can be quantified in hens, but this may cause further complications!

- *Objectivity Principle*: states that all business estimations and evaluations must be reasonable and equitable. To avoid bias, they must be founded on facts wherever feasible (Shanikat & Khan, 2013). For this reason, one-time costs are favored when calculating the value of an item. The fair market value is frequently used as a standard or

Remember

Various kinds of cloth, for instance, are trading goods for a textile trader, whereas racks designed to store and show the fabric are non-trading goods. Buses are trading goods for a transportation firm since they provide a service, whereas the sheds as well as tools used to maintain the vehicles are non-trading objects.

guidance. The value of a thing ought not to be judged by the amount a friend of a seller can pay for it but rather by the amount that a bunch of strangers is ready to pay. The closest companion is less probably to be impartial or objective. Since she is your friend, you could be prepared to offer her a very cheap cost. Or, since she is your closest friend, she may be ready to spend extra to assist you. Due to the possibility of favoritism, the transaction with your friend will be non-objective (Ruekert & Walker, 1987).

1.7.1. Double Entry System

There are two methods for maintaining records:

- single entry; and
- double entry.

Underneath the single-entry method, many transactions are not registered, while others are logged only partly. This makes the system unscientific, despite its apparent efficiency and cost-effectiveness. In contrast, the double entry system is built on scientific methods and is consequently utilized by most businesses. The system acknowledges that any transaction has two components and logs both facets. Under this arrangement, every transaction debits one account and credits another tab. The crux of accounting is determining which of two statements is influenced by a specific trade, which of such two accounts should be credited, and which should be rewarded (Ovunda, 2015).

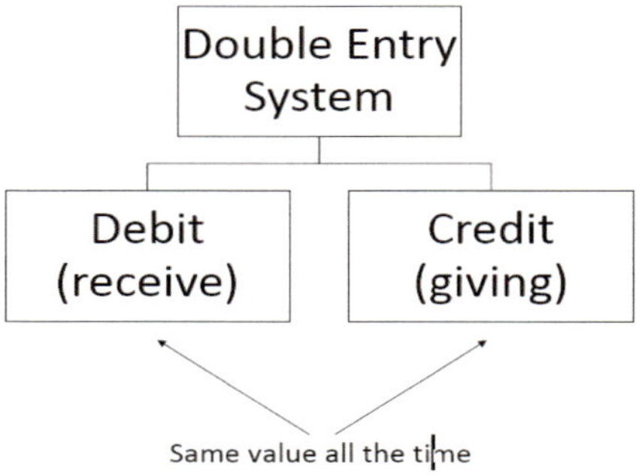

Figure 1.7. Diagram of Double Entry System (Source: Asia Bookkeeping, Creative Commons License).

Double Entry System features (Nobes, 1987):

- It meticulously documents all commercial transactions. Both personal and indifferent accounts are maintained. All information concerning asset values and revenues produced over the year is readily accessible.

- Because each debit has a matching credit, it checks the adequate precision of accounts.
- The statement of profit and loss can be generated to indicate yields gained or losses incurred at any time.
- The system enables the comparison of the current year's buys, sales, expenditures, profits, etc., with all those of past years, allowing a business owner to manage his business operations. At any specific time or date, the trial balance could be constructed to reflect the actual amounts of holdings, liabilities, and cash.
- It dramatically minimizes the likelihood of fraud, and if fraud does occur, it is simple to detect.
- The exact information on any account could be acquired without difficulty.

TIPS

While preparing financial statements revenue cannot be included as income

1.7.2. Rules of Debit and Credit

The left side of a bank is referred to as the debit column, while the right side is the credit side. A debit entry or debit is an item on the left of the account, while a credit entrance or crediting is an input on the right-hand side (Potts, 1974). Entering a statement on the left side of the balance sheet is known as debiting the bank, whereas making an item on the right-hand side is known as crediting the account. The checking account is the differential between the estimated debits and quantifies the amount. The double-entry system refers to the documentation of credit and debit card transactions.

GOLDEN RULES

Personal Accounts: "Credit the donor and debit the recipient."

Real Accounts: "Debit what is received and credit whatever is expended."

"Debit all losses and expenses and charge all profits and bonuses" is the rule for presenting a number.

1.7.2.1. Personal Accounts Debit and Credits

"Debit the recipient and pay the donor," or debit the recipient's bank and pay the donor. If one buys things on credit from Ram, the two systems concerned are the Goods (Purchase) Account and Ram's Account. The account in question is private. Ram is the donor in this exchange; hence, his bank will be paid. Likewise, Ram's Account would be credited if he receives cash as he is the recipient. Consequently, a person's account is deducted for every benefit they get and credited for every advantage they provide (Gupta, 2010).

Personal Accounts Debit

a) If the account is current, debit means that the individual in the account has been credited and is now the business's debtor.

b) If the account currently exists and the individual whose account has been charged is now a creditor of the firm, the new credit means that the amount owed by the individual has risen.

c) If a creditor's account is credited, it signifies that the balance owed to that debtor has lowered by the value of the credit. In that cash account, it is also possible for the debtor to turn into a debtor if the debit quantity increases the total for which that individual was a creditor before the credit (Levitin, 2005).

Personal Accounts Credit

a) If the bank is fresh, credit signifies that the account owner is now a creditor of the firm.

b) If a creditor's account is charged, the amount owed to that individual will increase by the quantity of the new credit. A debit entry in an enterprise's debtor's account indicates that the credit card's value has reduced the amount the debtor was obligated to the enterprise. After receiving credit, it is also feasible for a debtor to become a creditor.

Figure 1.8. Schematic of the rules of Debit and Credit (Source: Prince Kumar, Creative Commons License).

1.7.2.2. Real Accounts Debit and Credits

"Debit whatever goes in and credit what leaves out," or debit the record of what goes in now and credit the record of what leaves. For instance, when furniture is bought with cash, the furnishing, and the cash credit balance are debited.

Debit in Real Accounts: A debit in existing accounts signifies whether the amount of the asset to which the account has been credited has risen or the company has purchased more of that property.

Credit in Real Accounts: A credit in a real account suggests that the cost of the property for which the account has been charged has been reduced or that the firm has parted a portion or all of the asset for the value of the charge (Constantine, 2005).

1.7.2.3. Nominal Accounts Debit and Credits

Credit all losses and costs and credit all profits and gains; credit the balances of losses and expenses and credit the records of revenues and benefits (Warsono, 2015). For instance, if someone offers a clerk a salary, there are two meanings implicated: the salary account and the cash payments. Account for salaries is a numerical entity. This bank will be deducted because salaries paid are an expenditure for the company. Likewise, if interest is paid, the interest bank would be paid because interest is a source of income.

Debit in Nominal Accounts: A credit in a numerical account indicates that an item of expenditure or loss in the extent of the debit has occurred or that a specific revenue or gain has decreased by the extent of the debit.

Credit in Nominal Accounts: A credit in nominal accounting denotes a revenue, gain, or reduction in an item of expenditure or loss equal to the value of the credit.

1.7.3. Accounting Conventions

An accounting convention relates to globally accepted procedures for documenting and displaying the accounting information of a commercial entity. They are observed as customs, traditions, etc. (Yamey, 2014). International accounting standards have evolved via consistent and regular practice to ease uniform entry in the

KEYWORD

Credit is the trust which allows one party to provide money or resources to another party wherein the second party does not reimburse the first party immediately, but promises either to repay or return those resources at a later date.

account books. International accounting standards facilitate the comparison of accounting data from various business units or a single unit for multiple periods. These have evolved throughout the years. The most significant long-standing conventions include the following:

- Convention of consistency.
- Convention of full disclosure.
- Convention of materiality.
- Convention of conservatism.

1.7.3.1. Convention of Consistency

KEYWORD

Financial statements are written records that convey the business activities and the financial performance of a company.

The consistency rule dictates that the exact accounting standards should be utilized each year while generating financial statements (Ball et al., 1991). Whenever financial accounts of an identical company are compared across time, it is possible to make valuable conclusions. Nonetheless, this is only achievable if the enterprise's accounting standards and processes are consistent and stable. If various accounting techniques and practices are utilized for financial reporting for successive years, the resulting financial statements may not be equivalent.

1.7.3.2. Convention of Full Disclosure

The convention of disclosing information stipulates that all essential and pertinent information on financial statements must be presented in full. Full disclosure signifies that accounting information must be disclosed completely, fairly, and adequately (Semieniuk & Weber, 2020). Adequate refers to a sufficient quantity of information disclosed. Fair suggests an equal behavior of consumers. The term 'full' denotes a comprehensive information presentation. Thus, according to the norm of full disclosure, every financial report should fully reveal all relevant information. Let's make the business connection. The company delivers financial data to all appropriate parties, including investors, lenders, creditors, and shareholders.

1.7.3.3. Convention of Materiality

According to the convention of physical reality, only material facts, critical and pertinent data, should be provided to users of accounting data to provide relevant financial statements. Here, the question of what a material fact emerges. The significance of a fact relies on its type and magnitude. Material existence refers to facts affecting a user's decision (Robb, 1987).

1.7.3.4. Convention of Conservatism

This tradition is founded on the maxim, "Anticipate no profit, but plan for all potential losses." It offers direction for transaction records in the accounting books. It is predicated on a conservative approach to demonstrating profit. This convention's primary purpose is to establish a minimum profit (Copeland, 1949).

1.7.4. Accounting Equation

The accounting equation is a fundamental equation that governs the reporting of company transactions in accounts books. Whichever assets a firm has financed by the owner or outside sources. This equation demonstrates the equality of assets, outsider claims (receivables), and ownership or founders.

Formulized mathematically,

Assets=Liabilities + Capital

When a business acquires an asset, a matching responsibility also arises. A company possesses no funds of its own (O'Bryan et al., 2000).

However, It can be said that:

When a business acquires an asset, a matching responsibility also arises. A company possesses no funds of its own.

However, It can be said that:

1. The business neither owns nor owes anything.
2. What it Owns is What it Owes

Now examine how company transactions impact the financial statement. Such transactions either raise or reduce the value of the assets, liabilities, and capital. Each company possesses some assets.

For example, Sunita began her business with a Capital investment of INR 2,000,000. Cash might be considered a newly-created asset for the firm (Juárez, 2015).

Consequently,

KEYWORD

Liabilities are debts or obligations a person or company owes to someone else.

Cash INR 2,00,000

Capital INR 2,00,000

Sunita later gets 20,000 INR worth of furniture and 60,000 INR worth of machinery. The current status of the properties is as follows:

From the primary commercial operations, it can be concluded that:

Capital	=	Cash	+ Furniture	+ Machinery
2,00,000	=	1,20,000	+ 20,000	+ 60,000
		(2,00,000 - 80,000)		

Capital = Assets or

Assets = Capital

Remember

Assets are reported on a company's balance sheet. They're classified as current, fixed, financial, and intangible.

Increasing or decreasing capital will lead to a rise or reduction in assets. For instance, Sunita invests an additional 50,000 rupees.

Then,

Capital	=	Cash	+	Furniture	+	Machinery
2,00,000	=	1,20,000	+	20,000	+	60,000
+ 50,000		+ 50,000				
2,70,000	=	1,70,000	+	20,000	+	60,000

Every corporate entity typically borrows funds from outside sources to operate. In other words, all businesses owe money to third parties. Such assets are funded by funds contributed by their owners and third parties. Liability refers to the term for borrowed funds (Phillips & Heiser, 2011).

The three fundamental parts of every business deal are assets, liabilities, and capital, and their connection is expressed by way of a financial statement that is always identical. Individual support, liabilities, and capital can fluctuate at any time, but the two parties of the accounting stay equal. Analyze the fact by considering other transactions and determining how some change the accounting equation.

Suppose Rajni begins her business, as well as the subsequent transactions occur:

She started her business with a monetary investment of INR5,000,000.

	Assets cash	= Liabilities	+	Capital
Effect of the transaction	Rs. 5,00,000	= 0	+	Rs. 5,00,000

This transaction signifies that Rajni has contributed 5,000,000 INR in cash to the business as its initial investment. On the one side, an asset (money) in the amount of INR 5,000,000 has been produced.

She acquired merchandise from Rohit for INR40,000 (Scofield & Dye, 2009).

	Assets			=	Capital +	Liabilities
	Cash	+ furniture	+ Goods	=	Creditors	
Old Equation	4,40,000	+ 50,000	+ 10,000	=	5,00,000 +	0
effect	0	+ 0	+ 40,000	=	0 +	40,000
New Equation	4,40,000	+ 50,000	+ 50,000	=	5,00,000 +	40,000

In this transaction, products were acquired on credit from Rohit, resulting in a rise of INR 40,000 in assets (goods) and a rise of INR 40,000 in creditors, as the business now gives money to Rohit.

1.7.5. Accounting Standards

Accounting as the "language of business" conveys a company's financial statements to various parties through financial statements, which must present a "true and fair" picture of its financial condition. Like every other language, accounting possesses its own complex set of regulations. Nonetheless, these guidelines must be applied with sufficient flexibility following an organization's circumstances and the changing economic climate, human benefits, regulatory requirements, and technical improvements. Therefore, these regulations cannot be utterly rigorous or arbitrarily enforced (Barth et al., 2008).

Accounting standards (ASs) are codified policy guidelines published by a professional accounting organization, the government, or any other regulating agency. Accounting Standards address the recognition, measuring, reporting, and exposure of accounting

Did you get it?

The American Institute of Certified Public Accountants (AICPA) describes accountancy as "the art of documenting, categorizing, and presenting in a meaningful way and regards to money, transactions, and occurrences that are, at partially, of a financial nature, and evaluating the outcomes thereof.

transactions within financial statements. These are general principles, with implementation left to the expert's discretion.

An accounting standard may be viewed as a type of law – a guide for action, an established premise or basis for behavior or practice (Levitt, 1998). The purpose of establishing standards is to achieve uniformity in financial statements and to assure the accuracy and comparability of enterprise-published data. On April 21, 1977, the Institute of Chartered Accountants of India (ICAI) established the Accounting Standards Board (ASB) to harmonize India's accounting regulations and procedures. The ICAI has thus far released 32 Accounting Standards and 29 Accounting Standards Interpretations.

1.7.6. Accounting Policies

Accounting policies relating to the precise accounting principles and ways of implementing these principles that the company has adopted to create and present financial reports. Various accounting principles, principles, and traditions are the basis for policies (Christensen et al., 2002).

KEYWORD

Goodwill is a premium paid over fair value during a transaction and cannot be bought or sold independently.

Accounting standards produced by professional accounting organizations restrict and minimize the accounting policies from which a business may choose for assessing and reporting business transactions. An organization decides its unique accounting policies following broad financial accounting standards and practices. For instance, according to the idea of matching, degradation should be viewed as a cost of conducting trade and linked with the corresponding period's revenue. Following Accounting Standard No. 6, depreciation can be computed using the straight-line approach, the written-down value technique, etc. (Vergoossen, 1997). Therefore, the firm must establish a policy regarding its strategy. Similarly, the value of inventories, handling of goodwill, assessment of investments, evaluation of fixed assets, and so on are significant areas requiring standardization of accounting principles to ensure the accuracy and relevance of accounting data.

1.8. ACCOUNTING – A MEASUREMENT DISCIPLINE

Accounting is a measuring field since it works with the monetary measurement of resources, and as a consequence, it offers a framework for assessing the efficiency of a company's performance (Vickrey, 1970). The term "measurement" refers to assigning numerical numbers to particular features, qualities, or aspects of specific things or occurrences. It implies that the asset, liability, or shift in capital must be of a meaningful quality that can be stated in currency terms with good dependability. This applies whether the change is positive or negative.

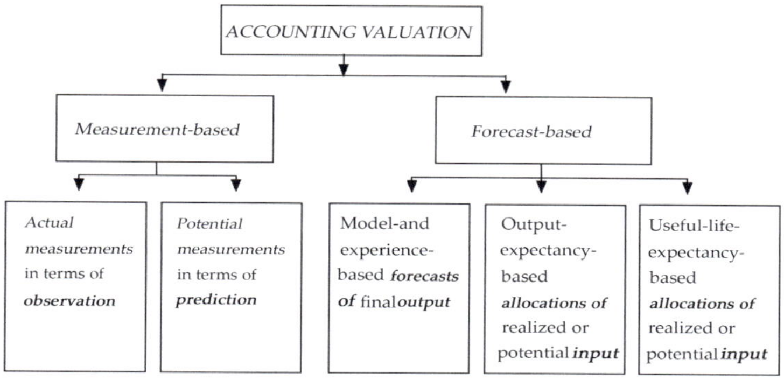

Figure 1.9. Schematic of measurement-based accounting valuation (Source: Petri Vehmanen, Creative Commons License).

The term "value" describes the advantages obtained from things, abilities, or ideas. The concept of valuation is primarily associated with economists. The use that an economic resource provides to the person who benefits from its utilization is what gives it value. When doing accounting, the value of an item, ability, or idea is measured in terms of monetary units. Money is the standard unit for evaluating value (Harris & Smith, 2009). If the value of the machine is determined to be $200,000, then this represents only one form of value, which is commonly referred to as purchase price or historical cost. The idea of valuation is narrower than that of measure. The concept of measurement encompasses the practice of value.

The four different bases that are commonly acknowledged in financial parlance are:

- Historical Cost
- Present Cost
- Realizable Worth
- Current Value

1.8.1. Historical Cost

The term "*historical cost*" refers to the initial purchase price of an asset, often known as the "acquisition price." When calculating liabilities, the quantity of profits obtained in return for the obligation is used (Bell 1987).

1.8.2. Current Cost

Assets are recorded at the quantities of cash or its equivalent required to be spent if identical or equal assets were purchased. This method ensures that assets are always recorded at the most accurate possible price. On the balance sheet, liabilities are recorded at an amount equal to the present value total of cash equals that will be necessary to satisfy the commitment at present.

Remember

The settlement value must be calculated as per the governing laws. FnF settlement should be made within a reasonable time.

1.8.3. Realizable Value

According to this valuation foundation, transactions are valued at the quantity of cash or comparable cash that might be recovered if the assets were sold commonly (Porter, 1992). This quantity is known as the realizable worth of the purchase. Similarly, liabilities are documented based on their final settlement valuations.

1.8.4. Present Value

According to the idea of current value, an asset is displayed in the income statement at the amount of discounted current total cash flows that the property is anticipated to produce in the normal process of company activities. This sum is referred to as the asset's "present value." Similarly, liabilities are revealed at the discounted present value of the future cash outflow anticipated to be needed to fulfill the liability in the normal or due process of business actions. This value is determined by discounting the future cash outflows to their sales price (Jones, 2000).

1.9. BALANCE SHEET

The balance sheet also referred to as the report of the situation or cash flow statement, displays a company's financial performance or health. It says the company's financial standing as of a specific date. The company's assets are typically shown on the left side of the page, while the debts and net worth are shown on the right-hand side. (Winjum, 1970): Assets are items that a company makes and are typically debit balances. Total assets and capital assets are the two fundamental divisions of assets. Any item that may be transformed into cash within a calendar year is considered a current asset. Long-term investments, also known as existing assets, are more durable items like large machinery and construction projects (Boys, 1995). Obligations are what a company owes and are typically credit balance sheets. Like investments, liabilities can be categorized into two main groups. They are represented as lengthy debt and interest expense, which refer to debt due within the following year. Bills for accounts receivable, inventory, rent, wages, etc., are considered current obligations (Abdukarimovich, 2020). Long-term debt consists of obligations that, by contrast, do not require immediate repayments, such as a loan or long-term note.

For publicly traded companies, net value, also known as stockholders' shares, is the sum of assets minus obligations. In other words, net worth is the amount that remains once all of the invoices and notes have been paid. Another definition of net worth is the amount owed to the company's owner(s) or stockholders after all obligations have been settled (Black, 2006).

Assets – Liabilities = Net Worth or

Assets = Liabilities + Net Worth

What does "Balance Sheet" mean exactly?

Balance is critical because cash reserves equal term debt plus net worth. This is true regardless of whether the obligations are more significant than the assets. In this situation, net worth is no longer buoyant and should be deducted from liabilities before being introduced. The concept of a double accounting equation is used in a balance sheet. Since every business action impacts two or more records, it is a double entry.

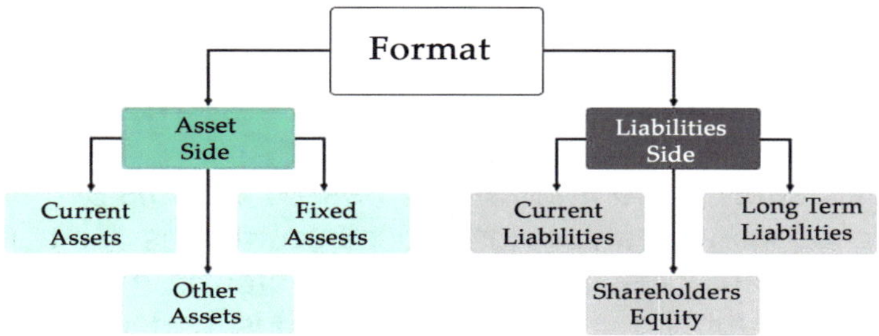

Figure 1.10. Illustration of the Balance Sheet (Source: Ashish Kumar Srivastav, Creative Commons License).

A sale might result in a rise in cash or receivable accounts but a fall in inventory, for instance. Amounts owed to you (accounts payable) or cash that is obligated to pay to you (accounts collectible) are all examples of accounts. Accrual accounts refer to accounts receivable and payable. Such accounts' balances represent money that needs to be earned by providers or that will do receive from clients at a later date.

The balance sheet is divided into sections with existing and fixed assets on the left side and existing and long-term obligations in addition to the net worth on the right. Remember that your assets, debts, and net worth must be managed (Farh et al., 1990).

Be aware that business activity changed three account balances on the asset section of the balance sheet: Inventory was reduced as a result of product sales; Cash increased as a result of the company receiving cash for a portion of the deal, and Trade receivables were added to or increased due to of a portion of the product being sold on borrowing (Kendrick, 1974).

1.10. LIMITATIONS OF ACCOUNTING

The following are accounting's limitations (Bay, 2011):

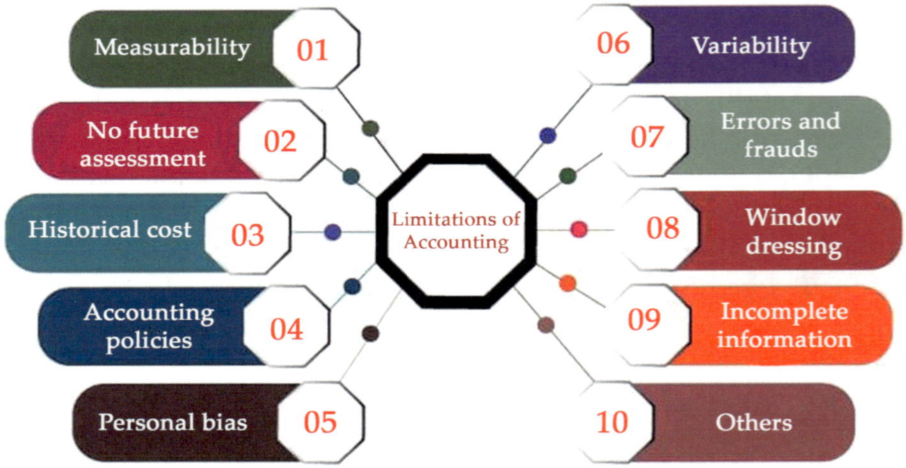

Figure 1.11. Illustration of the limitations of Accounting (Source: Java Point, Creative Commons License).

- *Accounting information is expressed in terms of money:* The accountant analyzes just those occurrences of a commercial intermediary suitable for being stated in monetary terms. In accounting, non-monetary goods and events are not quantified and documented.
- *Accounting information is based on estimates:* Certain accounting information relies on estimations, and these calculations may be wrong.

- *Accounting information may be biased:* Accounting information is not free of the accountant's direct influence or bias. In calculating income, accountants employ a variety of inventory valuation, depreciation, capital, revenue item treatment, etc. approaches. Therefore, the estimated payment might be inaccurate because of a lack of objectivity.
- *Fixed transactions are valued at their initial cost:* Because the worth of fixed assets can fluctuate over time, there may be a significant gap between some initial prices and the current purchase price. Cash flow might not always accurately reflect the financial status at a given period.
- *Accounting can be manipulated:* Accounting information cannot be regarded as the sole indicator of managerial performance because earnings could be controlled or overstated (Hasso & Duncan, 2013).
- *Money as a unit of evaluation fluctuates in value:* Its value is not constant. If price level fluctuations are not factored into the calculation of income, the financial statements would not accurately reflect the company's economic performance.

ACTIVITY 1.1.

The Household Aids Company assembles clip clothespins in three sections, and uses process costing. Under normal operating conditions, each section has a spoilage rate of 2%. However, spoilage can go as high as 5% and is usually discovered when a faulty pin enters process or on final completion by a section. The spring mechanism is the only material which can be saved from a spoiled unit. The production supervisor assigns a worker once or twice a week to remove the springs from spoiled units. The salvaged springs are placed in bins at the assembly tables in section No1 to be used again. No accounting entry is made of this salvage operation.

In the past, the controller has made no attempt to account for spoilage separately. Lost unit costs have been absorbed by the units transferred out of the section and those remaining in the process. However, because spoilage is increasing, a different method is needed.

SUMMARY

1. Financial accounting aims to find out the profit or losses of an accounting year and the assets and liabilities position by recording various transactions systematically.
2. Financial accounting aims to find an accounting year's results regarding profits or losses and assets and liabilities.
3. Trade means the purchase and sale of goods or/and services.
4. Tangible items such as furniture and machines can be touched, and their presence can be noted.
5. Current assets are held for a short time, generally a year only.
6. Non-current assets are those acquired for long-term use in the business.
7. Liabilities are the future obligations or debts payable by the business unit.
8. Internal liabilities are liabilities the business owes to the owners or proprietors.

REVIEW QUESTIONS

1. Explain the significant difference between cash and accrual accounting.
2. In what way does a business manager use accounting information?
3. Using examples, give a short description of five accounting principles or concepts.
4. Why is the rule for debit and credit entries the same for liability and owners' equity accounts?
5. Define the concept of depreciation.
6. What is the purpose of an accumulated depreciation account?
7. Explain the convention of consistency with an example.
8. Explain the accounting convention of conservatism with an example.
9. Explains the convention of materiality.
10. Distinguish between expense and expenditure.

MULTIPLE CHOICE QUESTIONS

1. Which of the following statements is incorrect?

a) Liabilities + Assets = Capital
b) Assets – Capital = Liabilities
c) Liabilities + Capital = Assets
d) Assets – Liabilities = Capital

2. **Which of the following is not an asset?**
   a) Cash balance
   b) A loan from K Harris
   c) Buildings
   d) Debtors
3. **Which of the following is a liability?**
   a) Motor Vehicles
   b) Cash at Bank
   c) Machinery
   d) Creditors for goods
4. **Which of the following best describes a trial balance?**
   a) Shows the financial position of a business
   b) It is a list of balances on the books
   c) It offers all the entries in the books
   d) It is a unique account
5. **Is it true that the trial balance totals should agree?**
   a) No, because it is not a balance sheet
   b) No, there are sometimes good reasons why they differ
   c) Yes, except where the trial balance is extracted
   d) Yes, always at the year-end
6. **Which of the following is correct?**
   a) Capital can only come from profit
   b) Profit increases capital
   c) Profit reduces capital
   d) Profit does not alter capital
7. **Which of the following should not be called 'Sales'?**
   a) Goods sold for cash
   b) Office fixtures sold
   c) Sale of the item previously included in _Purchases
   d) Goods sold on credit
8. **________aims at finding the results of an accounting year in terms of profits or losses and assets and liabilities.**
   a) Cost accounting
   b) Financial Accounting

c) Management Accounting

d) Both a and b

Answers to Multiple Choice Questions

1. (a) 2. (b) 3. (d) 4. (b) 5. (d)

6. (b) 7. (b) 8. (b)

REFERENCES

1. Abdukarimovich, O. A., (2020). Budget organization's formation and improving accounting for out-of-budget budgets. *International Journal of Advanced Science and Technology, 29*(8), 11–16.
2. Ascani, I., Ciccola, R., & Chiucchi, M. S., (2021). A structured literature review about the role of management accountants in sustainability accounting and reporting. *Sustainability, 13*(4), 235.
3. Bacheva, S., (2019). Conceptual basics of accounting theory–accounting rules. *Ikonomiceski I Sotsialni Alternativi*, (3), 97–107.
4. Ball, R., Thomas, R. E., & McGrath, J., (1991). Influence of R&D accounting conventions on internal decision-making of companies. *R&D Management, 21*(4), 261–270.
5. Barth, M. E., Landsman, W. R., & Lang, M. H., (2008). International accounting standards and accounting quality. *Journal of Accounting Research, 46*(3), 467–498.
6. Bay, C., (2011). Framing financial responsibility: An analysis of the limitations of accounting. *Critical Perspectives on Accounting, 22*(6), 593–607.
7. Bell, P. W., (1987). Accounting as a discipline for study and practice: 1986. *Contemporary Accounting Research, 3*(2), 338–367.
8. Benston, G. J., (1997). Accounting for derivates: Back to basics. *Journal of Applied Corporate Finance, 10*(3), 46–58.
9. Black, J., (2006). War, women, and accounting: Female staff in the UK army pay department offices, 1914–1920. *Accounting, Business & Financial History, 16*(2), 195–218.
10. Boháčková, I., & Brožová, I., (2012). We are assessing students' level of knowledge in profile courses of chosen economic study programs at the fem culs. *Journal on Efficiency and Responsibility in Education and Science, 5*(3), 148–156.
11. Boys, P. G., (1995). Samuel Pepys's accounts. *Accounting, Business & Financial History, 5*(3), 308–320.
12. Broadbent, J., (1998). The gendered nature of "accounting logic": Pointers to an accounting encompassing multiple values. *Critical Perspectives on Accounting, 9*(3), 267–297.

13. Christensen, P. O., Demski, J. S., & Frimor, H., (2002). Accounting policies in agencies with moral hazard and renegotiation. *Journal of Accounting Research, 40*(4), 1071–1090.
14. Collins, E., Lawrence, S., Roper, J., & Haar, J., (2011). Sustainability and the role of the management accountant. *CIMA Research Executive Summary Series, 7*(14), 1–11.
15. Constantine, L., (2005). The need for federal reserve and antitrust intervention in the failed US debit and credit card markets. In: *Proceedings of a Conference on Interchange Fees in Credit and Debit Card Industries: What Role for Public Authorities* (Vol. 1, pp. 4–6).
16. Copeland, M. A., (1949). Relevant accounting conventions to determine business income. *Journal of Accountancy (pre-1986), 87*(000002), 107.
17. Cuadrado-Ballesteros, B., Martínez-Ferrero, J., & García-Sánchez, I. M., (2017). Mitigating information asymmetry through sustainability assurance: The role of accountants and levels of assurance. *International Business Review, 26*(6), 1141–1156.
18. Daines, H. C., (1929). The changing objectives of accounting. *Accounting Review, 1*, 94–110.
19. De Bruyckere, S., & Everaert, P., (2021). The role of the external accountant in business planning for starters: Perspective of the self-determination theory. *Sustainability, 13*(6), 3014.
20. Drábeková, J., Pechočiak, T., & Matušek, V., (2018). Mathematical competencies of students entering university studies. Case study of Slovakia. *Mathematics in Education, Research, and Applications, 4*(1), 23–30.
21. Duffie, D., & Lando, D., (2001). Term structures of credit spread with incomplete accounting information. *Econometrica, 69*(3), 633–664.
22. Edogbanya, A., (2013). The impact of the global economic financial crisis on the role of the management accountants in an emerging economy. *Kuwait Chapter of the Arabian Journal of Business and Management Review, 2*(6), 49.
23. Faccia, A., & Mosteanu, N. R., (2019). Accounting and blockchain technology: From double-entry to triple-entry. *The Business & Management Review, 10*(2), 108–116.
24. Fagerberg, D., (1954). Spotlight on personal accounting. *The Accounting Review, 29*(3), 355–364.
25. Farh, J. L., Podsakoff, P. M., & Organ, D. W., (1990). Accounting for organizational citizenship behavior: Leader fairness and task scope versus satisfaction. *Journal of Management, 16*(4), 705–721.
26. Gray, R., (2013). Back to basics: What do we mean by environmental (and social) accounting and what is it for?—A reaction to Thornton. *Critical Perspectives on Accounting, 24*(6), 459–468.
27. Gupta, O. S., (2010). Single rule for debit and credit entries. *Indian Journal of Accounting, 40*(2), 1–5.

28. Harris, E. F., & Smith, R. N., (2009). Accounting for measurement error: A critical but often overlooked process. *Archives of Oral Biology, 54*, 107–117.
29. Hasso, T., & Duncan, K., (2013). Valuation of family firms: The limitations of accounting information. *Australian Accounting Review, 23*(2), 135–150.
30. Heath, L. C., (1988). Commentary: Accounting literature, the conceptual framework. *Accounting Horizons, 2*(2), 100.
31. Hoang, T. G., Nguyen, T. Q., & George, M., (2020). Business partner roles of management accountants through the emergence of sustainability disclosures. *The Journal of Asian Finance, Economics, and Business, 7*(12), 365–376.
32. Holthausen, R. W., (2009). Accounting standards, financial reporting outcomes, and enforcement. *Journal of Accounting Research, 47*(2), 447–458.
33. Hopwood, A. G., (2009). Accounting and the environment. *Accounting, Organizations and Society, 34*(3, 4), 433–439.
34. Ivanchenkova, L., Skliar, L., Stasiukova, K., Babich, I., Tsegelnik, N., & Tomchuk, Y., (2020). Improving the organization of accounting and control of payroll in budgetary institutions. *International Journal of Management (IJM), 11*(6), 718–727.
35. Jones, R., (2000). National accounting, government budgeting, and the accounting discipline. *Financial Accountability & Management, 16*(2), 101–116.
36. Juárez, F., (2015). The accounting equation inequality: A set theory approach. *Global Journal of Business Research, 9*(3), 97–104.
37. Kamla, R., Gallhofer, S., & Haslam, J., (2006). Islam, nature, and accounting: Islamic principles and the notion of accounting for the environment. In: *Accounting Forum* (Vol. 30, No. 3, pp. 245–265).
38. Kavanagh, M. H., & Drennan, L., (2008). What skills and attributes does an accounting graduate need? Evidence from student perceptions and employer expectations. *Accounting & Finance, 48*(2), 279–300.
39. Kendrick, J. W., (1974). The accounting treatment of human investment and capital. *Review of Income and Wealth, 20*(4), 439–468.
40. Keong, O., (2020). Determinants of intentions to engage in sustainability accounting & reporting (SAR) and moderating role of internal audit function: The perspective of accountants. *Arthatama, 4*(1), 33–43.
41. Klůfa, J., (2016). Comparison of the test variants in entrance examinations. *Journal on Efficiency and Responsibility in Education and Science, 9*(4), 111–116.
42. Kohanova, I., (2012). Analysis of university entrance test from mathematics. *Acta Didactica Universitatis Comenianae Mathematics, 12*, 31–46.
43. Košovská, I., Pietriková, M., & Váryová, I., (2020). The assessment of students' achievements from the subject basics of accounting in the study program accounting at FEM SUA in Nitra. *Mathematics in Education, Research, and Applications, 6*, 2.
44. Kučera, M., (2019). Analysis of student profile in terms of success in accounting study. In: *Annual Conference on Finance and Accounting* (Vol. 1, pp. 343–350_.

45. Laughlin, R. C., (1981). On the nature of accounting methodology: On the nature of accounting methodology. *Journal of Business Finance & Accounting, 8*(3), 329–353.
46. Levitin, A. J., (2005). The antitrust super bowl: America's payment system, no-surcharge rules, and the hidden costs of credit. *Berkeley Bus. LJ, 3*, 265.
47. Levitt, A., (1998). The importance of high-quality accounting standards. *Accounting Horizons, 12*(1), 79.
48. Maines, L. A., & Wahlen, J. M., (2006). The nature of accounting information reliability: Inferences from archival and experimental research. *Accounting Horizons, 20*(4), 399–425.
49. Makar, S., Wang, L., & Alam, P., (2013). The mixed attribute model in SFAS 133 cash flow hedge accounting: Implications for market pricing. *Review of Accounting Studies, 18*(1), 66–94.
50. Maksimović, S., & Boroja, I. V., (2016). The importance of preparation classes for taking the university entrance examination in mathematics. *Studies, 17*, 24–28.
51. Maskell, B. H., & Kennedy, F. A., (2007). Why do we need lean accounting, and how does it work? *Journal of Corporate Accounting & Finance, 18*(3), 59–73.
52. Mattessich, R., (1980). On the evolution of theory construction in accounting: A personal account. *Accounting and Business Research, 10*(sup1), 158–173.
53. Matušek, V., & Hornyák, G. R., (2019). Comparison of exam results in mathematics at faculty of economics and management, Slovak university of agriculture in Nitra. *Mathematics in Education, Research, and Applications, 5*(2), 78–83.
54. Michiels, A., Schepers, J., Vandekerkhof, P., & Cirillo, A., (2021). Leasing as an alternative form of financing within family businesses: The important advisory role of the accountant. *Sustainability, 13*(12), 6978.
55. Moyer, S. E., (1990). Capital adequacy ratio regulations and accounting choices in commercial banks. *Journal of Accounting and Economics, 13*(2), 123–154.
56. Muniroh, I., & Yuliati, A., (2021). Do cash flow and accounting profit information affect stock prices? *Journal of Accounting and Strategic Finance, 4*(1), 108–121.
57. Nobes, C. W., (1987). The pre-pacioli Indian double-entry system of bookkeeping: A comment. *Abacus, 23*(2), 182–184.
58. Nosofsky, R. M., (1988). Exemplar-based accounts of relations between classification, recognition, and typicality. *Journal of Experimental Psychology: Learning, Memory, and Cognition, 14*(4), 700.
59. O'Bryan, D., Berry, K. T., Troutman, C., & Quirin, J. J., (2000). Using accounting equation analysis to teach the statement of cash flows in the first financial accounting course. *Journal of Accounting Education, 18*(2), 147–155.
60. Országhová, D., & Horváthová, J., (2015). Pedagogical and statistical analysis of students' mathematical and language competencies. *Mathematics in Education, Research, and Applications, 1*(1), 28–35.

61. Ovunda, A. S., (2015). Luca Pacioli's double-entry system of accounting: A critique. *Research Journal of Finance and Accounting, 6*(18), 132–139.
62. Pandey, A., Tripathi, A., & Guhathakurta, K., (2022). The impact of banking regulations and accounting standards on estimating discretionary loan loss provisions. *Finance Research Letters, 44*, 102068.
63. Parker, R. H., (1993). The scope of accounting history: A note. *Abacus, 29*(1), 106–110.
64. Pechočiak, T., (2020). Education of mathematics during the coronavirus crisis. *Mathematics in Education, Research, and Applications, 6*, 2.
65. Perrin, J., (1998). Resource accounting and budgeting: From cash to accruals in 25 years. *Public Money and Management, 18*(2), 7–10.
66. Phillips, F., & Heiser, L., (2011). A field experiment examining the effects of accounting equation emphasis and transaction scope on students learning to journalize. *Issues in Accounting Education, 26*(4), 681–699.
67. Porter, T. M., (1992). Quantification and the accounting ideal in science. *Social Studies of Science, 22*(4), 633–651.
68. Potts, A. J., (1974). Teaching the rules of debit and credit. *Business Education World, 54*, 5–27.
69. Rapp, M. S., (2010). Information asymmetries and the value-relevance of cash flow and accounting figures–empirical analysis and implications for managerial accounting. *Problems and Perspectives in Management, 8*(2), 1–10.
70. Rayburn, J., (1986). The association of operating cash flow and accruals with security returns. *Journal of Accounting Research, 1*, 112–133.
71. Rebele, J. E., & Pierre, E. K. S., (2019). A commentary on learning objectives for accounting education programs: The importance of soft skills and technical knowledge. *Journal of Accounting Education, 48*, 71–79.
72. Robb, F. F., (1987). Accounting conventions. A cause of economic instability and company failure? *European Management Journal, 5*(2), 94–100.
73. Ronen, J., & Sorter, G., (1989). Reflections on "reflections on the FASB's conceptual framework for accounting and auditing." *Journal of Accounting, Auditing & Finance, 4*(1), 67–77.
74. Ruekert, R. W., & Walker, Jr. O. C., (1987). Marketing's interaction with other functional units: A conceptual framework and empirical evidence. *Journal of Marketing, 51*(1), 1–19.
75. Schaltegger, S., & Zvezdov, D., (2015). Gatekeepers of sustainability information: Exploring the roles of accountants. *Journal of Accounting & Organizational Change, 11*(3), 333–361.
76. Scofield, B. W., & Dye, W., (2009). Introducing the accounting equation with M&Ms. *American Journal of Business Education (AJBE), 2*(7), 127–138.

77. Scott, D. R., (1941). The basis for accounting principles. *Accounting Review, 1*, 341–349.
78. Semieniuk, G., & Weber, I. M., (2020). Inequality in energy consumption: Statistical equilibrium or a question of accounting conventions? *The European Physical Journal Special Topics, 229*(9), 1705–1714.
79. Shanikat, M., & Khan, A., (2013). Culture-specific forensic accounting conceptual framework: A skills set theoretical analysis. *International Journal of Business and Management, 8*(15), 112.
80. Taylor, J., (1996). What should be the role of the auditor-general in the context of managerialist government and new public management? *Australian Journal of Public Administration, 55*(4), 147–156.
81. Tillema, S., (2005). Towards an integrated contingency framework for MAS sophistication: Case studies on the scope of accounting instruments in Dutch power and gas companies. *Management Accounting Research, 16*(1), 101–129.
82. Tsiligiris, V., & Bowyer, D., (2021). Exploring the impact of 4IR on skills and personal qualities for future accountants: A proposed conceptual framework for university accounting education. *Accounting Education, 30*(6), 621–649.
83. Ulrychová, E., (2016). Students' mathematics knowledge–theory and exercises. *Journal on Efficiency and Responsibility in Education and Science, 9*(4), 103–110.
84. Vergoossen, R. G. A., (1997). Changes in accounting policies and investment analysts' fixation on accounting figures. *Accounting, Organizations and Society, 22*(6), 589–607.
85. Vickrey, D. W., (1970). Is accounting a measurement discipline? *The Accounting Review, 45*(4), 731–742.
86. Warsono, S., (2015). The relationality of rules of debit and credit. *The Indonesian Journal of Accounting Research, 18*(1), 1–20.
87. Winjum, J., (1970). Accounting in its age of stagnation. *The Accounting Review, 45*(4), 743–761.
88. Xiao, J. J., & Olson, G. I., (1993). Mental accounting and saving behavior. *Home Economics Research Journal, 22*(1), 92–109.
89. Yamaguchi, T., & Oba, M., (2020). Measurable interactive application to find out user recognition and strategy when problem-solving. *J. of Software, 15*(1), 12–22.
90. Yamey, B. S., (2014). The development of company accounting conventions. In: *Evolution of Corporate Financial Reporting (RLE Accounting)* (Vol. 1, pp. 243–252).
91. Yeung, K., Richards, J., Goemer, E., Lozano, P., Lapham, G., Williams, E., & Bradley, K., (2020). Costs of using evidence-based implementation strategies for behavioral health integration in an extensive primary care system. *Health Services Research, 55*(6), 913–923.
92. Yu, F., (2005). Accounting transparency and the term structure of credit spreads. *Journal of Financial Economics, 75*(1), 53–84.

93. Zulaiha, I., Miraza, M., & Muda, I., (2022). The mechanism of prepare closing entries and a post-closing trial balance. *Journal of Positive School Psychology, 6*(3), 2395–2400.

94. Zvezdov, D., Schaltegger, S., & Bennett, M., (2010). The increasing involvement of accountants in corporate sustainability management. *Journal of the Asia-Pacific Center for Environmental Accountability, 16*(4), 20–31.

CHAPTER 2

ACCOUNTING PROCESS AND ADJUSTMENT OF ACCOUNTS

UNIT INTRODUCTION

Financial statements aid individuals in understanding the company's condition at Rhino Foods, Inc. From the corrected balance sheet; we instantly created accounting information. However, it is simple to make mistakes because there are too many small details in the final accounting operations. A worksheet is one technique to reduce record-keeping errors and simplify the end-of-period processes.

The function of spreadsheets in accounting will be discussed in this chapter. The remaining processes in the accounting cycle, particularly the closing procedure, will also be covered, utilizing Pioneer Advertising Agency Inc. as an instance. After that, balance sheets will be categorized and rectified entries (Jorge et al., 2018).

Various modifications required after every accounting quarter are already known. These changes were needed to bring a firm's books and records up to date in preparation for calculating and documenting its revenue and financial situation. However, it is demonstrated how those modifications would be applied to the financial statements. That task will be the focus of this chapter.

Learning Objectives

At the end of this chapter, readers will be able to:

- Prepare a worksheet
- Explain the process of closing the books
- Describe the content and purpose of a post-closing trial balance
- State the required steps in the accounting cycle
- Explain the approaches to preparing to correct entries
- Identify the sections of a classified balance sheet
- Explain the time assumption
- Explain the accrual basis of accounting
- Explain the reasons for adjusting entries and identify the major types of adjusting entries
- Prepare to change access for deferrals
- Prepare to alter access for accruals
- Describe the nature and purpose of an adjusted trial balance

Key Terms

- Accrual-basis accounting
- Accruals
- Accrued expenses
- Accrued revenues
- Accrued revenues
- Adjusted trial balance
- Adjusting entries
- Book value
- Calendar year
- Classified balance sheet
- Correcting entries
- Current liabilities
- Stockholders' equity
- Worksheet

2.1. MAKING FINANCIAL STATEMENTS

Let's examine some of England Vacations Company's financial data to demonstrate the method for generating financial statements. Britain commenced operations early in 20X3. England concluded that the following modifying entries were necessary when completing its financial accounts for the year ended December 31, 20X3. The figures are all "supposed," therefore there is no need for worry (Ball et al., 2015).

12-31-X3	Depreciation Expense	5,000	
	Accumulated Depreciation		5,000
	To record annual depreciation expense for equipment with a 9-year life ($45,000/9)		
12-31-X3	Salaries Expense	2,000	
	Salaries Payable		2,000
	To record accrued salaries due to employees at the end of December		
12-31-X3	Interest Expense	1,200	
	Interest Payable		1,200
	To record accrued interest on note payable ($20,000 X 6%)		
12-31-X3	Unearned Revenue	1,800	
	Revenue		1,800
	Year-end adjusting entry to refect "earned" portion of tours sold in advance		

Figure 2.1. Schematic of making a financial statement (Source: Larry M. Walther, Creative Commons License).

The illustration compares England's balance sheet before and after the modifying entries discussed above. If England had constructed its financial accounts only based on the entire trial balance, the data that was provided would have been both inadequate and inaccurate (Hopkins, 1996). Instead, it is essential to use the corrected trial balance since it has been brought up to date to represent the year-end modifying entries; this is the case since the updated trial balance has been revised.

2.1.1. Actual Procedure for Adjustments

Typically, a business will compile its trial balance, examine it for possible changes, and create a list of required modifying entries. It's not always obvious to determine what needs to be adjusted. Typically, it needs to be reviewed by a person with extensive business and accounting experience (McCracken, 1998). Practically speaking, a corporation should not permit unlimited access to its accounting system to input year-end modifications because this will result in an excessive number of mistakes and erroneous entries. Instead, a business typically has a set procedure where submitted entries are recorded on the form. A chief controller receives these forms and analyzes and authorizes any recommended entries. The data input into the accounting system is then approved using the authorized journal vouchers as supporting documentation. After the modifying entries are made in the journal and transferred to the correct ledger accounts, the corrected trial balance can be created using the most recent ledger (Stewar et al., 2003).

2.1.2. Financial Statements

In most cases, the corrected trial balance is adequate to assist in compiling financial statements. Take time to trace the numbers from England's modified trial balance to the following financial information:

ENGLAND TOURS COMPANY
Income Statement
For the Year Ending December 31, 20X3

Revenues		
Tour services		$32,800
Expenses		
Salaries	$17,000	
Advertising	5,000	
Fuel	2,000	
Depreciation	5,000	
Interest	1,200	30,200
Net income		$2,600

ENGLAND TOURS COMPANY
Statement of Retained Earnings
For the Year Ending December 31, 20X3

Beginning ratained earnings	$ -
Plus: Net income	2,600
	$2,600
Less: Dividends	1,000
Ending ratained earnings	$1,600

ENGLAND TOURS COMPANY
Balance Sheet
December 31, 20X3

Assets		
Cash		$15,000
Accounts receivable		4,500
Equipment	$45,000	
Less: Accumulated depr.	(5,000)	40,000
Total assets		$60,000
Liabilities		
Accounts payable	$ 4,000	
Salaries payable	2,000	
Interest payable	1,200	
Notes payable	20,000	
Unearned revenue	1,200	
Total liabilities		$28,400
Stockholder's equity		
Capital stock	$30,000	
Retained earnings	1,600	
Total stockholders's equity		31,600
Total liabilities and equity		$60,000

Figure 2.2. Schematic of some examples of financial statements (Source: Larry M. Walther, Creative Commons License).

2.1.3. COMPUTERIZATION

Preparing financial statements is predominantly mechanical and may be automated easily (Stewar et al., 2003). Once the corrected entries have been generated and entered, all accounting software will quickly process the data to create financial statements. Consequently, one might well be tempted to disregard the need to know how to transfer numbers from a corrected trial balance to a financial statement set. In some ways, that is correct, just as it is correct that if a calculator is available, one does not have to comprehend how to add and subtract. The importance of knowing addition and subtraction is recognized, regardless of whether one uses a calculator. Assume, in the same vein, that knowing the flow of data into income statements is indeed a prerequisite for expanding the accounting expertise (Buell & Schicha, 1990).

2.1.4. A Worksheet Strategy

It's possible that, on occasion, you could want to generate financial statements that account for any necessary modifications without really amending the relevant journals and account balances. Why? Even if the company does not correctly create and record modifying entries each month, a manager could still want to see monthly financial reports; this can be accomplished through a worksheet technique. Before suggesting that the actual journal or ledger be revised, an auditor might employ a worksheet to generate financial information that considers suggested modifications (Deshpande & Modak, 2003). These statements would then be prepared after the auditor had proposed that the genuine journal or ledger be changed. At any given time, a request might be made to the accounting division to create financial statements. However, instead of interrupting their regular workflow and making book entries beyond the normal cycle, the accounting division could make the income statements using an informal worksheet.

KEYWORD

An auditor is a person or a firm appointed by a company to execute an audit.

The worksheet shown below is an example of one of these. The information initially given for England is consistent with the data and corrections. The uncorrected trial balance is the initial set of columns. The end-of-period modifications are shown in the following collection of columns. The corrected trial balance columns are created by combining the data in the initial two groups of columns. The worksheet's final three pairs of columns represent the relevant financial statement adaptations of the values in the queues for the corrected trial balance. Cash, for instance, is "suitably" stretched to the debit side of the financial statement pair of columns since it is an investment account with a debit balance. Similar to Service Revenue, which is expanded to the income statement credit column, it is a revenue statement account with a credit balance. This expansion of accounts must occur for each line item in the amended trial balance (Yamaguchi & Oba, 2020).

After extending all amounts from the modified trial balance to the relevant income statement columns, the financial statement sections are subtotaled. If credits surpass debits, earnings outweigh expenditures. An overabundance of debits over credits would result in a net deficit. To finish the worksheet, the total profit or loss is put in the lower part of the financial statement columns so that debits equal credits. The total revenue for England Tours was 2600 dollars, so a negative is required to equal the financial statement pair. A credit is recorded to offset the debit in the lower part of the maintained profits columns. This credit is the annual income that needs to be added to maintained incomes to conclude the official statement of retained profits. This sum is debited in the controlled profits columns and attributed in the balance sheet columns, balancing out both pairs of columns.

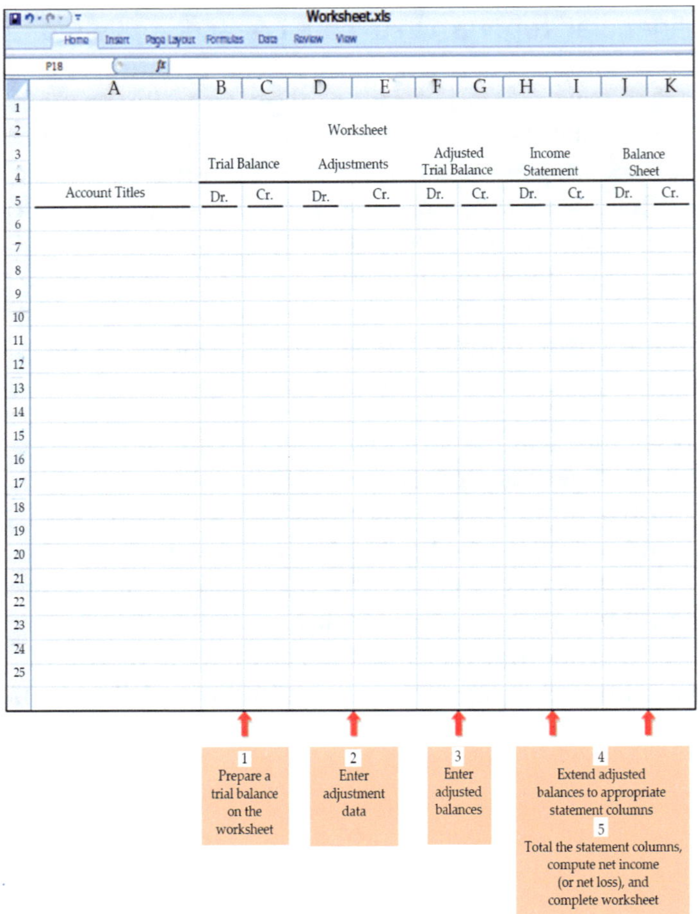

Figure 2.3. Graph representing a worksheet (Source: Larry M. Walther, Creative Commons License).

A worksheet is a multi-column form utilized in the process of adjustment and the preparation of financial statements. The worksheet, as the title suggests, is a tool for working. It is not an indelible accounting technique (Martínez et al., 2012). It is not a journal or a component of the ledger accounts. A worksheet is simply a tool for making modifying entries and financial statements. Worksheets are typically computerized by businesses that use an electronic spreadsheet tool like Excel.

The figure below depicts the basic layout of a worksheet and the five stages involved in its creation. Every step is carried out in the order that it was presented. The utilization of a spreadsheet is not required. When a corporation decides to use one, preparing financial statements from the spreadsheet begins. After completing the preparation of the income statement, it then journalizes and uploads the changes previously entered in the spreadsheet columns as part of the process. Worksheets make it easier to present leadership and other relevant individuals with the financial statements at an earlier period; this benefits everyone involved.

KEYWORD

A ledger is a book or digital record containing bookkeeping entries.

2.1.5. Steps in Making a Worksheet

To demonstrate how to create a worksheet, Pioneer Advertising Agency Inc.'s 31st October trial balance and modification data are used (Hughes et al., 2011). In the figures, every phase of the procedure is outlined, and examples of every step are provided.

2.1.5.1. Make Trial Balance on a Worksheet

In the column of account titles, insert the names of all ledgers with balances. In the trial balance columns, insert credit and debit values from the register. Pioneer Advertising Agency Inc.'s worksheet trial balance is depicted in the figure below.

2.1.5.2. Insert the Modifications in the Adjustments Columns

Enter all modifications in the adjustment columns of the worksheet. Utilize appropriate trial balance accounts for inputting modifications. If different accounts are required, add them directly below the trial balance totals (Salameh et al., 2019). For every adjustment entry, the credit and debit are denoted by a distinct letter. Keying is the phrase used to explain this operation. Companies do not record the modifications in the journal till after completing the spreadsheet and preparing the income statements.

The adjustments for Pioneer Advertising Agency Inc. have been entered in the adjustments columns of the spreadsheet as follows.

- Pioneer debits 1,500 dollars from Materials Expense and credits 1,500 dollars to Supplies expense for the price of supplies used.
- Pioneer debits $50 from an extra account, Insurance Expense, for the lapsed insurance and credits 50 dollars to Prepaid Insurance.
- The business needs two more declining balance accounts. Amortization for the month is debited from the Depreciation Expense of 40 dollars and credited to Consolidated Depreciation Equipment of 40 dollars.
- Pioneer pays back 400 dollars in Unearned Service Revenue for rendered services and credits 400 dollars in Service Revenue.
- Pioneer adds Service Revenue of 200 dollars and debits Accounts Receivable of 200 dollars for services rendered but not invoiced (Yeung et al., 2020).
- The business requires two more interest-related accounts. It deducts Interest Expense by 50 dollars and credits Interest Payable by 50 to account for accrued interest.
- Pioneer pays Salaries and Wages Expenses by 1,200 dollars for outstanding salaries and credits Wages and Salaries Payable by the same amount.
- After Pioneer has inputted all of the modifications, the columns of adjustments are added together to demonstrate their equivalence.

KEYWORD

Service revenue is the net income a company earns from the services provided.

2.1.5.3. Enter Modified Balances in the Modified Trial Balance Columns

The quantities entered into the first four columns of the spreadsheet for every account are added together to get the modified balance for the account (Joseph & Konrad, 2009). Pioneer does this. For instance, the Prepaid Insurance account seems to have a debit balance of 600 dollars and the credit balance of 50 dollars in the adjustments columns when looking at the trial balance columns of the spreadsheet. As a consequence, there is a debit balance of 550 dollars recorded in the columns of the corrected trial balance. The amount entered into the account's adjusted trial balance column will be entered into the ledger once the modifying entries have been journalized and posted to the log.

The columns of the corrected trial balance are summed to demonstrate equality once Pioneer has inputted all account balances. If the totals of columns do not match, the accounting information will be erroneous since the columns will not balance (Velázquez & Carrillo, 2013).

2.1.5.4. *Encompass Adjusted Trial Balance Amounts*

The 4th step is to add modified trial balance figures to the worksheet's financial statement and balance sheet columns. Pioneer populates the balance sheet credit and debit columns with balance sheet accounts. It inserts cash in the debit column of the balance sheet and Notes Due in the credit column of a balance sheet, for example. Pioneer adds Equipment Consolidated Depreciation to the credit column of the balance sheet. The reason for this is that consolidated depreciation is a credit-balanced counter-asset account.

TIPS

When total of debit column is higher than the credit column, The trial balance is temporarily balance by showing suspense account in Column.

Pioneer transfers any amounts in Common Stock and Cash Equivalents to the credit column of the balance sheet. Furthermore, since it is a stockholders' equity account having a debit balance, it moves the Dividend balance to the debit column of the balance sheet (Torres et al., 2014).

2.1.5.5. *Aggregate the Statement Columns*

The corporation should now sum every column of the financial information. The period's net earnings or loss is the disparity among the totals of the two columns on the income statement. If total credits surpass total debits, net income will result. In this situation, the company enters "Net Income" in the title space of the account. The amount is then entered into the debit column of the financial statement and the credit column of the balance sheet. The debit amount evens the columns of the income statement, while the credit amount evens the columns of the balance sheet. Additionally, the credit in the balance sheet column represents the boost in stockholders' equity caused by net income.

What if the overall debits in the financial statement columns surpass the total credits? The business has a massive loss (Al Shammari, 2017). The amount of the significant deficit is entered in the credit column of the financial statement and the debit column of the balance sheet.

2.1.6. Making Financial Statements from the Worksheet

After completing a worksheet, a business has all the information needed to prepare financial statements in its possession. The columns of the income statement are used to create the income statement. The balance sheet columns generate the balance sheet and retained inflows statement. The firm has not yet made any modifying entries or journalized any adjustments. As a result, certain accounts' ledger balances and financial statement amounts differ.

The total value displayed on the standard stock spreadsheet does not vary from the start to the completion of the period, except if the corporation distributes excess inventory during the time frame being analyzed (Mijušković, 2016). The account for Pioneer's retained earnings did not have any money, so the worksheet does not include a column for that particular account. This account will not have a balance after the first fiscal year of the firm unless dividends and net income have been recorded to retained earnings.

Figure 2.4. Statement of Income (Source: Christopher J. Skuosen, Creative Commons License).

PIONEER ADVERTISING AGENCY INC.
Income Statement
For the Month Ended October 31, 2015

Revenues		
Service revenue		$10,600
Expenses		
Salaries and wages expense	$5,200	
Supplies expense	1,500	
Rent expense	900	
Insurance expense	50	
Interest expense	50	
Depreciation expense	40	
Total expenses		7,740
Net income		$ 2,860

Figure 2.5. Statement of Retained Earnings (Source: Christopher J. Skuosen, Creative Commons License).

PIONEER ADVERTISING AGENCY INC.
Retained Earnings Statement
For the Month Ended October 31, 2015

Retained earning, October 1	$ –0–
Add: Net income	2,860
	2,860
Less: Dividends	500
Retained earnings, October 31	$2,360

PIONEER ADVERTISING AGENCY INC.
Balance Sheet
October 31, 2015

Assets		
Cash		$15,200
Accounts receivable		200
Supplies		1,000
Prepaid insurance		550
Equipment	$5,000	
Less: Accumulated depreciation-equipment	40	4,960
Total assets		$21,910
Liabilities and Stockholders's Equity		
Liabilities		
Notes payable	$5,000	
Accounts payable	2,500	
Interest payable	50	
Unearned service revenue	800	
Salaries and wages payable	1,200	
Total liabilities		$ 9,550
Stockholders' equity		
Common stock	10,000	
Retained earnings	2.360	
Total stockholders' equity		12,360
Total liabilities and stockholders' equity		$21,910

Figure 2.6. Illustration of a Balance Sheet (Larry M. Walther, Creative Commons License).

Before companies journalize and issue adjusting entries, businesses can create financial statements using a worksheet to track their data. Nevertheless, the filled worksheet is not intended to replace official financial statements (Torabi & Gholinia, 2010). The information in the financial statement columns is not presented in the exact format as the data that is shown in the financial statements themselves. The purpose of a worksheet is primarily for the accountant to use as a tool in their work; corporations don't typically share worksheets with management or other parties.

2.1.7. Creating Adjusting Entries from the Worksheet

A spreadsheet cannot be the foundation for posting to ledgers as it is not a journal. The business should journalize the changes and upload these to the log to modify the accounts (Shang & Chang, 2010). The worksheet's modified columns are used to create the adjusting entries. The descriptions of modifications at the bottom of the spreadsheet and reference letters in the modifications columns both aid in locating the adjusting entries. When a worksheet is employed, the journalizing and uploading of adjusting entries come after the creation of financial statements. The image implies England Tours was founded in early 20X3. As a result, there wasn't any initial retained earnings balance might wonder how a starting maintained earnings balance would affect the worksheet (AlAdwani et al., 2022). If you check England's 20X4 spreadsheet, you'll notice that the 1,600 dollars ending retained profits from 20X3 roll over to serve as the starting balance for 20X4.

2.2. THE CYCLE OF ACCOUNTING AND CLOSING METHOD

The accounting procedures discussed thus far illustrate the following main steps (Low & Song, 2014):

KEYWORD

The accounting cycle is a collective process of identifying, analyzing, and recording the accounting events of a company.

- transactions are documented in a journal
- journal entries are uploaded to suitable ledger accounts
- trial balance is made
- adjusting entries are created and forwarded
- a modified trial balance is made
- a production of formal financial statements takes place

It seems the accounting cycle is finished, which involves recording data on transactions and events, putting that data through a logical procedure that culminates in generating relevant financial statements, and then closing the books. And perhaps most crucially, there are extensive records that detail every transaction and the activity of every account that has been left over. There should not be any surprise that the fundamental components of this accounting approach have persisted for a long time (Low et al., 2016).

2.2.1. The Closing Method

There is still one final phase to do. The procedure is referred to as the closing phase. The closing procedure serves two purposes, which are as follows:

When an accounting period comes to a close, one of its functions is to ensure that the balance of the retained revenue account in the general ledger is identical to that of the end-of-period total. It is important to remember that documenting each line item of income, expenditure, or dividend doesn't naturally cause an updating charge or credits to retained earnings. As a result, the quantity of retained earnings at the start of the period continues to be recorded in the ledger till the procedure of closing "updates" the retained revenue account to reflect the influence of the activities during the period (Koshkin et al., 1998).

Accounts for income, expenses, and dividends reflect sums for the duration; after every period, these accounts should be "zeroed out." One has restored these accounts to 0 to start the subsequent accounting cycle. On the other hand, asset, liabilities, and equity accounts are referred to as real accounts since their balances are maintained from one period to the next. One does not, for instance, "start over" whenever collecting assets such as cash and other resources because their balances roll over (Sarkar et al., 2020).

Closing entails four steps: (i) close revenue accounts (to the non-financial statement account known as Income Summary), (ii) close expenditure accounts to Revenue Summary, (iii) close the Revenue Summary account to Retained Earnings, and (iv) close the Dividend account to Retained Earnings. As a result, all revenues and costs are "corralled" in the Income Summary. The revenue or loss is subsequently swept into Retained Earnings alongside dividends. Remember that concluding retained earnings equal starting retained earnings plus revenue fewer dividends; similarly, the closing procedure adjusts the starting retained earnings to move ahead to the final balance.

The following are the final entries for England Tours might find it helpful to verify the accounts and quantities shown below to those in the prior corrected trial balance (Fekete et al., 2016).

12-31-X3	Revenues	32,800	
	Income Summary		32,800
	To close revenues to income Summary		
12-31-X3	Income Summary	30,200	
	Salaries Expense		17,000
	Advertising Expense		5,000
	Fuel Expense		2,000
	Depreciation Expense		5,000
	Interest Expense		1,200
	To close expenses to income Summary		
12-31-X3	Income Summary	2,600	
	Retained Earnings		2,600
	To close income Summary to retained earnings (balance equals net income)		
12-31-X3	Retained Earnings	1,000	
	Dividends		1,000
	To close divideds		

Figure 2.7. Schematic of the closing entries (Larry M. Walther, Creative Commons License).

Note that the result of the entries mentioned above is to (a) upgrade the retained profits account and (b) bring the temporary (income, expenditure, and dividends) accounts to 0 balances. In addition, the Income Summary account is kept blank (32,800 dollars (cr) = 30,200 dollars (dr) + 2,600 dollars (dr)). The subsequent T-accounts illustrate the impact of closing entries on the different accounts:

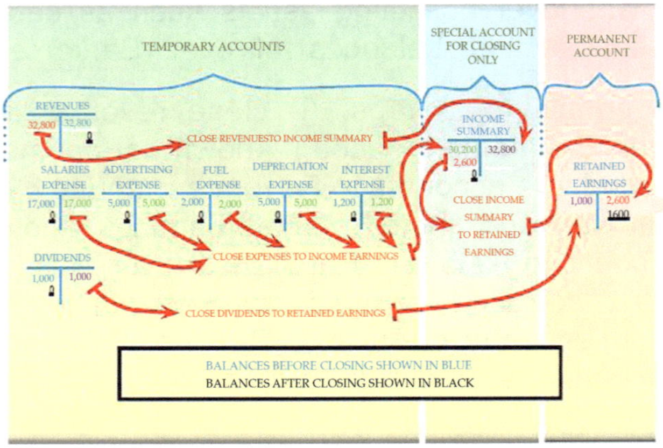

Figure 2.8. Diagram showing the closing entries' effects on the different accounts (Source: Christopher J. Skuosen, Creative Commons License).

2.2.2. Post-Closing Trial Balance

Only the accounts that appear on the financial statements are included in the post-close trial balance, indicating the account's state after the closing procedure has been completed (Asamoah, 2018). The post-closing trial balance is not a fair financial statement; instead, it is a method used to show that accounts are in the balance after they have been closed. This trial balance does not include income, cost, or dividend accounts because they were all cleared out with zeros when the books were closed.

Figure 2.9. Schematic of the Post-Closing Balance Sheet (Source: Christopher J. Skuosen, Creative Commons License).

ENGLAND TOURS COMPANY
Trail Balance
December 31, 20X3

	Debits	Credits
Cash	$15,500	
Accounts receivable	4,500	
Equipment	45,000	
Accumulated depreciation		$ 5,000
Accounts payable		4,000
Salaties payable		2,000
Interest payable		1,200
Notes payable		20,000
Unearned revenue		1,200
Capital stock		30,000
Retained earnings		1,600
	$65,000	$65,000

The business prepares the accounts for the following period after the accounting cycle. The books are closed at this point. The company distinguishes between interim and regular statements while closing the books (Ruata et al., 2018).

On the other hand, permanent accounts are related to one or more upcoming accounting cycles. They include all balance-sheet charges, including the accounting for stockholders' equity. Permanent accounts are not shut down periodically. Instead, the business forwards the permanent account balances to the following accounting cycle (Barral et al., 2021).

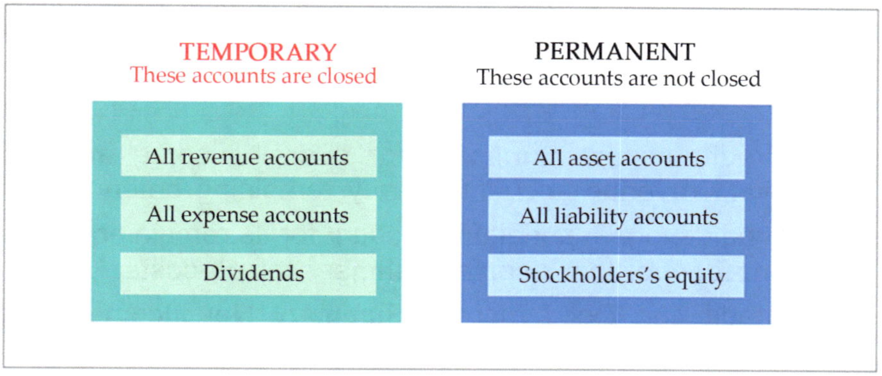

Figure 2.10. Schematic showing the accounts in every classification (Source: Larry M. Walther and Christopher J. Skuosen, Creative Commons License).

2.2.2.1. Making Closing Entries

The corporation uses closing entries to move transitory account balances to the everlasting shareholders' asset account, Retained Earnings, after the accounting cycle.

Closing entries officially record the shift of net income and Dividends to Retained Profits in the ledger. The consequences of these entries are shown in the retained revenue statement. Closing entries result in a 0 balance in all temporary accounts. The transitory accounts are then prepared to gather facts in the following accounting cycle, independent of the data from previous periods. Permanent accounts are not terminated (Zulaiha et al., 2022).

The accounting cycle must always begin with the preparation of the ledger and the uploading of closing entries. After preparing its financial information, the corporation moves on to the next phase. In contradiction to the processes in the cycle already seen, businesses typically do not journalize and post-closing entries until the end of the yearly accounting cycle; this is because corporations wait until

TIPS

Temporary accounts only have a specific accounting term in mind. They comprise the Dividend account as well as each income statement account. After the period, the corporation shuts all interim accounts.

then to close their books. Consequently, all transitory accounts will have data for the whole year within them.

When making closing entries, businesses can immediately close every account on the income statement to Retained Earnings (Clayton, 1969). On the other hand, doing so would result in a large amount of detail being recorded in the account that permanently tracks Retained Earnings. Instead, businesses move their expenses and revenue reports to a new transitory account known as the income summary. Then they move any net gain or loss from this account to the retained revenue account.

Typically, closing entries are derived from the ledger's modified balances. They could make separate closing entries for every nominal account, but the four entries below more effectively achieve the desired outcome (Baker, 1984):

- Credit Income Summary for overall income and debit every revenue account for any remaining balance.
- Credit every expenditure account for its remaining balance and deduct the Income Summary for all costs.
- Credit and Debit Income Summary Net income for the quantity of Retained Earnings.
- Credit Dividends for the outstanding balance in the Dividend ledger and debit Retained revenue for the same sum.

Did you get it?

In the general ledger, organizations keep closing entries. These entries are identified by the caption Closing Entries written in the diary between the last modifying entry and the initial closing entry. The closing entries are then posted to the accounting records.

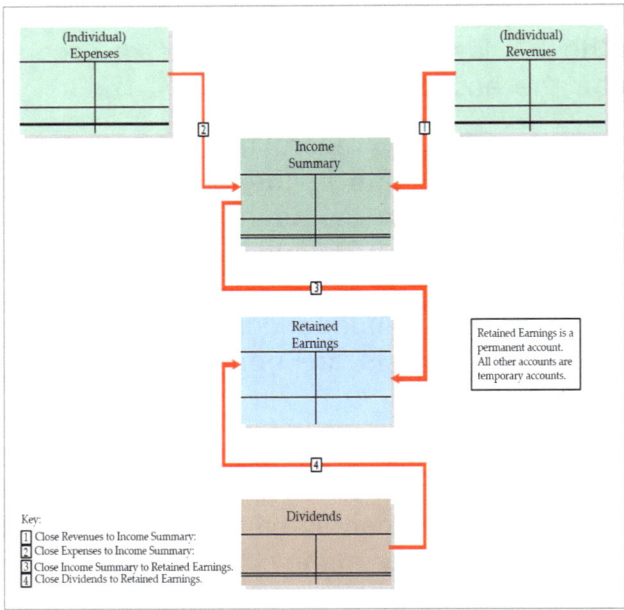

Figure 2.11. Illustration of the closing procedure (Source: Larry M. Walther, Creative Commons License).

If there were a massive loss (due to expenses exceeding revenues), the third entry in the worksheet would be altered:

In practice, corporations typically make closing entries just after the conclusion of the fiscal year. To demonstrate journalizing and submitting closing entries, it will be supposed Pioneer Advertising Agency Inc. ends its books monthly (Owen, 1949). The figure below depicts the deadline for entries on October 31.

GENERAL JOURNAL				J3
Date	Account TTutiles and Explanation	Ref.	Debit	Credit
	Closing Entries			
2015	(1)			
Oct. 31	Service Revenue	400	10,600	
	Income Summary	350		10,600
	(To close revenue account)			
	(2)			
31	Income Summary	350	7,740	
	Supplies Expense	631		1,500
	Depreciation Expense	711		40
	Insurance Expense	722		50
	Salaries and Wages Expense	726		5,200
	Rent Expense	729		900
	Interest Expense	905		50
	(To close expense account)			
	(3)			
31	Income Summary	350	2,860	
	Retained Earnings	320		2,860
	(To close net income to retained earnings)			
	(4)			
31	Retained Earnings	320	500	
	Dividends	332		500
	(To close dividends to retained earnings)			

Figure 2.12. Schematic of Closing Entries (Source: Larry M. Walther, Creative Commons License).

It is important to note that the overall numbers in the worksheet's debit and credit columns for the financial report correspond to the amounts in columns (1) and (2) for the Income Summary. Several words of caution should be taken into account when composing concluding entries: (1) one should take care not to 0 out the income and expenditure balances by accident since this will result in a doubling of both. (2) One should not close the Dividends account using the Income Summary interface. The payment of dividends is neither considered an expense nor is it taken into account when calculating net revenue (Peragallo, 1971).

2.2.2.2. Posting Closing Entries

The uploading of the closing entries and emphasizing the accounts are shown in the figure below. Once the closing entries are posted, you should take more notice that all transitory accounts have a balance of 0 must also be aware that the amount in Retained Earnings after the accounting cycle indicates the corporation's total cumulative unclaimed earnings. Pioneer only uses the Income Summary account at closing. It does not keep a journal throughout the year and upload entries to this account (Knost, 1948).

As part of the closing procedure, Pioneer totals, balances, and double outlines its transitory accounts, including Income, Expenditure, and Dividends. It does not close its regular reports, which include its resources, liabilities, and shareholders' equity. Pioneer instead puts a single underline underneath the existing entries for the permanent accounts. The balance of an account is then recorded underneath the single underline and carried over to the subsequent period (Dewangan & ikhar, 2018). (For instance, see Retained Earnings.)

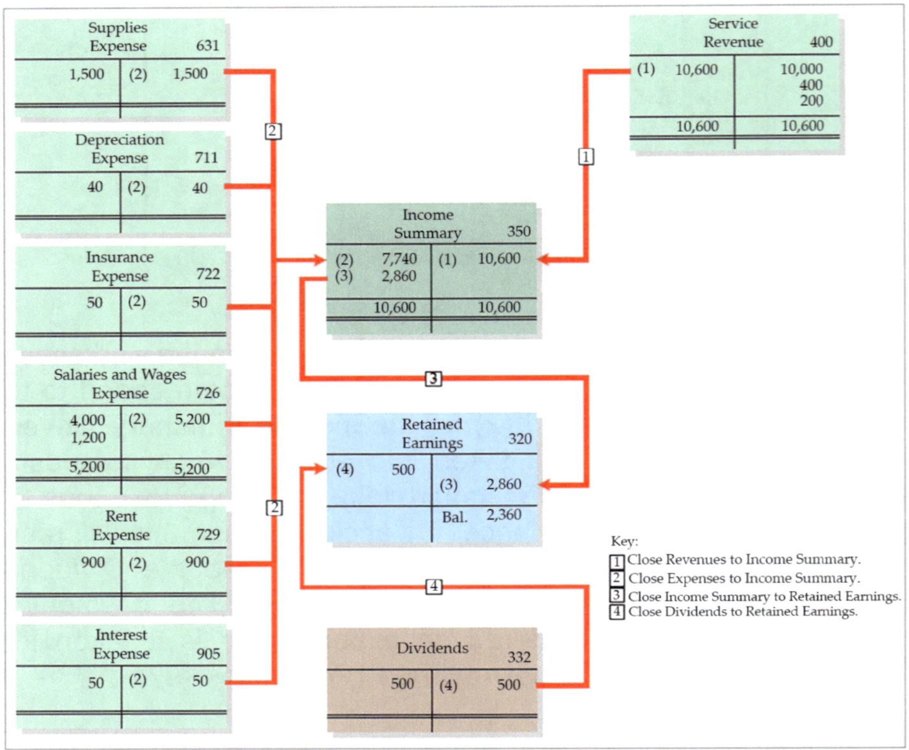

Figure 2.13. Pioneer totals, balances, and double outlines its transitory accounts (incomes, expenditures, and dividends) as part of the closing procedure (Source: Christopher J. Skuosen, *Creative Commons License).*

A second trial balance, known as a post-closing trial balance, is created from the ledger after Pioneer has journalized and recorded all closing entries (Peragallo, 1956). Following the journalizing and uploading of closing entries, the post-closing trial balance shows the everlasting accounts and their balances. This trial balance demonstrates the comparability of the balances carried over from one accounting cycle to the following in permanent accounts. Only permanent balance sheet accounts will be included in the post-closing trial balance because all transitory accounts will have 0 balances.

PIONEER ADVERTISING AGENCY INC.
Post-Closing Trial Balance
October 31, 2015

	Debit	Credit
Cash	$ 15,200	
Accounts Receivable	200	
Supplies	1,000	
Prepaid Insurance	550	
Equipment	5,000	
Accumulated Depreciation Equipment		$ 40
Notes Payable		5,000
Accounts Payable		2,500
Unearned Service Revenue		800
Salaries and Wages Payable		1,200
Interest Payable		50
Common Stock		10,000
Retained Earnings		2,360
	$21,950	$21,950

Figure 2.14. Pioneer Advertising Agency Inc.'s post-closing trial balance (Source: Christopher J. Skuosen, Creative Commons License).

A post-closing trial balance demonstrates that the closing entries were appropriately journalized and reported by the company. It also indicates that financial accounting is in the balance after the fiscal period. Moreover, it does not demonstrate, like the trial balance, that Pioneer has logged all occurrences or that the journal is accurate (Littleton, 1926). For instance, even if a payment is not journalized and submitted or is journalized and reposted, the post-closing trial balance will still balance.

2.2.3. Revisiting Computerization

Many different accounting software systems use database logic as their foundation. The user can query with relatively few limitations thanks to these practical tools. As a consequence of this, one was able to make a demand for financial outcomes for virtually any duration of time (e.g., the 45 days that ended on October 15, 20XX), even though the information pertained to a period that occurred many years before (Morrens et al., 2008). When circumstances like these arise, deleting the accounts becomes significantly less important. To explain it in the simplest terms possible, the computer can mine all activity data and extract the accounts and quantities corresponding to nearly any desired period.

2.3. REVERSING ENTRIES

A different accounting method that could help to streamline records management is reversing entries. Modifying access is "undone" by a reversing entry; a journal entry will soon be observed how streamlining the procedure can be accomplished by changing entries (Whiting et al., 1999).

Let's start with this illustration, which does not use reversing entries. After 20X3, an adjustment entry was created to account for 2 thousand dollars in accrued salary. The following payday was on January 15, 20X4, when 5 thousand dollars was distributed to the workforce. On that day, a debit had to be made to Wages Payable and Wages expense.

Figure 2.15. Drawing deprived of Reversing Entries (Source: Larry M. Walther and Christopher J. Skuosen, Creative Commons License).

20X3			
12-31-X3	Salaries Expense (20X3)	2,000	
	Salaries Payable		2,000
	Adjusting entry for accrued salaries due to employees at the end of December		
	Note: closing would "zero-out" all expense account at the end of 20X3		
20X4			
1-15-X4	Salaries Expense (20X4)	3,000	
	Salaries Payable	2,000	
	Cash		5,000
	To record payroll, part of which related to prior year service		

The total effect of these methods is to document the right amount of wage expenditure for 20X4 (2 thousand dollars credit and 5 thousand dollars debit results in the appropriate net pay cost debit of 3,000 dollars). You might find it peculiar to credit an expenditure account on January 1, as it does not make sense on its own (Draper et al., 1996). The credit is meaningful only in conjunction with the ensuing deduction on January 15. Observe from the accompanying figure that the outcomes of both strategies are the same.

Reversing entries will expedite the accounting procedure in practice. For instance, on the first day of pay after the reversing entry, a "regular" journal entry can be produced to record the entire amount of salary paid as cost – without taking into account the consequences of any previous modifying entry. Reversing entries are typically used for modifying entries that include the accounting of accumulated income and expenses, notably those involving future cash flows. The same outcome is obtained whether or not reversing entries are utilized.

2.3.1. Reversing Entries—Noncompulsory Step

Sure, accountants choose to reverse specific adjustment entries at the start of the subsequent accounting cycle. A reversing entry is the opposite of the prior period's modifying entry. Reversing entries are a discretionary bookkeeping technique; they are not essential for the accounting process (Patzig et al., 2011).

KEYWORD

Bookkeeping is the recording of financial transactions, and is part of the process of accounting in business and other organizations.

2.3.2. Altering Entries—A Preventable Step

Regrettably, there is a chance that mistakes will occur throughout the recording procedure. As early as errors are discovered, businesses must immediately repair them by journalizing and recording the appropriate entries in the relevant ledgers. If there are no mistakes in the accounting records, then there is no requirement for any rectifying entries to be made. There are several distinctions between adjusting entries and modifying entries, which one needs to be aware of. To begin, the accounting cycle would not be complete without changing entries.

In contrast, if there are no mistakes in the records, correcting any of the entries is not required. Second, businesses do not journalize and post changes until the last day of the accounting cycle. On the other hand, when companies find errors in their records, they update those records to reflect the corrections. In conclusion, altering entries will invariably affect one balance sheet account and one income statement account at a minimum (Izquierdo et al., 2006).

It is helpful to compare the inaccurate and accurate entries to identify the corrected ones; this makes it easier to determine which accounts and amounts need to be adjusted and which ones do not. The accountant compares and then enters a correction to the accounts. The following two Mercato Co. cases are examples of this strategy (Hille, 1973).

CASE 1

A customer's 50 dollars cash gathering on the account was journalized and recorded by Mercato Co. on May 10 as a 50 dollars debit to cash and 50 dollars credit to Service Revenue. The business realized the error when the consumer paid the final balance on May 20.

Incorrect Entry (May 10)			Correct Entry (May 10)		
Cash	50		Cash	50	
Service Revenue		50	Accounts Receivable		50

KEYWORD

Accounts receivable are the funds that customers owe your company for products or services that have been invoiced.

Comparing the wrong and accurate entries demonstrates that the 50 dollars debit to cash is exact. The 50 dollars credit to Service Revenue was intended for Accounts Receivable. In the accounting, Service Revenue and Accounts Receivable have been inflated. The subsequent correction is made by Mercato (Ornish et al., 1998).

Correcting Entry

May 20	Service Revenue	50	
	Accounts Receivable		50
	(To correct entry of May 10)		

CASE 2

On May 18, Mercato charged $450 worth of equipment to the customer's account. The purchase was recorded in a journal with a debit entry of 45 dollars to equipment and a credit entry of 45 dollars to Accounts Payable. When Mercato acquired the monthly report for May from the creditor on June 3, the day the error was found, it was for May.

When the two entries are compared, it is clear that two of the accounts are inaccurate. There is a discrepancy of 405 dollars between the reported amount for accounts payable and the reported amount for equipment. The following entry is a correction that was made by Mercato (Kuriyam et al., 1997).

It is feasible to delete the wrong entry and then create the entry that should have been there in its place. This is an alternative to creating a corrected entry. This strategy will lead to a more significant number of entries and reposting than would be the case with a simple correction entry; however, it will achieve the intended outcome.

2.4. CLASSIFIED BALANCE SHEETS

The balance sheet uncovers a company's assets, obligations, and justice. Always take into account that the elements mentioned on a financial statement are not essentially at fair market value when analyzing a balance sheet. Numerous assets are held at their historical cost, while others like the benefit of a company's branded product, patent applications, and other embedded operating assets) are not disclosed at all (Balanza et al., 2007).

Remember

A classified balance sheet is similar to a standard balance sheet and lists the same asset, liability and equity values.

Nonetheless, a comprehensive review of the financial accounts is essential for evaluating a business's financial health. Accountants frequently split the balance sheet into subgroups or classifications for accurate analysis. Significant groups of records can subsequently be recognized and subtotaled. Those very financial statements are referred to as "classified balance sheets."

The balance sheet outlines a company's financial state at a precise moment. Companies commonly use a categorized balance sheet to enhance users' comprehension of a company's economic location (Andres et al., 2022). A classified balance sheet employs a variety of standard categories and segments to group comparable assets and debts around each other. This is beneficial since goods inside a group hold common economic properties.

These classifications assist the reader in determining, for example, (1) if the company has sufficient assets to satisfy its liabilities as they mature, and

The assets of current and lengthy lenders are the entirety of the company's resources. The cash flow of Franklin Corporation contains a number of these classifications. In the subsequent sections, we clarify every one of these classifications (Lividini & Masters, 2022).

2.4.1. Assets

The asset section of the balance sheet (where relevant) might well be split into a total of as five separate components in the order listed:

1. Current assets are resources that can be transformed into cash or ingested quickly. Precisely, assets can be converted into money or utilized in one year or the business cycle, whatever is lengthy. The operating sequence of a business is the time required to transform funds into revenue (Bauman et al., 2016).
2. Back into money (i.e., buying assets, selling stock on funds, and gathering receivables); this is typically accomplished in less than a year. In this section's asset listing, the much more current cash must be mentioned first (i.e., cash, short-term savings, and receivables). These would be followed by inventories as well as expenditures paid in advance.
3. Long-term Holdings comprise land purchased for speculative purposes, monies reserved for a plant expansion plan, assets recoverable from insurance plans (such as the paid-up value of a life policy), and investments in other organizations.
4. Land, Plants, and Technology comprise the company's effectively utilized land, structures, and machinery.
5. Intangible Assets have no physicality and include goods such as bought patent laws, "goodwill" (the proportion of the purchase price of another firm outweighs that entity's capital resources), and essential products.
6. Other Assets are utilized to record asset accounts that do not fit anywhere else, like a particular long-term payable.

Remember

Current assets include cash, cash equivalents, accounts receivable, stock inventory, marketable securities, pre-paid liabilities, and other liquid assets.

Current assets are assets that a business intends to turn into money and use up within one year or during its operational cycle, whatever is greater (Cornaggia et al., 2013).

Franklin Corporation owned $22,100 in total assets. For most organizations, the categorization cutoff for total assets is a year from the balance sheet's date of publication (Normand & Wootton, 2001). For instance, accounts payable are considered current assets since they would be collected and converted to cash within a year. Supplies are valuable because the business anticipates using them in one year. Many companies designate assets and obligations as current over a longer timeframe than one year because their operating cycles are more significant than one year (Wilson & Stenson, 2008). A company's operating cycle is the average length required to buy inventory, sell it on credit, and recover cash from its clients. The majority of businesses complete this cycle in very little than one year. Hence they employ a one-year cutoff. However, this term could last more than one year for wineries and aircraft manufacturing industries. It will be presumed, unless otherwise specified, that corporations utilize a year to assess whether an item or obligation is long-term or current. Cash, investments (like short-term U.S. government securities), receipts (accrued liabilities, receivable accounts, and interest payables), stocks, and cash equivalents are frequent types of current assets (supplies and insurance). Companies typically put such things on the balance sheet in the sequence wherein they plan to turn them into cash (Song et al., 2019).

KEYWORD

The term depreciation refers to an accounting method used to allocate the cost of a tangible or physical asset over its useful life.

2.4.1.1. Long-Term Investments

Typically, long-term investments consist of

a) Investments in bonds and shares of other businesses that are managed to hold for several years,
b) Lengthy assets like buildings or land that a company is not presently using its financing tasks
c) Lengthy account liabilities.

Yahoo! Inc. reported lengthy financing on its balance sheet.

2.4.1.2. Property, Plant, and Machinery

Property, plant, and machinery are company property with a considerably longer service life that are presently being used. This classification includes land, houses, industrial machinery, shipping machinery, and décor (Dean et al., 2012).

Depreciation is the allocation of an asset's cost across a period. Companies achieve this by designating a percentage of an income statement as an annual expense (instead of expensing the total buying price in the year of buying). On the balance sheet, the depreciated items are represented at cost less cumulative depreciation. The depreciation expense account displays the total rate of depreciation that the business has incurred to date over the asset's life.

2.4.1.3. Intangible Assets

Most businesses have long-lasting, non-tangible assets that are frequently extremely valuable. Both are known as intangible assets. Goodwill is a substantial intangible asset. Other forms of intellectual property include licenses, rights, logos, and trade names that grant the corporation the first privilege of usage for a specific period (Zhu et al., 2021).

2.4.2. Liabilities

The liability portion of the balance sheet might well be segmented similarly to the asset part. Typically, the liability part is subdivided as follows: (Bauman & Shaw, 2016)

a) The liability part is typically subdivided as follows: Current liabilities are settled with current assets.

b) Typically, current liabilities are settled with total assets. Term loans, mortgage cards, and similar obligations are included in the category of liabilities. Significantly, many lengthy notes might well be partly classed as current and lengthy obligations. The portion designated as current is the principal payment amount within the following term (or an operating cycle, if longer). Some monies owed beyond that timeframe would be classified as a lengthy obligation.

KEYWORD

Long-term liabilities are a company's financial obligations that are due more than one year in the future.

Current obligations are the first category in the obligations and shareholders' equity portion of the balance sheet. Total liabilities are responsibilities that must be paid within one year or the company's operational cycle, whatever is more extended. Current liabilities, wages and salary receivable, payables, interest payments, and income taxes payments made are classic examples. Current liabilities also involve current deadlines of long-term liabilities or payments due on lengthy responsibilities within the next year (Gramlich et al., 2001).

Financial statement users look into the connection between current liabilities and current assets in great detail. This connection is essential for assessing a bank's profitability or capacity to fulfill the amount due in the coming year. When existing assets outweigh current assets, the liabilities will likely be satisfied. Whenever the opposite is true, the company might be unable to pay its brief creditors and eventually be compelled to declare bankruptcy.

Long-Term Obligations Bonds due, mortgages due, lengthy notes payable, leasing obligations, and pension obligations are included in this class of liabilities (Song et al., 2013). Numerous corporations report long debt maturing within a year as a single number in the balance sheet and present the loan's specifics in notes that include the financial statements. Others provide an overview of the numerous sorts of long-term obligations.

2.4.3. Equity

0The correct financial statement format for stock varies based on the type of business entity for whom the statement is produced. In practice, the examples in this chapter presuppose that the company is established. Consequently, the equity section includes (Bauman & Shaw, 2016):

1. Capital Stock consists of the money collected from shareholders for a particular value. The investors are becoming the company's shareholders, and their ownership stake is symbolized by stocks that may be sold to others (without further involvement by the company). In reality, the legalese of supply constraints can be rather complex, and you're likely to find extended capital stock-linked accounts (like preferred stock, regular stock, paid-in-capital above par, etc.).
2. You are acquainted with Retained Earnings, which represents the accumulated income minus payouts. In essence, it is the personal savings that have been returned in the growth of the company.

KEYWORD

Stocks are a type of security that gives stockholders a share of ownership in a company.

Stockholders' (Owners') Equity: The part on stockholders' (owners') equity differs depending on the type of corporate organization. There is only a capital account for a sole proprietor. There is a financial ledger for every collaboration member (Baladouni, 1990). Ordinary Shares (also known as Capital Stock) and Retained Earnings are the two frameworks into which corporations split their shareholders' equity. Companies record shareholders' stakes in the company by subtracting an account balance and paying the Common Stock accounts. In the Retained Earnings category, they record revenue kept for use within the business. The Common Stock and Retained Earnings accounts are combined and reported as shareholders' equity on the balance sheet. Lately, Nordstrom, Inc. reported the following for its shareholders' Equity section.

There is no requirement that a small business is undertaken via a company. A sole proprietorship is a company held by a single individual (Engel et al., 1999). Suppose the preceding example was indeed created for a sole proprietorship. In that case, the only difference is that the ownership part would comprise the owner's cash book (rather than capital stock and retained earnings). It is probably a partner if multiple people are involved in an unincorporated business. Likewise, the balance sheet will remain the same, except for the equity section, which will be separated into separate bank accounts for every partnership (indicating every partner's remaining financial stake). Recently, a flurry of legislation has created versions of such corporate types (limited liability businesses, limited liability partners, etc.). Still, the general structure of the balance sheet has been relatively unchanged. The nomenclature used to define corporate formations and appropriate capital arrangement also differs widely around the globe. However, the income statement's essential qualities, appearance, and substance are identical (Ruggles, 1987).

KEYWORD

An investor is a person who allocates financial capital with the expectation of a future return (profit) or to gain an advantage (interest).

2.5. BUSINESS LIQUIDITY AND THE OPERATING CYCLE

Financial statements might not tell the complete story. Numerous crucial aspects of a company could not be defined in monetary terms on the balance sheet. Notes are utilized to determine accounting rules, significant business events, pending litigation, and other operational aspects. The concept of full disclosure entails that financial statements are prepared relatively and that all material facts that could impact investors' and creditors' evaluations of the company are disclosed in the financial statements or related notes (Richards & Laughlin, 1980).

As stated previously, analyzing a company's financial health requires a careful investigation of the balance sheet; the categorized balance sheet aids in this analysis. Creditors and shareholders must consider the liquidity of a business. Liquidity is a company's capacity to meet its short-term responsibilities as they mature. Insufficient liquidity can spell disaster even in a business with promising lengthy opportunities and substantial noncash investments (VU et al., 2020).

Working Capital: The distinction between current liabilities and current assets is the cash flow. Finances for Classy Company were depicted to be $500,000, while total liabilities were $150,000. Consequently, the cash flow is $300,000 ($450,000 minus $150,000). One might hope to discover a good level of working capital for understandable reasons. If not, this could indicate financial strain.

One should exercise caution before drawing broad conclusions about a company's health using a single amount. Could a company have negative cash reserves and remain in excellent condition? Yes! For example, the company may maintain a backup letter of credit at a bank, allowing it to borrow the money as required to fulfill short-term obligations (Michalski, 2016). Or many businesses are in excellent shape while having working capital problems. Consider a fast food business with virtually no liabilities (most transactions are for cash) and insufficient stock (you understand that bread and milk do not keep well). Cash, a few inventories, and a few prepaid things may be the sole cash flows.

Nonetheless, they might have considerable current liabilities and brief debt as assets. How do they sustain? Their money flow rate could be pretty high if they can turn significant revenue volumes at large profit margins. This allows the generation of sufficient free funds to repay liabilities as they mature and to spend on expanding new business locations. Therefore, monitoring working capital is essential. Just be cautious about drawing broad inferences based on one metric (Fallah & Hashemi, 2017).

KEYWORD

Cash flow is simply a measure of the money coming into your business versus the money going out of it.

Is $1,000,000 in working capital an excessive amount? Maybe, perhaps not. For a corporate titan, $1,000,000 is a slight drop in the bucket, and that working capital figure might spell doom. On the contrary, a "mom-and-pop" business could thrive with significantly less than $1,000,000 in revenue. Therefore, it is contingent upon the current and current assets and liabilities ratio. The current balance is utilized to describe the relative current capital amount. By dividing current assets by existing debts:

Current ratio = Current Assets/Current Liabilities

The current ratio of Classy Company is 3:1 ($450,000/$150,000). Note that ratios are susceptible to manipulation. If Classy desired to improve its current ratio, it could reduce its debt load. The current updated ratio will "increase" to 4:1 (($450,000 -$50,000)/($150,000 -$50,000)) if they cleared off $50,000 of accounts due with money (Schiling, 1996).

A corporation could have a large amount of stock that is difficult to sell. Therefore, the current ratio (incorporating inventory) may indicate no issue, even though the company is not making its payments. A more difficult ratio is ratio analysis. This ratio gives a more demanding test of a company's ability to repay its debts by dividing current assets by current liabilities.

Quick Ratio = (Cash Plus Short-Term Investments Plus Receivables) / Current Liabilities The current ratio of Classy Company is 1.5:1 (($100,000 + $)):

Quick ratio = (Cash + Short-term Investments + Accounts Receivable)/Current Liabilities Classy Company has a quick ratio of 1.5:1 (($100,000 + $).

2.6. ADJUSTMENT OF ACCOUNTS

2.6.1. Fiscal and Calendar Years

Occasionally, large and small businesses' financial statements and reports review their economic well-being and operations results. Typically, accounting timeframes are a month, a quarter, or a year. Monthly and quarterly intervals are referred to as interim periods. Most large businesses must prepare yearly and quarterly financial declarations (Marinheiro, 2006).

A one-year accounting period is referred to as a fiscal year. A fiscal year typically begins at the beginning of the month and concludes at the end of the month 12 months after. Most businesses use the calendar year as their accounting cycle (January 1 – December 31). Others do not. Delta Air Lines and Walt Disney Productions have fiscal years that vary from the calendar year. Their budgetary years end on June 30 and September 30, respectively. Occasionally, a company's year-end may differ from one year to the next. PepsiCo's fiscal year, for instance, concludes on the Friday nearest to December 31, which would have been December 31 in 2011 and December 29 in 2012 (Brown, 1956).

Remember

The cash basis is a contrast to the accrual basis.

2.6.2. Accrual- versus Cash-Basis Accounting

This chapter will teach about accrual-based accounting. Under the accrual basis, transactions that impact a firm's financial statements are recorded in the period that they occur. Used this accrual method to calculate net income; for instance, corporations register revenue whenever they offer work (instead of when they receive cash) (Roska, 2017). It also involves recording expenses as they are spent (rather than whenever paid).

Under cash-basis accounting, revenue is recorded when money is received. Whenever cash is paid out, an expense is recorded. The cash basis is enticing due to its seeming ease, yet it frequently results in misleading income reports. It fails to register income for a business that has rendered services but has not yet received the money. As a result, expenses and revenues are not matched. Cash accounting is contrary to commonly recognized accounting rules (GAAP).

Several individuals and small businesses employ cash-basis accounting. Cash-basis accounting is appropriate for small organizations because they typically have minimal payments and receivables. Large and medium-sized companies use accrual-based accounting (Joudeh et al., 2021).

2.7. RECOGNIZING REVENUES AND EXPENSES

It might be hard to identify when expenditures and revenues should be reported. This work is aided by the income recognition concept as well as the expense recognition concept.

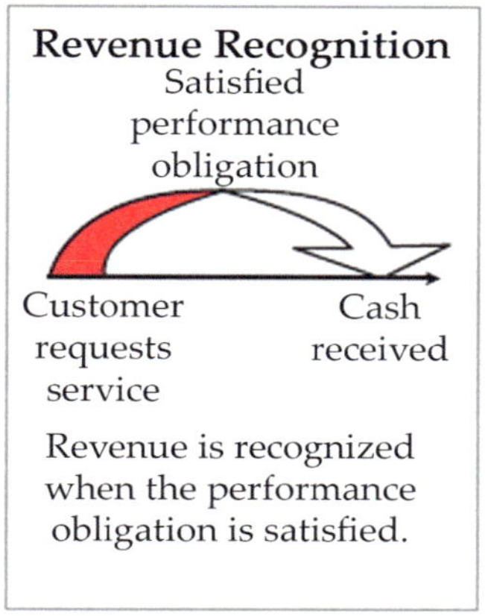

Figure 2.16. Diagram representing Revenue Recognition (Source: Jerry J. Weygandt, Creative Commons License).

Revenue Recognition Principle: A performance obligation exists whenever a corporation undertakes to execute a function or offer a product to a consumer. Whenever the company satisfies this obligation, revenue is recognized. Companies are required by the revenue recognition principle to record revenue in the accounting cycle when the valid contract is comfortable (Sa'eed et al., 2020). Consider that Dave's Dry Cleaning cleans garments on June 30, but clients do not assume and expect to be paid for until the beginning of July. Dave's should record income in June, whenever it fulfilled the requirement (executed the service), as opposed to

July, whenever it did receive the money. For the rendered service, Dave's would record a credit balance on its balance sheet and income on its financial statements as of June 30 (Warfield et al., 1995). According to a simple rule, accountants recognize expenses "Expenses should follow revenues." Consequently, expense recognition is dependent on recognizing revenue. In the laundry service instance, this implies that Dave's should record the salary expenditure incurred to undertake the cleaning service on June 30 in a similar period that it realizes the net income. The most crucial aspect of expense recognition is determining how the expense contributes to income (Erickson et al., 2004). This could or could not coincide with the period in which the cost is incurred. If Dave's does not entirely pay the compensation accrued on June 30 till July, it will list the pay rates receivable on its balance sheet as of June 30.

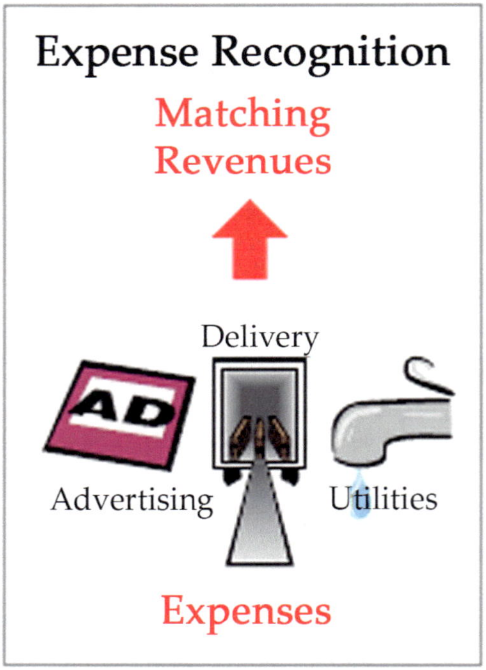

Figure 2.17. Diagram representing Expense Recognition (Source: Jerry J. Weygandt, Creative Commons License).

This method of expense recognition is known as the principle of expense recognition (often referred to as the matching principle). It requires that efforts (expenses) be proportional to outcomes (revenues) (Dutta & Reichelstein, 2005).

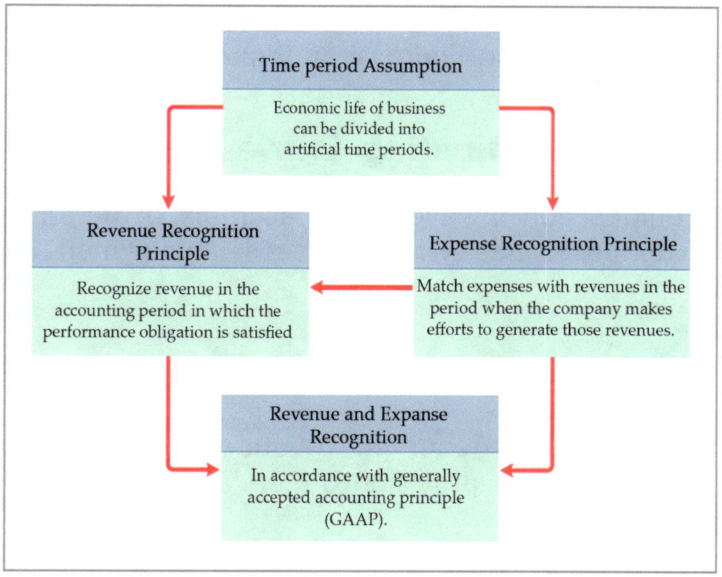

Figure 2.18. Illustration of the Revenues and expenses recognition (Source: Paul D. Kimmel, Creative Commons License).

2.8. THE BASICS OF ADJUSTING ENTRIES

Companies create adjusting entries to ensure that profits are recognized when the services are provided and that expenditures are accounted for in the time they are paid. Adjusting entrances guarantee adherence to the rules of recognizing revenue and cost recognition (Novita, 2022):

Since the trial balance—the initial compilation of the transaction records not include precise and complete information, adjusting inputs are required. This is accurate for several reasons:

1. Since it is not practical to capture certain events daily, they are not. Instances include the usage of goods and workers' receipt of payment.
2. Since they fail over time instead of as a consequence of everyday transactions, a few expenses are not documented during the accounting period. Instances include fees for using facilities and machinery, rent, and insurance.
3. A few goods might not be documented—an illustration of a utility bill that will not get until the following accounting period.

Every time a business produces financial information, an accounting cycle is necessary. So every account in the financial statement is examined by the company to see if it is complete and current for financial statement reasons (Abdul Manaf, & Wan-

Hussin, 2011). Each existing account includes one balance sheet account or one from the financial statements.

2.8.1. Types of Adjusting Entries

Adjusting entries can involve either accruals or deferrals. Every one of such classes has two subclasses (Musselman 1969).

Deferrals:

1. Expenses are those that are paid for entirely before being used or spent.
2. Completely undeserved revenues: Funds received in advance of the provision of services.

Accruals:

1. *Accrued revenues*: Payments for rendered services that have not yet been recognized or received in money.
2. *Accrued expenses:* Costs that have been spent but have not yet been reported or received in cash.

KEYWORD

A fund is a collection of different people's money, collected & managed by high market professionals.

Instances of every form of modification are provided in the following sections. Each example is derived from Pioneer Advertising Agency Inc.'s October 31 balance sheet. Pioneer Advertising is thought to follow a one-month accounting cycle. So, modifying entries are made each month. Dated October 31 are the items (Dunn, 1960).

2.8.2. Adjusting Entries for Deferrals

Defer is another word for postponing or postponing. Deferrals are costs or profits that are recorded at a time after the original date wherein money was transferred. Prepayments and unearned income are the two categories of deferrals.

Prepaid Expenses: Businesses record an asset known as accrued expenses or prepayments whenever they register expenditures of expenditures that would profit from more than an income statement. An asset account is raised (debited) whenever costs are paid to reflect the benefit or service the business will eventually get. Extra payments are frequently made for insurance, equipment, advertising, and rent. Additionally, enterprises prepay for their purchases of machinery and buildings (Ermaliza et al., 2022).

Prepaid costs are those that either run out with time (like rent as well as insurance) or via usage (e.g., supplies). Such expenditures do not need to be entered daily, as this would be needless and impracticable. As a result, businesses wait to recognize these cost expirations after creating their financial statements (Laitinen, 1994). They create adjusting entries at every statement date to reflect the costs associated with the current income statement and display the existing assets' balances.

Assets are exaggerated, and expenditures are undervalued before correction. As an outcome, an adjusting entry for prepaid expenses causes an increment (a debit) to an expense report and a reduction (a credit) to an investment account.

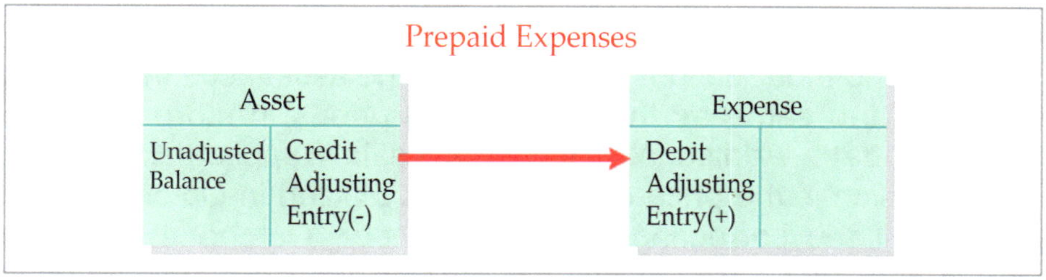

Remember

An accounting period may consist of weeks, months, quarters, calendar years, or fiscal years.

Supplies An asset account is increased (debited) when supplies like paper and envelopes are bought. The firm utilizes supplies at the time of the accounting period. Companies acknowledge supply costs at the end of the fiscal year instead of recording them as the materials are consumed. The business calculates the remaining supply after the accounting period (Phillips & Schmidt, 2010). The uncorrected balance in the resources (asset) category and the actual price of goods on hand show the goods consumed (an expenditure) for that period.

On October 5, Pioneer Advertising Agency Inc. spent $2,500 on goods. Pioneer increased (debited) the asset Supplies to reflect the transaction. In the balance sheet as of October 31, this bank has a balance of $2,000. At the end of operations on October 31, an inventory count shows that there is still $1,000 worth of supplies available. Therefore, the price of the materials used is $1,500 (Musselman 1967). This utilization of supplies reduces a supply-related asset. Additionally, it lowers stockholders' equity by raising the Supplies Expenditure expense account (Dewangan & ikhar 2018).

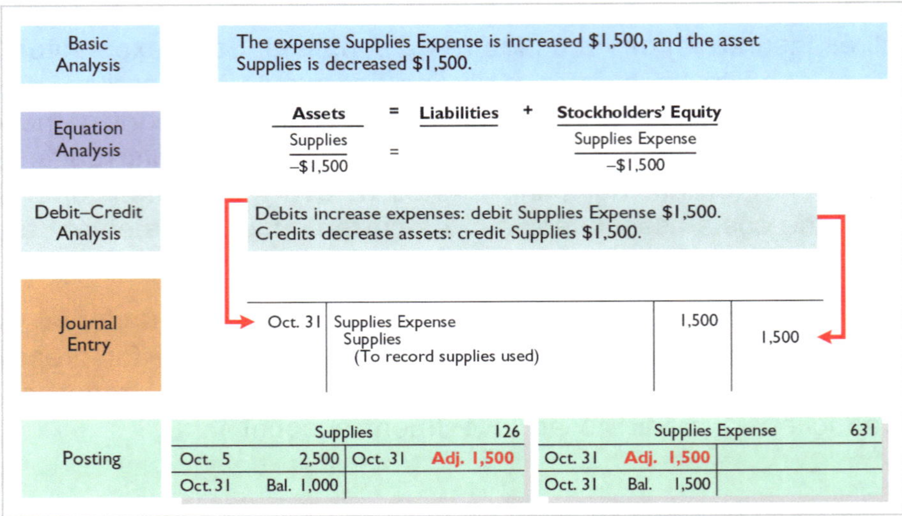

Figure 2.19. Illustration of the entries adjustment for deferrals (Paul D. Kimmel, Creative Commons License).

Following modification, the balance in the asset account Supplies is $1,000, the same as the price of the goods in store as of the statement date. Additionally, the balance in Supplies Expense is $1,500, which is the price of the supplies utilized in October. In the absence of the correcting entry by Pioneer, October's expenses are inflated by $1,500, while net income is overstated (Habibie et al.,2022. Additionally, on the balance sheet as of October 31, assets and stockholders' capital will be overvalued by $1,500.

Insurance Companies buy insurance to shield themselves from damages brought on by fire, theft, and other circumstances. Insurance premiums must be paid upfront, frequently for several years. The asset account Prepaid Insurance records the price of the insurance (premiums) paid upfront as an increase (debit). For the insurance cost that has ended at the time of the period, corporations raise (debit) Insurance Expenses and reduce (credit) Prepaid Insurance as of the company's financial period (Malau et al., 2022).

Pioneer Advertising bought a year's worth of fire insurance on October 4 for $600. On October 1, programming commenced. Pioneer added (debited) Prepaid Insurance to reflect the purchase. In the trial balance as of October 31, this account has a balance of $600. So monthly, a $50 insurance policy ($600 4 12) expires (Seipel, 1998). Prepaid insurance's expiration reduces its value as an asset. Additionally, it lowers stockholders' equity by raising the Insurance Expenditure expense report. The Prepaid asset Insurance displays a balance of $550, which shows the price for the next 11 months of insurance. In addition, the insurance cost that ended in October is equivalent to the sum in the *Insurance Expense*. If Pioneer need not execute this correction, October's expenses will be $50 overstated, and October's net profits will be $50 exaggerated. Additionally, on the balance sheet as of October 31, assets and shareholders' ownership would be overvalued by $50 (Rhodes & Smith, 2004).

Depreciation: usually a business possessing a range of long-lived assets, like buildings, machinery, and automobiles. The duration of service is known as the lifespan of the asset. Since the building is anticipated to offer assistance for several years, it is recognized as an asset instead of a cost on the date of acquisition. According to the historical cash basis, companies must report these assets at a price. To adhere to expenditure recognition, businesses designate a part of this price as an expenditure throughout every period of the asset's useful life. Depreciation is allocating an asset's cost to expenses throughout its life span (Garrison, 1981).

KEYWORD

An appraisal is a process of determining the value of real properties, antiques, or collectibles.

Required Adjustment: The purchase of long-lived goods is a lengthy payment in advance for the asset's usage. Depreciation requires an adjustment entry to identify the price that has been utilized (an expenditure) throughout the term and to recognize the price that has not been used (an asset) after the period. A crucial element to comprehend is that depreciation is a notion of allocation, not an appraisal. In other words, depreciation distributes the cost of an item to the periods during which it is utilized. Depreciation does not seek to reflect the asset's actual decline in value.

Suppose that Pioneer Advertising's equipment depreciation is $480 per year or $40 per month. Rather than simply decreasing (crediting) the asset account, Pioneer credits Accumulated Depreciation— Equipment. The account for Accumulated Depreciation is known as a counter-asset account. On the balance sheet, such an account is adjusted between an asset account. Consequently, the Accumulated Depreciation—Equipment account balances the Equipment account balance. This account tracks the depreciation expenses incurred during the asset's useful life. To maintain accounting equilibrium, Pioneer diminishes shareholders' equity by adding a cost item, Depreciation Expense. Every month, the sum in the Accumulated Depreciation—Equipment account would rise by $40, but the Equipment account balance would stay at $5,000 (Harianja et al., 2022).

Declarative Presentation. As noted, the Accumulated Depreciation—Equipment account is a counter asset. It is subtracted from the equipment on the financial statement. A counter asset account's regular balance is a debit. Theoretically, an option for utilizing a contra-asset account would be to lower (credit) the asset account by the depreciation each month. However, the contra account is superior for a simple reason: it reveals both the initial price of the machine and the total expenses incurred to date. Pioneer deducts Accumulated Depreciation—Equipment from the associated asset's value in its balance sheet (Simanjuntak et al., 2022)

Book value distinguishes between a depreciable asset's cost and cumulative depreciation. The machine's book value at the time of the balance sheet is $4,960. Generally, the purchase price and the fair market value of an item are two different numbers. As stated before, the objective of depreciation is not an assessment but rather cost allocation.

Remember

A cost object can be a specific product or product line, a particular service you offer, a production-related activity or a department or division in your company.

Depreciation expenditure represents the part of an asset's cost that died during the period covered by the charge (in this scenario, in October). Without such adjustment addition, the accounting equation reveals that financial assets, total shareholders' equity, and net earnings are each overestimated by $40, while depreciation expenditure is underestimated by $40.

Unearned Revenues: Whenever corporations receive payment before the performance of services, they register an obligation by raising (crediting) an unearned revenue liability position. In other words, a firm is now obligated to provide a product to one of its consumers. Unearned income could include rent, magazine subscriptions, and consumer deposits for future support. For example, airlines like United, American, and Delta consider ticket sales as unearned money till the flying service is offered (Tjandra et al., 2022).

Prepaid costs are the reverse of unearned earnings. Unearned income on the accounts of one firm is probably a booked expenditure on the records of the business that made the additional payment. For instance, assuming similar accounting years are maintained, a landlord with a prepaid rental will have unpaid rent income.

When a corporation gets money for goods to be rendered in a future accounting period, it adds (credits) a deferred revenue (liability) account to record the obligation. Whenever the service is delivered, the corporation realizes future revenues. It is impractical to record everyday transactions while the business assists during the accounting period. Instead, the corporation waits for revenue recognition till the adjustment procedure is complete. The firm then makes an adjustment entry to reflect the money for services provided throughout the accounting cycle and to reflect the remaining obligation after the term. Usually, liabilities are exaggerated, and earnings are underestimated before correction. The adjusting entry for income reduces (debits) a liabilities account and increases (credits) a revenue account (Zulaiha et al., 2022).

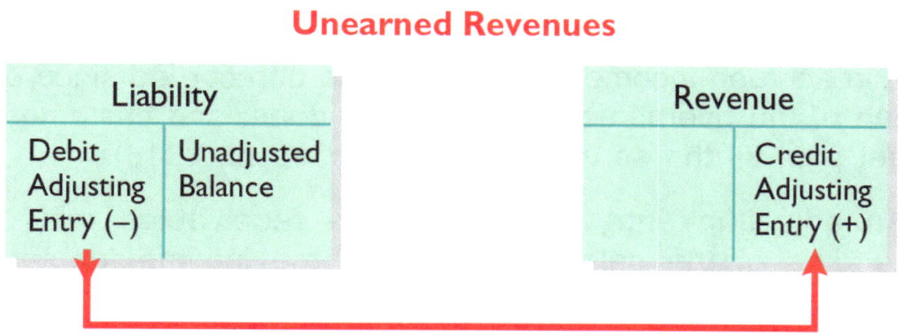

Figure 2.20. Schematic of the Unearned Revenues (Source: Donald E. Kieso, Creative Commons License).

R. Knox paid $1,200 to Pioneer Advertising on October 2 for advertising obligations to be delivered by December 31. The payment was paid to Unearned Service Revenue by Pioneer. This account for liabilities reflects a balance of

$1,200 in the balance sheet as of October 31. Based on examining the service Pioneer delivered for Knox in October, the business concludes that it should record $400 in profit for the month. Thus, the obligation (Unearned Service Revenue) decreases, and shareholders' equity (Service Revenue) rises (Caroline & Muda, 2022). The Unearned Service Revenue obligation now has a balance of $800. This sum indicates the advertisements that are anticipated to be provided in the future. Similarly, Service Revenue displays $10,400 in total revenue received in October. Without such an adjustment, the income statement understates profits and net profit by $400. In addition, on the October 31 balance sheet, liabilities would be overestimated by $400, and shareholders' equity would be underestimated by $400 (Sormin et al., 2022).

2.8.3. Adjusting Entries for Accruals

Accruals are the two most common forms of adjusting entries. Before an accrual adjustment, either the revenue account (and its corresponding asset account) or the expenditure budget (and its corresponding debt account) is underestimated. Consequently, the accruals adjustment entry would raise both an income statement and a balance sheet position.

Revenues for services rendered that have not been recognized at the financial statement date are accrued profits. As with interest revenue, accrued earnings may build up over time. Such activities are not recorded since interest accrual does not entail everyday transactions. Businesses do not report interest income daily as it is frequently difficult to do so. Commissions and fees are activities that have already been done but not yet paid or paid, which might result in accrued income. These could go unrecorded since only a fraction of the overall service has been done, and customers will not get paid till the service is finished (Cecchi, 2018).

An adjusting entry documents the receivables that occur at the date of the balance sheet and the income for services rendered at the time of the period. Overall assets and income are underestimated before adjustments. An accrued revenue adjustment entry causes a debit (a debit) to an asset's value and a rise (a credit) to an income statement.

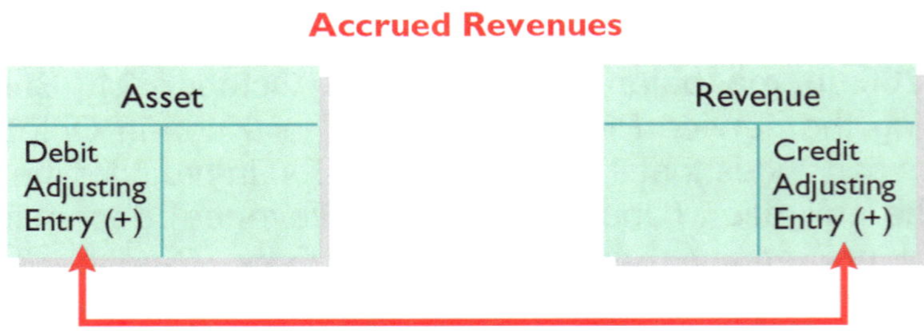

Figure 2.21. Schematic of the Accrued Revenues (Source: Donald E. Kieso, Creative Commons License).

Pioneer Advertising Agency, Inc. provided $200 worth of activities in October that were not invoiced to customers by October 31. Such actions are not documented since they are not invoiced. The accumulation of unrecorded service income increases the Accounts Receivable account balance. It also enhances owners' equity by raising the Service Revenue accounts receivable (Laitinen, 1994).

The Accounts Receivable asset indicates that customers pay Pioneer $200 as of the date the balance sheet was created. The Service Revenue balance of $10,600 corresponds to all profit from services rendered by Pioneer throughout the month ($10,000) ($400) ($200). Even without adjusting entry, the resources and shareholders' equity on the income statement and the earnings and net earnings on the financial statements would be understated (Dixon, 1952).

On November 10, Pioneer received $200 in funds for services rendered in October and recorded the amount as follows. The company debits (increases) cash and credits (decreases) Account Receivable upon collecting the receivables.

Accrued Expenses: Accrued costs are those racked up yet to be earned or noted as of the date of the statement. Interest, taxes, and wages are instances of typical accumulated expenses.

Adjustments: are made to accounts payable to reflect the commitments that occur at the time of the balance sheet and to realize the expenditures that pertain to the current fiscal year. Both obligations and expenses are underestimated even before adjustment. An accrued expenditure adjusting entry causes a debit (a bank card) to an expense report and a raise (a credit) to an amount payable (Musselman, 1967).

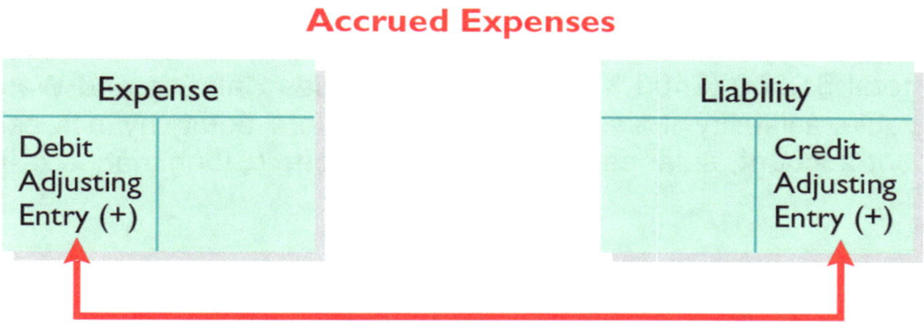

Figure 2.22. Illustration of the Accrued Expenses (Source: Paul D. Kimmel, Creative Commons License).

Let's examine a few particular accrued expenses in greater detail, starting with accrued interest.

Compounded Interest: On October 1, Pioneer Advertising signed a $5,000 note due over three months. The note stipulates that Pioneer must pay an annual rate of return of 12%.

Three criteria influence the rate of payment recorded:

a) The cost price of the notes;
b) The rate of interest, which is usually indicated as an annualized rate
c) The period the note remains outstanding.

The final amount due by Pioneer on the $5,000 note at its maturity date in 3 months is $150 ($5,000 3 12% 3 3), or $50 per month. (Wallace, 1933). The accrual of tax on October 31 raises the Interest Payable obligation account. It also reduces shareholders' equity by increasing the Interest Expenditure expense report.

Interest Expense: displays the interest expenses for October. Interest Payable shows the interest the business gives at the time of the financial statement. Pioneer would not pay interest till three months have passed and the note is due (O'Bryan et al., 2000). Rather than crediting Notes Payable, businesses use the Interest Payable account to reflect the principal and interest commitments in their financial statements and records. Without such an adjustment, obligations and interest expenditure would be understated, while operating earnings and shareholders' equity would be exaggerated.

Accrued Wages and Salaries: Many expenditures, such as staff wages and salaries, are paid for once the goods have been rendered. Pioneer salaries and compensation for the first two months of employment on October 26. (Talley et al., 2012).

The wages and salaries for such three days are an accumulated charge and liability for Pioneer as of October 31. The employees' full pay and salaries for a five-day workday amount to $2,000, or $400 per day. Therefore, salary and earnings accrued as October 31 total $1,200 ($400 3 3). An accrual raises Salaries and Wages Payable, a liability. It also reduces stockholders' equity by increasing a cost account, salaries, and wage expenses (Stoehlmache et al., 2004).

ACTIVITY 2.1.

Mayes Company records all prepayments in income statement accounts. At April 30, the trial balance shows Supplies Expense $2,800, Service Revenue $9,200, and zero balances in related balance sheet accounts. Prepare the adjusting entries at April 30 assuming (a) $700 of supplies on hand and (b) $3,000 of service revenue should be reported as unearned.

Prepare adjusting entries under alternative treatment of deferrals.

After such adjustment, the remainder of $5,200 (13 days x $400) in Salaries and Wages Costs is the real wage and salaries expenditure for October. As of October 31, the $1,200 sum in Wages and Salaries Payable represents Pioneer's responsibility for wages and salaries. Without the $1,200 correction for wages and salaries, Pioneer's expenses and obligations are each underestimated by $1,200.

Pioneer Advertising provides wages and salaries every two weeks. Therefore, the next paycheck would be November 9, when the corporation gives a total of $4,000 in wages and compensation. The payment comprises $1,200 in wages and salaries paid on October 31 and $2,800 in wages and salary expenses for November (7 days of work, as indicated on the November calendar). So, on November 9, Pioneer created the following entrance:

This entry cancels the obligation for wages and salaries Payable that Pioneer entered in the existing account for October 31 and entered the correct amount of Salaries and Wages Expenditure between November 1 and November 9 (Gong et al., 2016).

SUMMARY

- Spend some time reviewing and analyzing the adjustment entries. Each modification impacts one balance sheet account and one income statement account.
- On October 31, pictures 3–23 (below) and 3–24 (on page 122) depict the journaling and posting of adjusting entries by Pioneer Advertising Agency, Inc. Because they were recorded on page 2 of the general diary, all modifications have the designation J2 because they were recorded there. The center caption "Adjusting Entries" may be inserted between the last transaction record and the first adjusting item in the journal.
- After journalizing and publishing all adjustment entries, a company creates a second trial balance from the ledger accounts. Adjusted trial balance describes this trial balance. It shows the account balances after the accounting period, including any changes. An adjusted trial balance aims to demonstrate that the debit and credit balances of the general ledger are equal after any modifications. Because the accounts include all the necessary information for financial statements, the adjusted trial balance serves as the basis for creating financial statements.
- The amended trial balance of Pioneer Advertising Agency, Inc. is obtained from the ledger accounts. Different hues are assigned to the quantities influenced by the variable inputs. As a consequence of the adjusting entries made at the end of the month, the trial balance has additional accounts after being adjusted.

REVIEW QUESTIONS

1. Define two generally accepted accounting principles that relate to adjusting the accounts.
2. "Adjusting the historical cost principle of accounting requires entries." Do you agree? Explain.
3. Why may a trial balance not contain up-to-date and complete financial information?
4. Distinguish between the two categories of adjusting entries, and identify the adjustments applicable to each.
5. Why can financial statements be prepared directly from an adjusted trial balance?
6. A company fails to recognize an expense incurred but not paid. Indicate which of the following accounts is debited and which is credited in the adjusting entry: (a) asset, (b) liability, (c) revenue, or (d) expense.

MULTIPLE CHOICE QUESTIONS

1. The revenue recognition principle states that:

a) Revenue should be recognized when a performance obligation is satisfied in the accounting period.

b) Expenses should be matched with revenues.

c) The economic life of a business can be divided into artificial periods.

d) The fiscal year should correspond with the calendar year.

2. Does every adjusting entry affect it?

a) Income statement account only

b) Balance sheet account only

c) Both A & B

d) None

3. If a business pays for only 11 months' rent during a financial year, what accounting term is given to the outstanding one month's rent?

a) Repayment

b) Prepayment

c) Underpayment

d) Payable

4. Adjusting Entries?

a) Assign revenue to the period in which they are earned

b) Help to measure the period's Net Profit / Loss properly

c) Bring asset and liability accounts to correct balances

d) All of about statements are true regarding Adjusting Entries

5. The accounting cycle begins by recording ____________ in the form of journal entries.

a) Business Transactions

b) Financial Information

c) Corporate Minutes

d) Business Contracts

6. Reports that can be prepared from the adjusted trial balance

a) General Purpose Financial Statements

b) Expense Reports

c) Inventory Reports

d) Payroll Spending Reports

7. Accounts with balances that are carried over to future years.

a) Temporary Accounts

b) Permanent Accounts

c) Expense Accounts

d) Withdrawal Accounts

Answers to Multiple Choice Questions

1. (a) 2. (c) 3. (d) 4. (d) 5. (a) 6. (a) 7.(c)

REFERENCES

1. Abdul, M. N. A., & Wan-Hussin, W. N., (2011). Application of problem-based learning (PBL) in a course on financial accounting principles. *Malaysian Journal of Learning and Instruction, 8*, 21–47.
2. Aisyah, E. S., Maimunah, M., & Martono, A., (2017). Effectiveness of book closing using web-based accounting online system 2.0 to know the company's financial ratios. *APTISI Transactions on Management (ATM), 1*(1), 56–60.
3. Al Shammari, F. M. R., (2017). Developing Saudi EFL student's reading skills through schema-based techniques. *Culture & Development, 112*, 1–38.
4. AlAdwani, A., AlFadley, A., AlGasab, M., & Alnwaiem, A. F., (2022). The effect of using KWL (know-want-learned) strategy on reading comprehension of 5th grade EFL students in Kuwait. *English Language Teaching, 15*(1), 79–91.
5. Andres, J., Bosca, J. E., Ferri, J., & Fuentes-Albero, C., (2022). Households' balance sheets and the effect of fiscal policy. *Journal of Money, Credit and Banking, 54*(4), 737–778.
6. Asamoah, G., (2018). Developing an accounting information system for a restaurant and understanding its potential impact on the business. *Interdisciplinary Research Journal of Theology, Apologetics, Natural & Social Sciences, 1*, 359–362.
7. Baker, R. E., (1984). Belcher and stickney, "business combinations and consolidated financial statements" (book review). *The Accounting Review, 59*(1), 141.
8. Baladouni, V., (1990). An early attempt at balance sheet classification and financial reporting. *The Accounting Historians Journal, 1*, 27–45.
9. Balanza, R., García-Lorda, P., Pérez-Rodrigo, C., Aranceta, J., Bonet, M. B., & Salas-Salvadó, J., (2007). Trends in food availability determined by the Food and Agriculture Organization's food balance sheets in Mediterranean Europe in comparison with other European areas. *Public Health Nutrition, 10*(2), 168–176.
10. Ball, R., Li, X., & Shivakumar, L., (2015). Contractibility and transparency of financial statement information prepared under IFRS: Evidence from debt contracts around IFRS adoption. *Journal of Accounting Research, 53*(5), 915–963.
11. Barral, N., Husillos, R., Castillo, E., Cánovas, M., Lam, E. J., & Calvo, L., (2021). Volumetric quantification and quality of water stored in a mining lake: A case study at Reocín mine (Spain). *Minerals, 11*, 212.
12. Bauman, M. P., & Shaw, K. W., (2016). Balance sheet classification and the valuation of deferred taxes. *Research in Accounting Regulation, 28*(2), 77–85.

13. Bima, P. M., Gulo, W. V. A., & Muda, I., (2022). Use of journal in the recording process in accounting system. *Journal of Positive School Psychology, 6*(3), 2368–2374.
14. Brown, E. C., (1956). Fiscal policy in the thirties: A reappraisal. *The American Economic Review, 46*(5), 857–879.
15. Buell, U., & Schicha, H., (1990). Nuclear medicine to image applied pathophysiology: Evaluation of reserves by computerized emission tomography. *European Journal of Nuclear Medicine, 16*(3), 129–135.
16. Caroline, S. D. B. S., & Muda, I., (2022). The five financial statements based on IFRS and how they are prepared. *Journal of Positive School Psychology, 6*(3), 2343–2354.
17. Cecchi, M., (2018). The accrual anomaly: The dampening effect of adjusting entries. *Corporate Ownership & Control, 16*(1), 94–106.
18. Clayton, D., (1969). Dramatize steps in the accounting cycle. *The Journal of Business Education, 45*(1), 10.
19. Cornaggia, K. J., Franzen, L. A., & Simin, T. T., (2013). Bringing leased assets onto the balance sheet. *Journal of Corporate Finance, 22*, 345–360.
20. Coupland, C., (2001). Accounting for change: A discourse analysis of graduate trainees' talk of adjustment. *Journal of Management Studies, 38*(8), 1103–1119.
21. Dean, P. C., Mckenna, K., & Krishnan, V., (2012). Accounting for human capital: Is the balance sheet missing something? *International Journal of Business and Social Science, 3*(12), 3–9.
22. Deshpande, V. S., & Modak, J. P., (2003). Maintenance strategy for tilting table of rolling mill based on reliability considerations. *Reliability Engineering & System Safety, 80*(1), 1–18.
23. Dewangan, S., & Ikhar, M. K., (2018). Role of ethics and governance in the accounting practices in present Indian businesses with special reference to the Satyam scandal. *Indian J. Sci. Res., 21*(1), 33–37.
24. Dewangan, S., & Ikhar, M. K., (2018). Role of ethics and governance in the accounting practices in present Indian businesses with particular reference to the Satyam scandal. *Indian J. Sci. Res., 21*(1), 33–37.
25. Dixon, D. R., (1952). Pyramiding income in changing from a cash to an accrual method of accounting. *Tax L. Rev., 8*, 355.
26. Draper, G., Gutiérrez, G., & Lewis, J. F., (1996). Thrust emplacement of the Hispaniola peridotite belt: Orogenic expression of the mid-cretaceous Caribbean arc polarity reversal? *Geology, 24*(12), 1143–1146.
27. Dunn, C. L., (1960). The teaching of adjusting and reversing entries in the elementary accounting courses. *The Accounting Review, 35*(1), 135–137.
28. Dutta, S., & Reichelstein, S., (2005). Accrual accounting for performance evaluation. *Review of Accounting Studies, 10*(4), 527–552.
29. El Serafy, S., (1997). Green accounting and economic policy. *Ecological Economics, 21*(3), 217–229.

30. Engel, E., Erickson, M., & Maydew, E., (1999). Debt-equity hybrid securities. *Journal of Accounting Research, 37*(2), 249–274.

31. Erickson, M., Hanlon, M., & Maydew, E. L., (2004). How much will firms pay for earnings that do not exist? Evidence of taxes paid on allegedly fraudulent earnings. *The Accounting Review, 79*(2), 387–408.

32. Ermaliza, R., Lubis, S., & Muda, I., (2022). Prepare adjusting entries for deferrals cases. *Journal of Positive School Psychology, 6*(3), 2355–2360.

33. Fallah, S., & Hashemi, S. A., (2017). The effects of inflation and operating cycle on cash holdings (liquidity) of listed companies in Tehran stock exchange. *Asian Economic and Financial Review, 7*(1), 43–51.

34. Fekete, B., Palkó, M., Mándity, I., Haukka, M., & Fülöp, F., (2016). A domino ring-closure followed by retro-Diels–alder reaction for the preparation of pyrimido [2, 1-a] isoindole enantiomers. *European Journal of Organic Chemistry, 2016*(21), 3519–3527.

35. Garcia-Vedrenne, A. E., Orland, C., Ballare, K. M., Shapiro, B., & Wayne, R. K., (2020). Ten strategies for a successful transition to remote learning: Lessons learned with a flipped course. *Ecology and Evolution, 10*(22), 12620–12634.

36. Garrison, L. L., (1981). Adjusting entries: An overview. *The Journal of Business Education, 56*(5), 176–178.

37. Gong, J., Maia, M. C., Dizman, N., Govindarajan, A., & Pal, S. K., (2016). Metastasis in renal cell carcinoma: Biology and implications for therapy. *Asian Journal of Urology, 3*(4), 286–292.

38. Goodwin, J., Ahmed, K., & Heaney, R., (2008). The effects of international financial reporting standards on the accounts and accounting quality of Australian firms: A retrospective study. *Journal of Contemporary Accounting & Economics, 4*(2), 89–119.

39. Gramlich, J. D., McAnally, M. L., & Thomas, J., (2001). Balance sheet management: The case of short-term obligations reclassified as long-term debt. *Journal of Accounting Research, 39*(2), 283–295.

40. Habibie, M., Rais, R. R., & Muda, I., (2022). Describe the nature and purpose of an adjusted trial balance. *Journal of Positive School Psychology, 6*(3), 2522–2529.

41. Harianja, F., Hutabarat, S. F. T., & Muda, I., (2022). The building blocks of accounting: Ethics, principles, and assumptions. *Journal of Positive School Psychology, 6*(3), 2324–2332.

42. Hille, B., (1973). Potassium channels in myelinated nerve: Selective permeability to small cations. *The Journal of General Physiology, 61*(6), 669–686.

43. Hopkins, P. E., (1996). The effect of financial statement classification of hybrid financial instruments on financial analysts' stock price judgments. *Journal of Accounting Research, 34*, 33–50.

44. Hughes, B., Forbes, A. B., & Sun, W. J., (2011). *Good Practice for Deploying and Using iGPS/iSPACE: NIMTech Deliverable 3.1 (2)*, 2–10.

45. Izquierdo, A., Wiedholz, L. M., Millstein, R. A., Yang, R. J., Bussey, T. J., Saksida, L. M., & Holmes, A., (2006). Genetic and dopaminergic modulation of reversal learning in a touchscreen-based operant procedure for mice. *Behavioral Brain Research, 171*(2), 181–188.

46. Jorge De, J. M. A., & Jorge, S. M., (2014). From governmental accounting into national accounts: Adjustments diversity and materiality with evidence from the Iberian Countries' Central Governments. *Innovar, 24*(54), 121–138.

47. Jorge, S., Jesus, M. A., & Laureano, R., (2018). Budgetary balance adjustments from governmental accounting to national accounts in EU countries: Can deficits be prone to management? *Public Budgeting & Finance, 38*(4), 97–116.

48. Joseph, L. M., & Konrad, M., (2009). Teaching students with intellectual or developmental disabilities to write a literature review. *Research in Developmental Disabilities, 30*(1), 1–19.

49. Joudeh, O. A. A., Barakat, F. S., & Mahmoud, O. A., (2021). The effect of using accounting measurement bases (cash and accrual) on the performance of the industrial companies listed on the Palestine stock exchange. *International Journal of Financial Research, 12*(3), 393–406.

50. Knost, R., (1948). A classroom teaching procedure in bookkeeping. *The Journal of Business Education, 24*(1), 17–26.

51. Koshkin, A. A., Rajwanshi, V. K., & Wengel, J., (1998). Novel convenient syntheses of LNA [2.2. 1] bicyclo nucleosides. *Tetrahedron Letters, 39*(24), 4381–4384.

52. Kuriyam, S., Tomonari, H., Yoshida, H., Hashimoto, T., Kawaguchi, Y., & Sakai, O., (1997). Reversal of anemia by erythropoietin therapy retards the progression of chronic renal failure, especially in nondiabetic patients. *Nephron, 77*(2), 176–185.

53. Laitinen, E. K., (1994). Traditional versus operating cash flow in failure prediction. *Journal of Business Finance & Accounting, 21*(2), 195–217.

54. Lande, E., (2000). Macro-accounting and micro-accounting relationships in France. *Financial Accountability & Management, 16*(2), 151–165.

55. Littleton, A. C., (1926). Italian double entry in early England. *Accounting Review, 3*, 60–71.

56. Lividini, K., & Masters, W. A., (2022). Tracing global flows of bioactive compounds from farm to fork in nutrient balance sheets can help guide intervention towards healthier food supplies. *Nature Food, 3*(9), 703–715.

57. Low, J. S. C., Lu, W. F., & Song, B., (2014). Product structure-based integrated life cycle analysis (PSILA): A technique for cost modeling and analysis of closed-loop production systems. *Journal of Cleaner Production, 70*, 105–117.

58. Low, J. S. C., Tjandra, T. B., Lu, W. F., & Lee, H. M., (2016). Adaptation of the product structure-based integrated life cycle analysis (psila) technique for carbon footprint modeling and analysis of closed-loop production systems. *Journal of Cleaner Production, 120*, 105–123.

59. Malau, A., Teguh, M., & Muda, I., (2022). The accrual basis of accounting and the reasons for adjusting entries. *Journal of Positive School Psychology, 6*(3), 2401–2404.
60. Marinheiro, C. F., (2006). The sustainability of Portuguese fiscal policy from a historical perspective. *Empirica, 33*(2), 155–179.
61. Martínez, B., Pato, L. S., & Rico, J. M., (2012). Nutrient uptake and growth responses of three intertidal macroalgae with perennial, opportunistic, and summer-annual strategies. *Aquatic Botany, 96*(1), 14–22.
62. McCracken, L. M., (1998). Learning to live with the pain: Acceptance of pain predicts adjustment in persons with chronic pain. *Pain, 74*(1), 21–27.
63. Michalski, G., (2016). Full operating cycle influence on the food and beverages processing firms' characteristics. *Agricultural Economics-Zemedelska Ekonomika, 62*(2), 2–10.
64. Mijušković, M., (2016). Comprehending the text through the use of metacognitive strategies. *ANGLISTICUM. Journal of the Association-Institute for English Language and American Studies, 2*(6), 48–53.
65. Morrens, M., Hulstijn, W., Lewi, P., & Sabbe, B., (2008). Bleuler revisited: Psychomotor slowing in schizophrenia as part of a catatonic symptom cluster. *Psychiatry Research, 161*(1), 121–125.
66. Musselman, V. A., (1967). Let's update our bookkeeping teaching. *The Journal of Business Education, 42*(4), 143–144.
67. Musselman, V. A., (1969). The theory of adjusting entries. *The Journal of Business Education, 45*(2), 56–57.
68. Normand, C., & Wootton, C. W., (2001). The recognition and valuation of current assets on the balance sheet in the United States, 1865–1940. *Accounting Historians Journal, 28*(2), 63–108.
69. Novita, S. K., (2022). Efforts to improve student understanding on the basic competency of making adjustment journal through working papers. *Indonesian Journal of Education Teaching and Learning (IJETL), 2*(1), 51–58.
70. O'Bryan, D., Berry, K. T., Troutman, C., & Quirin, J. J., (2000). Using accounting equation analysis to teach the statement of cash flows in the first financial accounting course. *Journal of Accounting Education, 18*(2), 147–155.
71. O'Donnell, E., & Schultz, Jr. J. J., (2005). The halo effect in business risk audits: Can strategic risk assessment bias auditor judgment about accounting details? *The Accounting Review, 80*(3), 921–939.
72. Ornish, D., Larry, W. S., James, H. B., Lance, G. K., Terri, A. M., Stephen, S., William, T. A., et al., (1998). Intensive lifestyle changes for reversal of coronary heart disease. *JAMA, 23*, 2001–2007.
73. Owen, H., (1949). Teaching bookkeeping by the daily recitation method. *The Journal of Business Education, 24*(6), 24.

74. Patzig, J., Jahn, O., Tenzer, S., Wichert, S. P., De Monasterio-Schrader, P., Rosfa, S., & Werner, H. B., (2011). Quantitative and integrative proteome analysis of peripheral nerve myelin identifies novel myelin proteins and candidate neuropathy loci. *Journal of Neuroscience, 31*(45), 16369–16386.

75. Peragallo, E., (1956). Origin of the trial balance. *The Accounting Review, 31*(3), 389–394.

76. Peragallo, E., (1971). A commentary on viganó's historical development of ledger balancing procedures, adjustments, and financial statements during the fifteenth, sixteenth, and seventeenth centuries. *Accounting Review, 1*, 529–534.

77. Phillips, F., & Schmidt, R. N., (2010). Creating early success in financial accounting: Improving performance on adjusting journal entries. *Accounting Perspectives, 9*(2), 87–96.

78. Rhodes, K., & Smith, A., (2004). Using games to teach basics: Learn to love learning accounting. *Academy of Educational Leadership Journal, 8*(3), 67–75.

79. Richards, V. D., & Laughlin, E. J., (1980). A cash conversion cycle approach to liquidity analysis. *Financial Management, 1*, 32–38.

80. Roska, V., (2017). Cash principle of determining the tax in Croatia. *Economic and Social Development: Book of Proceedings,* 700–709.

81. Ruata, D. S., Tinangon, J. J., & Mawikere, L. M., (2018). Evaluasi perlakuan akuntansi aset tetap menurut PSAK No. 16 pada PT bank maluku malut cabang tobelo. *Going Concern: Jurnal Riset Akuntansi, 13*(02).

82. Ruggles, N. D., (1987). Financial accounts and balance sheets: Issues for the revision of SNA. *Review of Income and Wealth, 33*(1), 39–62.

83. Sa'eed, A., Gambo, N., Inuwa, I. I., & Musonda, I., (2020). Effects of financial management practices on the technical performance of building contractors in northeast Nigeria. *Journal of Financial Management of Property and Construction, 25*(2), 201–223.

84. Salameh, L. A., Salameh, Z. A., & Al-Emami, A. H., (2019). Measuring the effect of cognitive and metacognitive questioning strategies on EFL learners' reading comprehension in understanding, critical thinking, and the quality of schema at the university of hail-KSA. *International Journal of English Linguistics, 9*(5), 12–28.

85. Sarkar, S. K., Solel, E., Kozuch, S., & Abe, M., (2020). Heavy-atom tunneling processes during denitrogenation of 2, 3-diazabicyclo [2.2. 1] hept-2-ene and ring closure of cyclopentane-1, 3-diyl diradical. Stereoselectivity in tunneling and matrix effect. *The Journal of Organic Chemistry, 85*(14), 8881–8892.

86. Schilling, G., (1996). Working capital's role in maintaining corporate liquidity. *TMA Journal, 16*(5), 4–7.

87. Seipel, C., (1998). Using the cost of goods sold schedule to teach various accounting topics. *Accounting Educators Journal, 10*, 94–103.

88. Sembiring, H. R., Sinulingga, M. H., & Muda, I., (2022). Analysis of the effect of business transactions on the accounting equation. *Journal of Positive School Psychology, 6*(3), 2375–2379.
89. Shang, H. F., & Chang-Chien, I. J., (2010). The effect of self-questioning strategy on EFL learners' reading comprehension development. *International Journal of Learning, 17*(2).
90. Simanjuntak, Y. S. M., Ardiansyah, A., & Muda, I., (2022). Prepare a trial balance and the function. *Journal of Positive School Psychology, 6*(3), 2405–2410.
91. Song, M., Zhu, S., Wang, J., & Wang, S., (2019). China's natural resources balance sheet from the perspective of government oversight: Based on the analysis of governance and accounting attributes. *Journal of Environmental Management, 248*, 109232.
92. Sormin, K. S. B., Afrida, T. B., & Muda, I., (2022). Government accounting activities and users in Indonesia. *Journal of Positive School Psychology, 6*(3), 2380–2387.
93. Stewart, J. P., Kim, S., Bielak, J., Dobry, R., & Power, M. S., (2003). Revisions to soil-structure interaction procedures in NEHRP design provisions. *Earthquake Spectra, 19*(3), 677–696.
94. Stoehlmacher, J., Park, D. J., Zhang, W., Yang, D., Groshen, S., Zahedy, S., & Lenz, H. J., (2004). A multivariate analysis of genomic polymorphisms: Prediction of clinical outcome to 5-FU/oxaliplatin combination chemotherapy in refractory colorectal cancer. *British Journal of Cancer, 91*(2), 344–354.
95. Suresh, R., Huq, S. M., & Arunachalam, L., (2022). A study on financial performance analysis with reference to super auto forge Pvt Ltd. *Elementary Education Online, 19*(3), 4715–4715.
96. Talley, N. J., Locke, III. G. R., Herrick, L. M., Silvernail, V. M., Prather, C. M., Lacy, B. E., & Zinsmeister, A. R., (2012). Functional dyspepsia treatment trial (FDTT): A double-blind, randomized, placebo-controlled trial of antidepressants in functional dyspepsia, evaluating symptoms, psychopathology, pathophysiology, and pharmacogenetics. *Contemporary Clinical Trials, 33*(3), 523–533.
97. Tjandra, G., Marpaung, M., & Muda, I., (2022). How accounts, debits, and credits are used to record business transactions. *Journal of Positive School Psychology, 6*(3), 2311–2323.
98. Torabi, M. A., & Gholinia, E., (2010). The effect of teaching cognitive and metacognitive strategies on reading comprehension ability. *Journal of English Language Pedagogy and Practice, 4*(8), 208–227.
99. Torres, M. J., Rincón, M. E., Lentz, H. A., & González, C. L., (2014). Alternative energies in physics, a proposal for exploring the teaching of physics concepts with the solar water heater. *Energy Procedia, 57*, 975–981.
100. Velázquez, C. B., & Carrillo, J. T., (2013). Evaluation of two tutorial teaching programs intended to support English as a foreign language beginners' writing and listening skills development. In: *INTED2013 Proceedings* (Vol. 1, pp. 6255–6259).

101. Vu, T. M. T., Truong, T. V., & Dinh, D. T., (2020). Determinants of liquidity in manufacturing firms. *The Journal of Asian Finance, Economics, and Business, 7*(12), 11–19.

102. Wallace, W. C., (1933). Methods in advanced bookkeeping, part II. *The Journal of Business Education, 8*(9), 13, 14.

103. Warfield, T. D., Wild, J. J., & Wild, K. L., (1995). Managerial ownership, accounting choices, and informativeness of earnings. *Journal of Accounting and Economics, 20*(1), 61–91.

104. Whiting, D. A., Waldstreicher, J., Sanchex, M., & Kaufman, K. D., (1999). Measuring reversal of hair miniaturization in androgenetic alopecia by follicular counts in horizontal sections of serial scalp biopsies: Results of finasteride 1 mg treatment of men and postmenopausal women. In: *Journal of Investigative Dermatology Symposium Proceedings* (Vol. 4, No. 3, pp. 282–284).

105. Wilson, R. M., & Stenson, J. A., (2008). Valuation of information assets on the balance sheet: The recognition and approaches to the valuation of intangible assets. *Business Information Review, 25*(3), 167–182.

106. Xiao, J. J., & Olson, G. I., (1993). Mental accounting and saving behavior. *Home Economics Research Journal, 22*(1), 92–109.

107. Yamaguchi, T., & Oba, M., (2020). Measurable interactive application to find out user recognition and strategy when problem-solving. *J. of Software, 15*(1), 12–22.

108. Yeung, K., Richards, J., Goemer, E., Lozano, P., Lapham, G., Williams, E., & Bradley, K., (2020). Costs of using evidence-based implementation strategies for behavioral health integration in a large primary care system. *Health Services Research, 55*(6), 913–923.

109. Zhu, D. L., Duan, W. J., Zhang, H., & Du, T., (2021). Natural resource balance sheet compilation: A land resource asset accounting case. *Journal of Chinese Governance, 6*(4), 515–536.

110. Zulaiha, I., Miraza, M., & Muda, I., (2022). The mechanism of prepare closing entries and a post-closing trial balance. *Journal of Positive School Psychology, 6*(3), 2395–2400.

CHAPTER 3

ACCOUNTING FOR DEPRECIATION AND RECONCILIATION STATEMENTS

UNIT INTRODUCTION

Depreciation is the term used to describe the decrease in quality or loss of value of a fixed property due to wear and tear, the passage of time, and obsolescence brought on by advances in technology and the market, among other causes. With a few probable exceptions, such as land and artifacts, devaluation occurs in the context of all fixed assets, even though the practice may be subtle or gradual. Regardless of how frequently investments are repaired and maintained correctly, depreciation still occurs. Depreciation and the idea of business income are strongly intertwined. We cannot declare that the business income has been accurately determined unless it is credited against revenues; using long-term resources tends to deplete their economic value over time, rendering them unusable. To accurately quantify the firm's income, the monetary value that was so obsessed must be retrieved from its revenue. Therefore, the method accountants employ to recover the cost of permanent assets over time is the practice of charging depreciation.

Depreciation is the distribution of a stock's depreciable amount over the estimated usefulness of the item. According to AS-6, depreciation is a measurement of the value of a depreciable asset that is lost due to usage, the passage of time, or expiry due to technological and market developments. During the anticipated productive life of the assets, depreciation is assigned to charge a reasonable percentage of the depreciable amount in each accounting period. A specified asset's life span is amortized as part of depreciation.

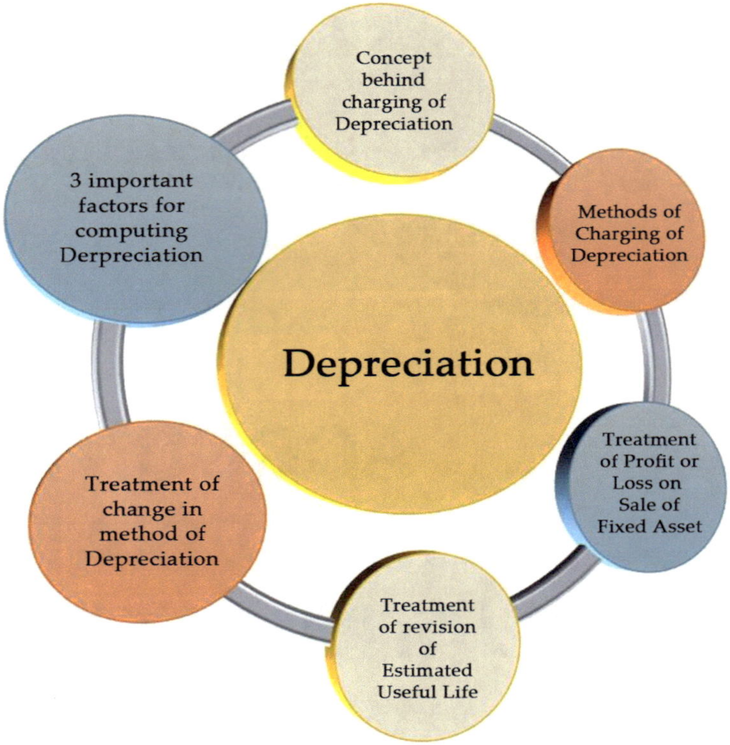

Figure 3.1. Schematic showing the concept of Depreciation (Source: Sanjay Kumar Sharma, Creative Commons License).

Depreciation is the distribution of a stock's depreciable amount over the anticipated use of the item. According to AS-6, depreciation is a measurement of the value of a depreciable asset that is lost due to usage, the passage of time, or expiry due to technological and market developments. During the anticipated productive life of the assets, depreciation is assigned to charge a reasonable percentage of the depreciable amount for each accounting period. A specified asset's life span is amortized as part of depreciation.

These definitions make it evident that during the asset's anticipated useful life, a fair percentage of the asset's depreciable amount should be allocated to each accounting period. The historical cost of an asset, less the expected residual value, is the depreciable amount. Finally, it can be said that depreciation is the steady loss of an asset's economic worth due to any factor.

Learning Objective

At the end of this chapter, readers will be able to learn:

- The concepts of depletion, obsolescence, and amortization.
- The causes of depreciation in accounting.

- Methods of calculating depreciation in accounting.
- The concepts of reserves and provisions in accounting.
- The idea of reconciliation statement.

Key Terms

- Depreciation
- Depletion
- Obsolescence
- Amortization
- Reserves
- Provisions
- Reconciliation Statement
- Income
- Bank Balance

3.1. DEPRECIATION, DEPLETION, OBSOLESCENCE, AND AMORTIZATION

There is often conflation between the terms depletion, depreciation, amortization, and obsolescence. Moreover, these many names have been created for accounting to describe this process for various asset categories. The following is a description of these terms:

Figure 3.2. Image showing the difference between Depreciation, Depletion, and Amortization (Source: Michael Brown, Creative Commons License).

Depreciation Depletion and Amortization

Depreciation	Wear and tear of a physical asset	Equipment
Depletion	Exhaustion of the supply of a resource	Coal mine
Amortization	Extinction of an intangible asset	Patent

3.1.1. Depreciation

Depreciation is adding the cost of fixed assets humans created to operations (and not determining asset value for the balance sheet). Depreciation is employed when the usefulness of a physical asset (a building, piece of equipment, or machinery) has expired and needs to be reported.

3.1.2. Depletion

This phrase describes taking a readily available yet permanent resource, like coal from a miner or oil from a well. In contrast to depreciation, which denotes a decrease in an asset's ability to perform its intended function, depletion indicates elimination of a natural resource.

3.1.3. Amortization

Amortization is the method of depreciating intangible assets. Copyrights, patents, goodwill, and leaseholds are examples of intangible assets recorded at cost in the books of account. Because many of these resources have a short shelf life, they are written off.

3.1.4. Obsolescence

It describes the shortening of an asset's useful life as a result of (i) technological breakthroughs, (ii) shifts in consumer demand, (iii) constraints imposed by law or other authorities, or (iv) improvements in the process of production.

3.2. CAUSES OF DEPRECIATION

The following factors contribute to the depreciation:

3.2.1. Constant Usage

Assets lose their functioning ability due to continual use, which also causes wear and tear. As a result, decreased capacity may cause a fall in the value of the assets. As they are used continuously, things like furniture and machines lose weight.

Remember

When applied to an asset, amortization is similar to depreciation.

3.2.2. Passage of Time

With time, many fixed assets depreciate; this is valid for fixed intellectual purchases, including copyrights, leasehold properties, and patents. The term amortization typically denotes the decline in such asset value.

3.2.3. Depletion

The value of some assets also declines due to depletion; this is valid for purchases like forest stands, oil wells, and mines being wasted. These assets reduce value over time due to the ongoing mineral or oil extraction until, eventually, they are fully depleted.

3.2.4. Obsolescence

The asset itself might not have undergone any destruction. Despite this, the emergence of a better approach, machine, or process may lead to a decrease in the usefulness of an asset. For instance, despite being in good functioning order, an old machine may need to be replaced with a new one since the latter is more effective and economical. The asset becomes outdated due to discoveries, advancements in manufacturing techniques, shifts in consumer demand, etc.

3.2.5. Accidents

If an asset is subjected to an accident, its value may be reduced.

3.2.6. Permanent Fall in the Market Value

Depreciation is the term used to describe a permanent drop in the value of some assets. Depreciation, for instance, could be considered the long-term reduction in the market value of investments and securities.

3.3. NEED FOR PROVIDING DEPRECIATION

Offering depreciation is necessary due to the following reasons.

KEYWORD

Financial Situation means the salary, wages, investments, savings or debt of a person.

3.3.1. To find out the Profits or Losses

When all of the expenses associated with generating income have been correctly deducted from them, genuine profits or losses can be determined. Fixed assets like buildings, plants, furniture, cars, and other items are crucial for generating revenue for a corporation. However, the fixed asset's cost is not reflected in the profit or loss for the accounting period in which the asset is acquired. As a result, the fixed asset's price, less its salvage value, must be equitably distributed among the periods that profit from its use. Depreciation is a type of company expense that must be allowed to match costs to revenue properly.

3.3.2. To Exhibit the Asset at Its Appropriate Demand

Over time, the assets lose value for various causes, including elapsed time, continuous use, accidents, etc. As a result, the investment will show up on the balance sheet with an exaggerated value if depreciation is not paid. This method is unethical since it would mask the financial situation on the balance sheet.

3.3.3. Assets Replacement

When a business asset's life expires, it becomes useless and must be replaced. Accounting for depreciation keeps the company's cash resources from being paid as dividends. If placed away annually, the saved resources might be sufficient to replace them when the asset's life span is up.

3.3.4. Reduction of Income Tax

As tax is charged on business income without taking depreciation into account, the amount paid will exceed the real income tax. The company suffers a loss as a result. Depreciation must be subtracted from income similar to other costs for tax purposes because it is a charged expense and generates a tax advantage.

3.4. FACTORS AFFECTING DEPRECIATION

The following three crucial variables should be taken into account when determining the value of depreciation to be assessed about an asset within a specific accounting period:

3.4.1. Asset Cost

Calculating the depreciation amount to be recorded to the account for profit and loss involves knowing the asset's cost. Moreover, the financial costs, including interest on borrowed money used to purchase the product, should not be figured into the asset's price.

3.4.2. Predicted Life of An Asset

In practice, estimated life refers to the years an asset could be maintained in a commercial setting while requiring essential maintenance and generating income. When calculating an asset's life span, one must first consider the asset's physical existence, any changes done, reasons for obsolescence, and previous experiences with similar assets. In practice, an asset's economic life is less than its physical life. Internal policies, including frequency, repairs, management, and replacement, primarily determine the physical life. On the contrary, economic life is driven mainly by external causes like obsolescence due to technological developments.

KEYWORD

Interest is payment from a borrower or deposit-taking financial institution to a lender or depositor of an amount above repayment of the principal sum, at a particular rate.

3.4.3. Scrap Asset Value

The value that will likely be realized from the asset's sale when its useful life is up is known as the asset's salvage value. The disposal charges should be subtracted from the asset's sale value before arriving at this figure. If the scrap value is regarded insufficient, it is typically taken to be zero.

3.5. METHODS OF CALCULATING DEPRECIATION

The nature of depreciation is subject to several concepts. Additionally, no two permanent assets can have the same kind of nature. Different techniques are discovered to arise for charging depreciation as a consequence. The methods can be categorized as follows:

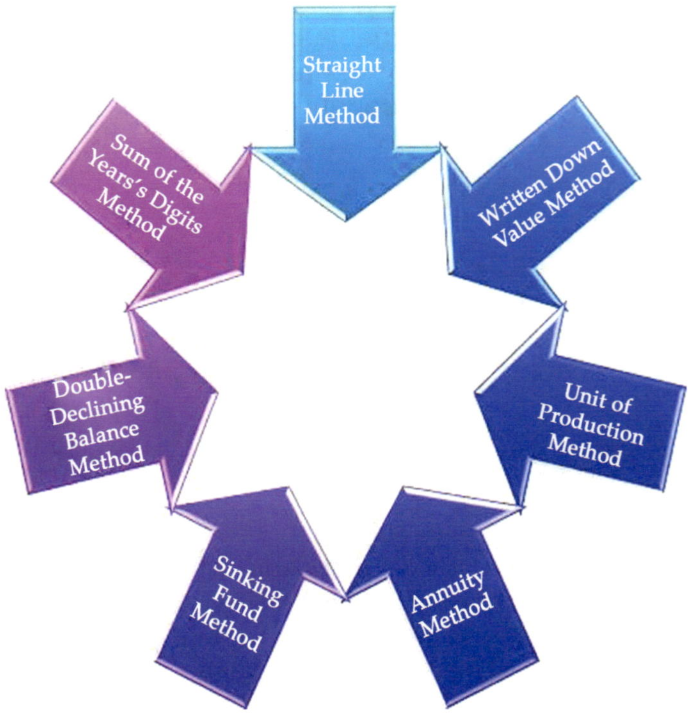

Figure 3.3. Illustrating different depreciation methods (Source: Anjali J, Creative Commons License).

3.5.1. Straight Line Method

The fixed installment system is another name for this. This system charges depreciation consistently each year. A straight line will result if the annual depreciation charged using this method is drawn on graph paper. Because of this, the straight-line technique assumes that depreciation is a time factor rather than use, meaning that each accounting period receives the same advantage from utilizing the asset as every other period. For each accounting period, the depreciation charge is calculated using the following formula:

$$\text{Amount of annual Depreciation} - \frac{\text{Original cost of the fixed assets - Residual value}}{\text{Estimated Life in Years}}$$

For example, if an asset cost Rs. 50,000 and it will have a residual value of Rs. 2000 at the end of its useful life of 10 years, the amount of annual depreciation will be Rs. 4800 and it will be calculated as follow:

$$\text{Depreciation} - \frac{\text{Rs. } 50{,}000 - 2000}{10 \text{ Years}} = \text{Rs. } 4800$$

There are many problems with this strategy. The first is that seasonal changes, booms, and busts are disregarded. The level of depreciation is the same whether the machine is used continually or sometimes for a few months. Second, it ignores the interest accrued on the money used to purchase that product. Third, the total cost of using the asset (i.e., depreciation and management) is going up despite though the assets might have been utilized each year consistently. For example, early years have significantly lower costs for repairs and depreciation than later years. Due to increasing repair expenditures, each consecutive year is burdened with more outstanding usage fees.

Did you get it?

Depreciation methods that provide for a higher depreciation charge in the first year of an asset's life and gradually decreasing charges in subsequent years are called accelerated depreciation methods.

3.5.2. Diminishing Balance Method

The Written Down Value Method (WDV) is another name for this. Depreciation is based annually on the lowering balance (lower cost depreciation) under the decreasing balance approach at a fixed rate. As a result, depreciation continues to decrease annually. According to this system, depreciation is likewise moved to account for profit and loss for each year, and the asset is reflected on the balance sheet at book value after depreciation has been subtracted from it. For instance, depreciation during the first year will be Rs. 2000 if an asset is bought for Rs. 10,000, and depreciation is to be charged at 20% p.a. on a declining balance method. It will be Rs. 1600 in the second year (20% of 8000), Rs. 1280 in the next year (20% of 6400), and so on.

Benefits of the Method of Reducing Balance:

i. Despite the early variance in the book value after depreciation, it is pretty simple to comprehend and compute the amount of depreciation.

ii. Because the amount of depreciation continues to decrease each year while the cost of repairs continues to rise, this method evenly distributes the cost of using the asset over each subsequent year.

iii. The act of income tax in force in India has also approved this procedure.

3.6. PROVISION

A provision is a portion of the profits set aside for a future obligation, the amount of which cannot be determined with certainty at the time the financial accounts are finalized. In any business, there may be certain foreseen or unexpected occurrences that the businesspeople must manage without further postponing them. Accordingly, every corporate firm needs to operate responsibly, according to the convention of conservatism. When the financial statements are prepared, the required provisions and reserves must be established.

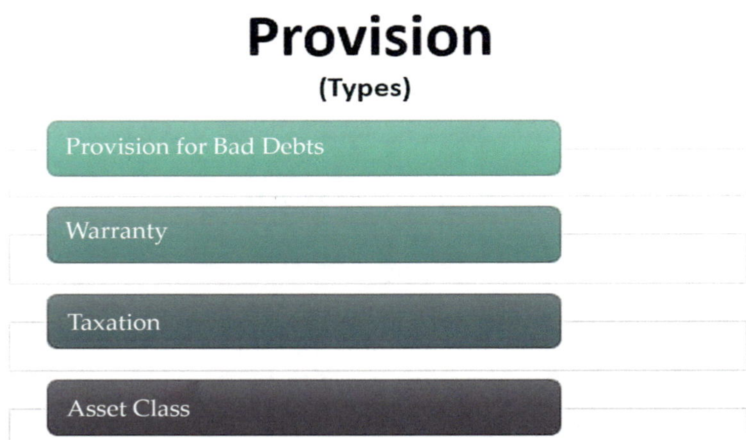

Figure 3.4. Illustration of the different types of Provision (Source: Ashish Kumar Srivastav, Creative Commons License).

A liability that will undoubtedly be paid but whose exact amount is unknown must be provided. If the precise sum can be determined, it changes from a provision to a liability. A few examples of conditions include "Provision for Depreciation," "Provision for Legal Damages," "Provision for Doubtful Debts," "Provision for Taxation," and "Provision for Discount on Debtors."

The concept that a provision is a charge against earnings implies that it must be included in the financial statements whether or not a business firm is making a reasonable profit. Provisions must be made, even if the company enterprise is experiencing severe losses. It is important to note that since the formation of conditions is an internal operation, they have no impact on cash flow.

A "provision" is defined as "any amount written off or maintained by way of paying for depreciation, repairs, or diminishment assets value, or maintained by way of covering for any known liability of which the amount cannot be determined with substantial accuracy" in Part III, Schedule VI of the Companies Act, 1956.

Did you get it?

Depreciation methods that provide for a higher depreciation charge in the first year of an asset's life and gradually decreasing charges in subsequent years are called accelerated depreciation methods.

3.6.1. Provisions Objectives

(i) *To determine the True Net Profit:* To calculate the business's genuine net profit, expenses from that year, whether paid or unpaid, must be displayed in the loss and profit account. Additionally, a provision should be made for any costs or liabilities whose precise amount is ambiguous or impossible to estimate. For instance, requirements for doubtful debts and debtor discounts have been made.

(ii) *To determine the True Financial Position:* Only when the company makes sufficient allowances for all losses and expenses will the balance sheet reflect a genuine and accurate picture of its financial situation.

(iii) *To determine the Known Future Losses:* Actions should be taken to offset some of the profits to cover an unknowable future liability. As an illustration, consider making provisions for taxes, bad debts, repairs, etc.

(iv) *To determine the continuous Charge on Income Statements:* Provisions must be established to distribute costs and losses equally throughout all years to perform accurate analysis. For instance, Rs. 10,000 was to be spent during the machine's expected 10-year lifespan.

In this instance, it would be better to divide the Rs. 10,000 into ten equal payments over ten years rather than debiting it all at once so that the Account for Profit and Loss would be loaded following the advantages obtained from using the machine over ten years.

3.6.2. Treatment and Types of Provision in Accounting

As a result, establishing provisions guarantee accurate synchronization of expenses and revenues and accurate profit computation. When producing financial statements, the following conditions are made:

Remember

Doubtful debts may be the result of either objective evidence (as in the case of Bad Debts) or it may be subjective, based on current information received or conduct of the account, that may not yet warrant the account be classified as Bad.

(i) *Provision for Bad and Doubtful Debts:* In practice, there are a few debts that cannot be collected from debtors or receivables for various reasons, including debtor death, bankruptcy, insolvency, or untraceable debtors. These debtors and receivables are classified as bad debts in the books.

(ii) *Provision for discount to debtors:* We must offer a discount to all our different debtors and receivables to receive payment earlier. Therefore, it is necessary to make a provision for the value to debtors or receivables in the current year.

(iii) *Provision for Discount from Creditors:* To receive payment faster, the creditors or payables will also offer us a concession. Therefore, it is necessary to make a provision for the benefit from creditors or payable in the current year. Moreover, in reality, one should only offer a concession from creditors if there is a contract between the company and the creditors for some provision of discount or cash back (as in the case of modern digital transactions). The concession provision is stated in the contract or is offered in advance as a rate.

(iv) *Provision for Taxation:* The requirement for taxes is to cover anticipated income tax owed on income received in the current year.

(v) *Provision for Depreciation:* The requirement for a depreciation account, which is displayed either on the "liabilities side" of the balance sheet or by way of a reduction from the initial cost of the asset in question on the asset side of the balance sheet, contains the depreciation that has been paid to date.

3.7. RESERVE

Reserve refers to utilizing profits or other balances to increase the business's liquid resources rather than cover obligations, liabilities, or contingencies.

The amount reserved from profits and other surpluses that is not in any way designated to fulfill any specific obligation known to be present as of the balance sheet date is referred to as a reserve, according to William Pickles.

The money set aside from earnings or surpluses to reserves, which will support the company during a challenging financial moment, actually applies to the owner and the capital the proprietor has contributed. It is an ownership of profits rather than a levy against them. This implies that reserves cannot be built in the event of a loss. Reserves strengthen the financial standing of the company enterprise.

They were not established to cover any liabilities, obligations, or eventualities. It is vital to note that while the company cannot set aside money in case of losses, it can do so in the event of a loss. The term "Reserve Fund" refers to the amount of reserve invested in external securities. Reserves are recorded in the Profit and Loss Appropriation Account rather than the Profit and Loss Account because they constitute an allocation rather than a charge against profits.

3.7.1. Reserve Types

There are generally two types of reserves:

(i) Revenue reserves and

(ii) Capital Reserves

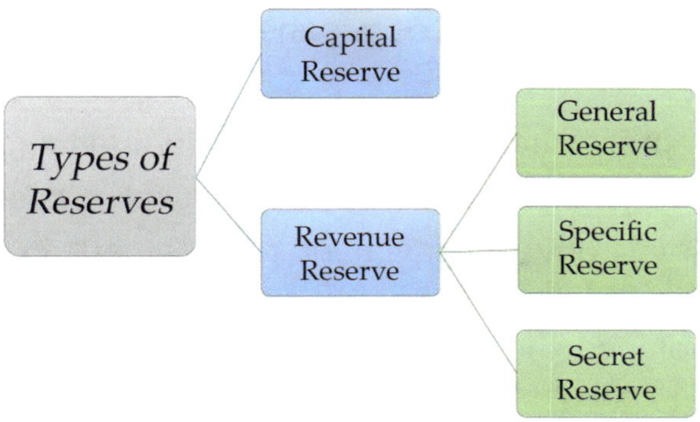

Figure 3.5. Schematic of different types of reserves (Source: Anjali J, Creative Commons License).

3.7.2. Revenue Reserves

Profits made in the regular course and from the normal operations of the business concern are used to generate revenue reserves.

Revenue reserves can also be categorized as

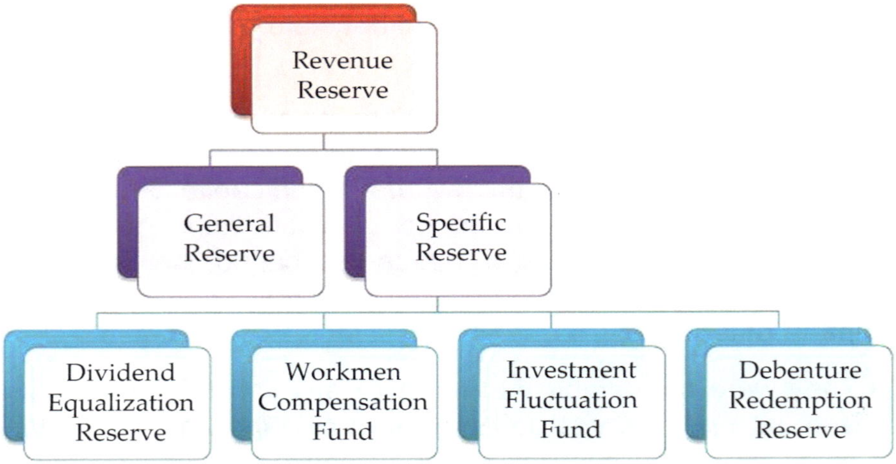

Figure 3.6. Schematic of different types of Revenue Reserves (Source: Surbhi S, Creative Commons License).

a) General Reserve
b) Specific Reserve and
c) Secret Reserve.

3.7.3. General Reserve

The amount of profits known as a general reserve is set aside for public purposes rather than being produced for any particular use. These are typically kept on hand to help the business's financial position and give it access to more working capital as required. This reserve is also referred to as a "Contingency Reserve" or "Free Reserve" because it can be used for any unforeseen reason.

Any corporate firm creates a general reserve for the following reasons:

a) To improve the company's financial standing
b) To always have more working capital accessible
c) To cover any obligation or replacement in the event of unanticipated events
d) To balance the dividend rate over time in the event of insufficient profits.

3.7.4. Specific Reserve

For some particular uses, specific reserves are made. These reserves may only be used for the intended reason they were established. Specific reserves might be used, at the board of directors' judgment, for purposes other than those they originally intended if the articles of association permit.

Here are a few instances of particular reserves:

a) Workmen Compensation Fund
b) Investment Fluctuation Reserve
c) Dividend Equalization Reserve
d) Debenture Redemption Reserve

3.7.4.1. Workmen Compensation Fund

The Workmen Compensation Fund was established to cover the requests of the employees if they sustain injuries in an accident.

Remember

Both corporations and governments frequently issue debentures to raise capital or funds.

3.7.4.2. Investment Fluctuation Reserve

Businesses occasionally invest their excess cash in debentures, shares, or other instruments outside their core operations. Additionally, the cost of these assets constantly fluctuates, depending on various market factors, governmental regulations, etc. Businesses set aside a portion of their profits as an Investment Fluctuation Reserve to cover any losses they may incur should the value of these investments decline. This reserve is then used to cover any losses that may occur.

3.7.4.3. Dividend Equalization Reserve

A reserve for dividend equalization is established to balance the dividend rate throughout the years. Typically, a part of profits is moved into this account in years of high and sufficient profits, and in years with low yields, the money held in this account can be utilized to pay dividends to shareholders.

3.7.4.4. Debenture Redemption Reserve

A debenture redemption reserve is established for the intention of redemption debentures after a given period. In this regard, a fixed amount from the distributable profits is set up in this reserve each year. The sum is to be put toward buying securities. The needed amount, which must be paid to debenture holders, is the sum generated with compound interest.

3.7.4.5. Secret Reserve

A reserve that does not appear on the balance sheet is a private reserve. It can be built during years of increased profits and combined with gains throughout years of low yields. The following are ways to construct private reserves:

a) Stock undervaluation
b) Establishment of more provisions than essential,
c) Addition of capital expenses to revenue.
d) Representation of future liabilities as current liabilities of the company.

The outer world is unaware of the existence of the private reserve. It is advised that a private reserve be constructed within reasonable bounds while keeping in mind the case's requirements.

> **KEYWORD**
>
> **Capital expense** is the money an organization or corporate entity spends to buy, maintain, or improve its fixed assets, such as buildings, vehicles, equipment, or land.

3.7.4.6. Capital Reserves

The reserves produced from capital gains are known as capital reserves. Here are some examples of objects that could make up capital reserves:

a) Gain from Fixed Asset Sales
b) Profit on Fixed Asset Revaluation
c) The Securities Premium is obtained upon the issuance of bonds or shares.
d) Profit from Debenture Redemption.
e) Profit made before incorporation,
f) profit made from the reissuing of forfeited shares, etc.

Capital losses may be written off using cash holdings. Moreover, the capital reserves of a joint stock company may also be used to grant paid entirely bonus shares to the members. Shareholders typically do not have access to capital reserves for revenue sharing.

Moreover, if the following requirements are met, some capital reserves, like the profit from the sale of fixed assets, may be used for dividend distribution:

If the corporation is allowed to do so according to its articles of association, it must have acquired cash profits from the sale of fixed assets, and such gains persist after the revaluation of all assets and liabilities, not just investments.

3.8. CONCEPT OF INCOME

"Concept of Income" is one of the essential accounting principles. Similarly, an accountant's ability to measure a company's income is crucial. In practice, money obtained in exchange for goods or services is income. For instance, a worker's wage counts as income. There are many various types of earnings, including gross, net, national, and personal incomes; however, our focus here is mainly on company income. Business income is the amount of revenue that is earned more than expenses.

KEYWORD

Personal income includes compensation from a number of sources, including salaries, wages, and bonuses received from employment or self-employment, dividends and distributions received from investments, rental receipts from real estate investments, and profit sharing from businesses.

3.8.1. Net Income Objectives

The fundamental objectives of a net income are as follows:

The foundation for future estimates is the historical income figure.

a) A net income must be determined to provide a percentage of the profit to the employees.
b) It facilitates the evaluation of initiatives that maximize the use of limited resources. It contributes to a company's wealth growth.
c) Determining a net income is helpful for any firm that wants to pay dividends to its shareholders.
d) Return on capital employed provides insight into a business's general efficiency.

3.8.2. Income Definition

The most accurate definition of income is provided by the American Accounting Association, which states that realized net income "measures an enterprise's effectiveness as an operative unit and is the change in its net assets arising out of an (a) excess or deficiency of revenue compared with the related expired cost, and (b) other gains or losses to the enterprise from sales, exchange or another conversion of assets."

The American Accounting Association states that money must be realized to qualify as company income. For instance, merely increasing a company's asset worth is insufficient to allow business revenue; the asset must have been sold.

A period is needed to assess any financial needs rather than a point in time. All parties that demand periodic accounting reports must provide them at suitable intervals, including owners, creditors, investors, and the government. The most extended period between assessments is one year, as it enables a business person to take any remedial action. To quantify the income of the concerns, we must have both the matching idea and the realization idea, which are closely tied to an accounting period concept. The gain or loss for the accounting period will be established by comparing the costs in a specific accounting period (often a year) with the revenues (depending on the realization principle).

KEYWORD

A gain is a general increase in the value of an asset or property.

3.8.3. Accounting Concept and Income Measurement

Various accounting ideas and procedures apply to the calculation of accounting income. The following table provides based-on accounting principles and conventions for calculating accounting income.

3.8.3.1. Conservatism

The "conservatism approach" is used when an income from one interval may be transferred to another to calculate payment.

The conservative convention dictates that while calculating a business income, the "playing it safe" policy is used, and an accountant works to ensure the recorded profit is accurate. One of the critical instances when it comes to applying the concept of income measurement is measuring stock at cost or market price, whatever is less. However, it must be ensured that there are no excess reserves, doubtful debt provisions, or depreciation allowances.

3.8.3.2. Consistency

This idea holds that the consistency principle should be maintained in accounting procedures, such as how assets, obligations, expenses, and revenues, are handled, to ensure that accounting records from one period may be compared to those from another.

As a result, financial statements must be prepared to assume that the data provided are comparable with those of the prior year following the accounting profession and the corporate laws of most nations.

3.8.3.3. Entity Concept

An entrepreneur and a business are separate entities based on the idea of entities. For instance, interest on capital is a business expense, yet it provides income to the entrepreneur. We cannot, therefore, treat corporate revenue as personal income or the opposite.

KEYWORD

Capital is typically cash or liquid assets being held or obtained for expenditures.

3.8.3.4. Going Concern Concept

This idea assumes that business will endure for a very long time. This idea is the foundation for allocating depreciation to a Fixed Asset.

3.8.3.5. Accrual Concept

This idea states that an income must be recorded during the time it was generated and that costs must be equal to the revenue of time.

3.8.3.6. Accounting Period

Using a calendar year or an actual business year to track business performance is preferable.

3.8.4. Computation of Business Income

To calculate business income, the two following methods are used:

3.8.4.1. Balance Sheet Approach

The balance sheet approach compares a company's closing values (Assets fewer external liabilities) to its opening values at the start of the accounting period. When calculating the business revenue of a company, a capital increase will be removed from the above amount, and addition of drawings will be added. As income is determined using the balance sheet, the term "balance sheet approach" is used.

3.8.4.2. Transaction Approach

Most transactions are tied to manufacturing, buying, and selling things, and each of these transactions is directly or indirectly linked to revenue or cost. As a result, income measurement is the excess revenue collected through the sale of commodities, overspent during production, or purchased outright. The businesses that use the double entry technique largely adhere to it.

3.8.5. Measurement of Business Income

The following factors can be used to estimate one's income:

a) Revenues – Making money is made through the sale of goods and the provision of services. Thus, it can be described as compensation that the company receives in exchange for providing goods and services to its clients.

b) *Expenses* – Costs that have expired are expenses. The costs that were expended in the process of generating income are referred to as expired costs. Expenditures show the assets depleted as a byproduct of a business's services.

KEYWORD

Commodities are basic goods and materials that are widely used and are not meaningfully differentiated from one another.

3.8.6. Measurement of Revenue

The notion of accrual accounting is used to measure revenue. The period during which revenue accrues is the accounting period. As a result, receiving money and earning money are two separate things. According to this definition, revenue is only considered earned when it is truly realized, not usually when it is received.

3.8.7. Measurement of Expenses

When things are delivered to clients, the revenue is directly correlated. Office salaries and rent have a tangential relationship with income.

The following four sorts of occurrences should be carefully considered as expenses for a certain period, as well as any expenditures and cash payments related to those items:

a) Expenditures are outlaid for the current fiscal year.

b) Some before this period expenses have now been included in the current year's expenses.

c) In the following accounting periods, an item incurred this year becomes an expense. As an illustration, consider the purchase of fixed assets and depreciation in the upcoming years.

d) Costs incurred this year will be reimbursed in subsequent accounting years. For instance, an outstanding expenditure

3.9. RECONCILIATION STATEMENT

3.9.1. Bank Reconciliation purpose

Considering the overall goal of comprehending the reason for bank reconciliation is essential. To enable the preparation of final accounts, financial records are kept. The entire financial records must be trustworthy since the primary objective of final accounts would be that they fairly portray the company's income, financial condition, and expenditures. This implies that proper recording of all transactions is required.

KEYWORD

A bank statement is a list of all transactions for a bank account over a set period, usually monthly.

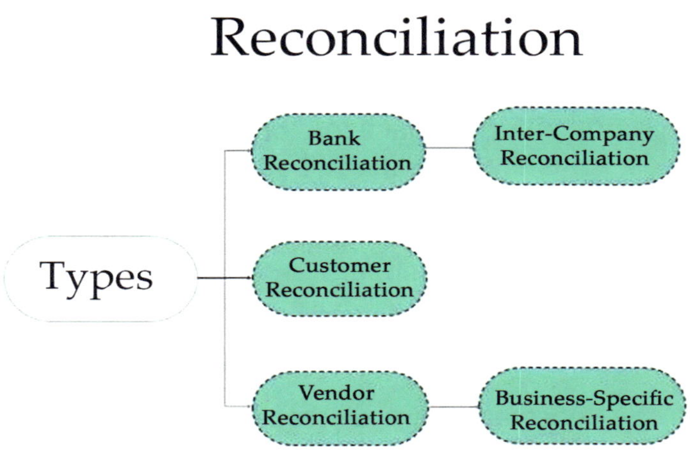

Figure 3.7. Diagram showing different types of Reconciliation (Source: Ashish Kumar Srivastav, Creative Commons License).

Thus, a bank reconciliation aims to confirm the accuracy of the records for bank transactions; this indicates that completing a bank reconciliation requires more than just accurate arithmetic. A statement that compares the balance on the bank account in the entity's accounting and the bank statement is insufficient. Instead, this is crucial to ensure the ledger balance is accurately described by adding any necessary corrections so that the rectified ledger balance may be compared to the balance on the bank statement. Conduct a reconciliation between the statement balance and the rectified ledger balance, as stated in outcome 12 (e).

So, the goal of a bank reconciliation is to verify that the bank balance is accurately represented in the final accounts and to verify the validity of the bank balance in the entity's ledger.

3.9.2. Reporting the Bank Balance

The bank balance to be recorded in the final accounts is the rectified ledger balance, as inferred from the description above. If the rectified balance is a debit balance, the entity will have money in the bank, which needs to be listed as a current asset on the balance sheet. The bank account is overspent if the adjusted balance is positive; this needs to be listed as a present obligation on the balance sheet.

KEYWORD

Lodgement means any deposit of money into the Account.

3.9.2.1. Process

Comparing the two sets of records (the entity's ledger and the bank statement) and spotting any discrepancies constitute the process of performing a bank reconciliation. Both documents will contain a significant proportion of transactions, but there will unavoidably be discrepancies. An exam question will often begin with one of these differences. Therefore, choosing how to handle each variation is the exam's duty. Examining the causes of disparities may be the most straightforward approach.

3.9.2.2. Time differences

These are the most apparent discrepancies since they are just transactions reported differently in each set of records at different times. They appear since the entity will note the issuance of checks or deposit requests to the bank when the activity starts. Moreover, due to the structure of the financial system, presenting a statement to the bank or having a deposit verified by the bank may take longer than expected.

These discrepancies are merely things for reconciliation. As a result, no ledger entry is needed; however, such things should be listed on the bank reconciliation.

3.9.2.3. Transactions initiated by the bank

The bank may start a transaction for several reasons. The bank may have assessed interest or fees or compensated the company, with interest being the most obvious possibility.

When the paying bank does not recognize a check submitted by the business, the bank starts a less visible form of transaction. In these situations, the bank will create a debit charge to cancel the deposit and another debit charge to cover the bank's costs. The business often would not be made aware of such transactions until it receives the bank statement. These transactions must be entered into the entity's ledger and considered when calculating the adjusted bank balance if the final accounts are to be trusted.

It is essential to consider that the bank statement is a copy of the transaction log that the bank keeps. As a result, transactions are documented from the viewpoint of the bank. A lodgment will therefore appear as a credit entry on the bank statement because it raises the bank's obligation to the account owner. A lodgment will be recorded in the account holder's books as a debit item in the general ledger for the bank account. Like this, bank fees issued checks and charges will appear as debit entries on the bank statement but will be recorded as credit entries in the account holder's general ledger. A balance at the bank will therefore appear as a credit balance on the bank statement and a debit balance on the account in the account holder's general ledger.

Omitted transactions by the entity: It goes without saying that if a transaction is missing, an entry must be recorded in the ledger to keep the record accurate. The transaction type that has been missing will determine the nature of the entrance.

Incorrect recording of transactions: These are likely the most challenging issues to resolve. The first thing to consider is whether the bank or the company made a mistake. A ledger record must be created if the entity is responsible for the error. A correction will be issued to the reconciliation statement if the bank is to blame for the inaccuracy. The value will be the combined result of erasing the erroneous entry and restoring the actual access in both situations.

ACTIVITY 3.1.

ROLTA India limited is an Indian company operating in India and overseas. It provides software/information technology based engineering and geospatial solutions and services to customers across the world and has executed projects in more than 35 countries.

A company's balance sheet discloses the financial position or rather health of the company. The financial position of an enterprise is influenced by the economic resources, financial structure, liquidity, solvency and its capacity to adapt to changes in the environment. However, it is becoming increasingly clear that intangible assets have a significant role in defining the growth of a company. So often, the search for the added value invariably leads us to calculating and evaluating the intangible assets of the business.

What do you understand by measuring the intangibles assets?

SUMMARY

- Depreciation is a strategy used in accounting to divide the expense of a physical or item acquired with the goal of the asset's useful life. Depreciation indicates the extent to which an asset's worth has been consumed. It helps businesses to generate income from the resources they control by compensating for them over time. Because firms are not required to account for them in the year they are acquired fully, the initial cost of possession is significantly lowered. Depreciation can have a significant impact on a company's profits. Long-term investments can also be depreciated for both accounting and tax purposes. Comparable to depreciation is amortization, which accounts for the fluctuation in the value of intangible assets over time.
- A reconciliation statement is a report that starts with a firm's track of a current account, inserts and deducts reconciling elements in a set of options in order, and then uses these changes to arrive at the third party's record of the same account. The purpose of the reconciliation statement is to give an independent verification of the account balance's truthfulness and to highlight the distinctions between the two forms of the account.

REVIEW QUESTIONS

1. Define and explain the concepts of depletion, obsolescence, and amortization.
2. What are the causes of depreciation in accounting?
3. Describe any two methods of calculating depreciation in accounting.
4. Define and explain the concepts of reserves and provisions in accounting.
5. What is a reconciliation statement? Explain some types of reconciliation statements.

MULTIPLE CHOICE QUESTIONS

1. Which of the following are financial charges responsible for reducing economic profits?

a) Discount on debentures or bonds

b) Stamp duty and other expenses on the issuance and transferring of bonds, shares, or stocks

c) Losses on capital assets

d) All of the above

2. Which statements are genuine about reconciling the cost and financial accounts?

a) Reconciliation of the cost and financial accounts doesn't facilitate internal control

b) Reconciliation of the cost and financial accounts facilitates internal control

c) Reconciliation of the cost and financial accounts facilitates external control

d) All of the above

3. Which of the following statements is true about the interest on investments?

a) The interest on investment increases profits in the cost account

b) The interest on investment increases profits both in the financial and the cost accounts

c) The interest on investment increases earnings in the financial account

d) The interest on investment does not increase profits either in the financial or the cost accounts

4. In the reconciliation statement, ___________.

a) The expenses shown only in the financial accounts are added to the economic profits

b) The costs shown only in the financial accounts are deducted from the financial profits

c) The expenses shown only in the financial accounts do not affect the financial profits

d) The prices shown only in the financial accounts are removed from the costing profits

5. Which of the following methods is commonly used to calculate depreciation?

a) Straight-line method

b) FIFO method

c) LIFO method

d) Weighted average method

Answers to Multiple Choice Questions

1. (d) 2. (b) 3. (c) 4. (a) 5. (a)

REFERENCES

1. Abadir, K., & Talmain, G., (2001). Depreciation rates and capital stocks. *The Manchester School, 69*(1), 42–51.
2. Abeler, J., Falk, A., Goette, L., & Huffman, D., (2011). Reference points and effort provision. *American Economic Review, 101*(2), 470–92.
3. Adams, C. A., Weetman, P., & Gray, S. J., (1993). Reconciling national with international accounting standards: Lessons from a study of Finnish corporate reports. *European Accounting Review, 2*(3), 471–494.
4. Adkerson, R. C., (1979). Can reserve recognition accounting work? *Journal of Accountancy (pre-1986), 148*(000003), 72.

5. Ashari, N., Koh, H. C., Tan, S. L., & Wong, W. H., (1994). Factors affecting income smoothing among listed companies in Singapore. *Accounting and Business Research, 24*(96), 291–301.
6. Asplund, R., (2004). *The Provision and Effects of Company Training: A Brief Review of the Literature, 1*(1), 2–12.
7. Bagchi, A., (1971). Depreciation and current repairs in income-accounting: Independent or interdependent? *Economic and Political Weekly*, 2011–2016.
8. Bakri, M. H., Azman, H., & Dabas, N., (2021). Factor affects customer behavior during currency depreciation in Johor Bahru. *The Journal of Technology Management and Technopreneurship (JTMT), 9*(1), 48–55.
9. Barnea, A., Ronen, J., & Sadan, S., (1975). The implementation of accounting objectives: An application to extraordinary items. *The Accounting Review, 50*(1), 58–68.
10. Barrar, P., Wood, D., Jones, J., & Vedovato, M., (2002). The efficiency of accounting service providers. *Business Process Management Journal, 2*(1), 2–12.
11. Beckman, J., Brandes, C., & Eierle, B., (2007). German reporting practices: An analysis of reconciliations from German commercial code to IFRS or US GAAP. *Advances in International Accounting, 20,* 253–294.
12. Bell, T. B., (1983). Market reaction to reserve recognition accounting. *Journal of Accounting Research, 2*(1), 1–17.
13. Bierman, H., (1966). A further study of depreciation. *The Accounting Review, 41*(2), 271–274.
14. Billings, M., & Capie, F., (2009, March). Transparency and financial reporting in mid-20th century British banking. In: *Accounting Forum* (Vol. 33, No. 1, pp. 38–53).
15. Borio, C., & Lowe, P., (2001). To provision or not to provision. *BIS Quarterly Review, 9*(3), 36–48.
16. Burkhanov, A., (2020). *Factors Affecting the Development of the Light Industry in Uzbekistan, 1*(22), 4–10.
17. Cairns, W., (1919). Depreciation and depletion in tax returns. *Journal of Accountancy (pre-1986), 28*(000003), 204.
18. Canetti, E., & Greene, J., (1992). Economic growth and exchange rate depreciation as causes of inflation in African countries: An empirical analysis. *Journal of African Development, 1*(1), 37–62.
19. Chen, Q., Filardo, A. J., He, D., & Zhu, F., (2012). *International Spillovers of Central Bank Balance Sheet Policies* (Vol. 2, No. 1, p. 66). BIS Paper.
20. Connor, J. E., (1979). Reserve recognition accounting: Fact or fiction? *Journal of Accountancy (pre-1986), 148*(000003), 92.
21. Cordazzo, M., (2013). The impact of IFRS on net income and equity: Evidence from Italian listed companies. *Journal of Applied Accounting Research, 14*(1), 54–73.
22. Cusano, F., Marinelli, G., & Piermattei, S., (2021). Learning from revisions: A tool

for detecting potential errors in banks' balance sheet statistical reporting (No. 611). Bank of Italy, *Economic Research and International Relations Area, 1*(1), 2–12.

23. Cusano, F., Marinelli, G., & Piermattei, S., (2022). Learning from revisions: An algorithm to detect bank balance sheet statistical reporting errors. *Quality & Quantity, 1*(1), 1–35.
24. De Menezes, N. J. A., & Aguiar, V. R. L., (2019). Redesign of the bank reconciliation interface of the ContaAzul software. In: *Handbook of Research on Human-Computer Interfaces and New Modes of Interactivity* (Vol. 3, No. 1, pp. 119–137).
25. Devaney, S., (2022). Depreciation: Old concept and new causes. *Journal of Property Investment & Finance, 40*(6), 529–531.
26. Doran, B. M., Collins, D. W., & Dhaliwal, D. S., (1988). The information of historical cost earnings relative to supplemental reserve-based accounting data in the extractive petroleum industry. *Accounting Review, 1*, 389–413.
27. Epple, D., & Romano, R. E., (1996). Public provision of private goods. *Journal of Political Economy, 104*(1), 57–84.
28. Feng, W., & Figliozzi, M., (2013). An economic and technological analysis of the critical factors affecting the competitiveness of commercial electric vehicles: A case study from the USA market. *Transportation Research Part C: Emerging Technologies, 26*, 135–145.
29. Firth, M., (1997). The provision of non-audit services by accounting firms to their audit clients. *Contemporary Accounting Research, 14*(2), 1–21.
30. Gallego-Alvarez, I., Martínez-Ferrero, J., & Cuadrado-Ballesteros, B., (2016). Accounting treatment for carbon emission rights. *Systems, 4*(1), 12.
31. Gallemore, J., (2022). Bank financial reporting opacity and regulatory intervention. *Review of Accounting Studies, 1*, 1–46.
32. Georgescu, O. M., & Laux, C., (2007). *Financial Reporting, Financial Regulation, and Financial Stability: Evidence from German Bank Failures, 4*, 20–30.
33. Ghicas, D., & Pastena, V., (1989). The acquisition value of oil and gas firms: The role of historical costs, reserve recognition accounting, and analysts' appraisals. *Contemporary Accounting Research, 6*(1), 125–142.
34. Giudice, V. D., Manganelli, B., & Paola, P. D., (2016, July). Depreciation methods for a firm's assets. In: *International Conference on Computational Science and Its Applications* (Vol. 3, No. 1, pp. 214–227).
35. Grimes, J. A., (1928). The income tax-depletion and depreciation. *Accounting Review*, 161–176.
36. Gyamfi-Yeboah, F., & Ayitey, J., (2009). Assessing depreciation for valuation purposes–a decompositional approach. *Journal of Science and Technology (Ghana), 29*(2) 5–10.
37. Haig, R. M., (2020). The concept of income—economic and legal aspects. In: *Forerunners of Realizable Values Accounting in Financial Reporting* (Vol. 3, pp. 140–167).

38. Haldane, A. G., (2012). Discussion of 'financial instruments, financial reporting, and financial stability by Christian Laux 2012. *Accounting and Business Research, 42*(3), 261–266.

39. Halpern, B. S., Regan, H. M., Possingham, H. P., & McCarthy, M. A., (2006). Accounting for uncertainty in marine reserve design. *Ecology Letters, 9*(1), 2–11.

40. Hatfield, H. R., (1936). What they say about depreciation. *The Accounting Review, 11*(1), 18–26.

41. Ijiri, Y., & Kaplan, R. S., (1969). Probabilistic depreciation and its implications for group depreciation. *The Accounting Review, 44*(4), 743–756.

42. Kaul, I., Conceiçao, P., Le Goulven, K., & Mendoza, R. U., (2003). *How to Improve the Provision of Providing Global Public Goods: Managing Globalization, 1*, 21.

43. Kiger, J. E., & Williams, J. R., (1977). An emerging concept of income presentation. *The Accounting Historians Journal, 1*, 63–77.

44. Klein, J. J., (1935). Depreciation and obsolescence charges in the chemical industry-how affected by the new deal. *Tax Mag., 13*, 457.

45. Kohn, M. E., (1977). Accelerated depreciation: Rehabilitation of low-income neighborhoods through appropriate allocation of capital toward obsolescence and exhaustion. *Louis ULJ, 21*, 726.

46. Kurtanović, S., (2012). Software support to DuPont model of flexible change management of accounting policy provisions to achieve the management's objectives. *Ekonomski Pogledi,* (2), 108–121.

47. Kurunmäki, L., & Miller, P., (2008). Counting the costs: The risks of regulating and accounting for health care provision. *Health, Risk & Society, 10*(1), 9–21.

48. Lane, J., & Willett, R., (1997). Depreciation need not be arbitrary. *Accounting and Business Research, 27*(3), 179–194.

49. Littleton, A. C., (1937). Concepts of income underlying accounting. *The Accounting Review, 12*(1), 13–22.

50. Luciano, R., (2003). EBITDA [earnings before interest, tax, depreciation, and amortization] as an indicator of earnings quality. *JASSA*, (1), 29–34.

51. Magliolo, J., (1986). Capital market analysis of reserve recognition accounting. *Journal of Accounting Research, 1*, 69–108.

52. McAnally, H. T., (1948). *Curbing the Effect of Our Erratic Dollar in Pricing Inventories and Providing for Depreciation* (Vol. 18, No. 000008, p. 573). New York Certified Public Accountant (pre-1986).

53. McKinley, S., Pany, K., & Reckers, P. M., (1985). Examine the influence of CPA firm type, size, and MAS provision on loan officer decisions and perceptions. *Journal of Accounting Research, 1*(2), 887–896.

54. Mills, L. F., & Newberry, K. J., (2005). Firms' off-balance sheet and hybrid debt financing: Evidence from their book-tax reporting differences. *Journal of Accounting Research, 43*(2), 251–282.

55. Mills, L. F., & Plesko, G. A., (2003). Bridging the reporting gap: A proposal for more informative reconciling of book and tax income. *National Tax Journal, 56*(4), 865–893.
56. Nechaev, A., & Rasputina, A., (2020). Integrated depreciation management system. In: *IOP Conference Series: Earth and Environmental Science* (Vol. 421, No. 3, p. 032011).
57. Newlove, G. H., (1927). Depreciation. *Journal of Accountancy, 44*(6), 4.
58. Nicholson, M., (1989). Bank reconciliation statements. In: *Accounting Skills* (Vol. 3, No. 1, pp. 271–284).
59. Nieh, C. C., & Lee, C. F., (2001). The dynamic relationship between stock prices and exchange rates for G-7 countries. *The Quarterly Review of Economics and Finance, 41*(4), 477–490.
60. Nurnberg, H., (1989). Depreciation in the cash flow statement of manufacturing firms: Amount incurred or expensed? *Accounting Horizons, 3*(1), 95.
61. Okoh, V. P., Ebi, U., & Dada, A. O., (2017). Causes of depreciation in process plants in the paper industry: Analysis of the perception of practicing estate surveyors and valuers in Lagos and Ogun States. *International Journal of Research in Business Management (Impact: IJRBM) ISSN (E), 2*(1) 2347–4572.
62. Onuoha, L. N., & Amponsah, E. B., (2012). Bank reconciliation is a due process imperative for effective financial management. *Canadian Social Science, 8*(3), 52–56.
63. Parker, R. H., (1990). Regulating British corporate financial reporting in the late nineteenth century. *Accounting, Business & Financial History, 1*(1), 51–71.
64. Philips, G. E., (1963). The accretion concept of income. *The Accounting Review, 38*(1), 14.
65. Pinnuck, M., (2012). A review of the role of financial reporting in the global financial crisis. *Australian Accounting Review, 22*(1), 1–14.
66. Prendergast, C., (1999). The provision of incentives in firms. *Journal of Economic Literature, 37*(1), 7–63.
67. Preston, A. M., (1992). The birth of clinical accounting: A study of the emergence and transformations of discourses on costs and practices of accounting in US hospitals. *Accounting, Organizations and Society, 17*(1), 63–100.
68. Procházka, D. A., (2009). *Hicks' Concept of Income and its Relevancy for Accounting Purposes, 1*, 37–60).
69. Raman, K. K., & Tripathy, N., (1993). The effect of supplemental reserve-based accounting data on the market microstructure. *Journal of Accounting and Public Policy, 12*(2), 113–133.
70. Restrepo, J. F., & Galiana, F. D., (2007). Secondary reserve dispatch accounting for wind power randomness and spillage. In: *2007 IEEE Power Engineering Society General Meeting* (Vol. 1, pp. 1–3).
71. Saito, S., & Fukui, Y., (2019). Whither the concept of income. *Accounting, Economics, and Law: A Convivium, 9*(1), 3–12.

72. Schmidt, R. A., & Wright, H., (1996). Reconciliation of financial statements. In: *Financial Aspects of Marketing* (Vol. 4, pp. 31–36).
73. Scholes, M. S., Wilson, G. P., & Wolfson, M. A., (1990). Tax planning, regulatory capital planning, and financial reporting strategy for commercial banks. *The Review of Financial Studies, 3*(4), 625–650.
74. Shearer, T. L., & Arrington, C. E., (1993). Accounting in other wor (l) ds: Feminism without reserve. *Accounting, Organizations and Society, 18*(2, 3), 253–272.
75. Singer, F. A., (1957). "Depreciation"-better left unsaid. *Accounting Review, 1*, 406–412.
76. Solomons, D., (1961). Economic and accounting concepts of income. *The Accounting Review, 36*(3), 374–383.
77. Stafievskaya, M. V., Sarycheva, T. V., Nikolayeva, L., Vanyukova, R. A., Shakirova, R. K., Ryzhova, L. I., & Norkina, K. V., (2016). Provision for accounting risks. *The Social Sciences (Pakistan), 11*(8), 1776–1779.
78. Suojanen, W. W., (1954). Accounting theory and the large corporation. *The Accounting Review, 29*(3), 391–398.
79. Taggart, H. F., (1926). Cheaper depreciation. *Accounting Review, 1*, 31–44.
80. Taggart, H. F., (1940). Accounting for functional depreciation. *The Accounting Review, 15*(4), 463–469.
81. Toma, M., Ionescu, L., & Founanou, M., (2018). The analysis applied to the impact of depreciation methods of immobilized assets on financial performance. *Journal of Science and Arts, 18*(4), 985–992.
82. Wright, T. P., (1936). Factors affecting the cost of airplanes. *Journal of the Aeronautical Sciences, 3*(4), 122–128.
83. Young, T. N., & Peirson, C. G., (1967). Depreciation-future services basis. *The Accounting Review, 42*(2), 338–341.

CHAPTER 4

ACCOUNTING FOR MERCHANDISING OPERATIONS

UNIT INTRODUCTION

Retailing and Merchandising are the most critical sectors in the US. Some of you may gain work with a merchandiser. Therefore, it is essential to have a solid grasp of the financial statements that merchandising organizations publish. After reading this chapter, you will gain a fundamental understanding of how to report merchandising transactions. In addition, you will be guided through preparing and analyzing a multiple-step income statement, a type of income statement used frequently. The following is an outline of both the contents and the structure of the chapter (Sweeney, 1973):

Corporations like Amazon.com, Wal-Mart Stores, and Inc. are considered merchandising companies as their primary source of revenue comes from the sales and purchase of goods rather than the performance of services. Retailers are businesses that deal in consumer goods and make purchases to resell them to end users. Wholesalers are businesses that deal in merchandise and sell it to retailers at retail stores. As an illustration, the retail establishment Walgreens may purchase products from the wholesaler McKesson. The wholesaler, United Stationers, may sell office supplies to the retailer Office Depot. The company's sale, also known as sales revenue, is the principal source of income for organizations that deal in merchandising. Expenses for a merchandising business can be broken down into two classes: the price of items sold and operating expenses (Earl et al., 1999).

The entire cost of the products sold throughout the period is what is referred to as the "cost of goods sold." This expenditure is inextricably linked to the revenue accumulated from the sale of goods. The steps involved in calculating a merchandising company's income are illustrated in Figure 4.1. The contents of the blue boxes are proprietary to a retail organization.

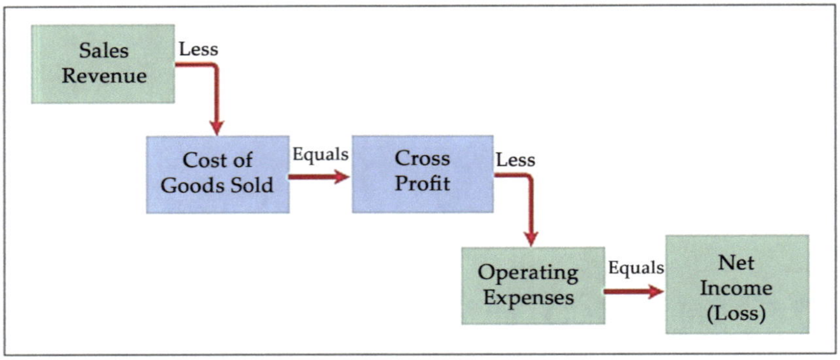

Figure 4.1. The procedure for calculating a company's profit in the merchandising industry (Source: Jerry J. Weygandt, Creative Commons License).

Learning Objectives

At the end of this chapter, readers will be able to:

- Recognize the distinctions between retail businesses and services.
- Describe how to record purchases in a perpetual inventory system.
- Describe how a perpetual inventory system records sales revenue.
- Describe the stages in a merchandising company's accounting cycle.
- Differentiate between a multiple-step income statement and a single-step income statement.

Key Terms

- Operating Cycle
- Flow of Costs
- Perpetual System
- Periodic System
- Merchandise
- Freight Costs
- Allowances and returns
- Discounts

4.1. OPERATING CYCLES

A retail company's operating cycle is longer than a service organization's. The acquisition of goods for subsequent sale extends the process (Lebrun, 1990).

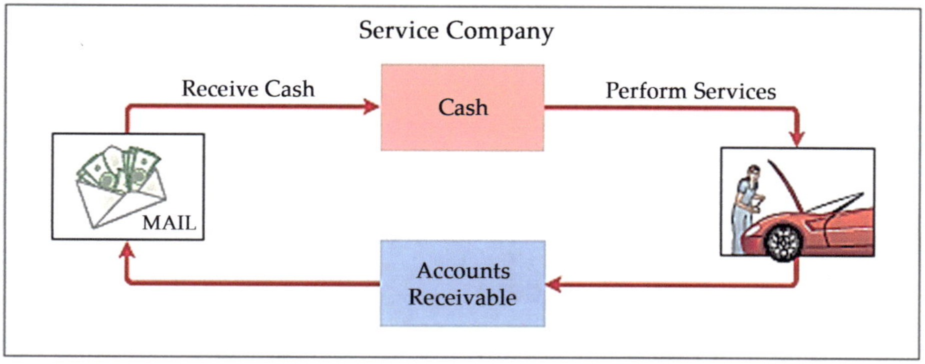

Figure 4.2. Illustration of a service company's operational cycle (Source: Jerry J. Weygandt, Creative Commons License).

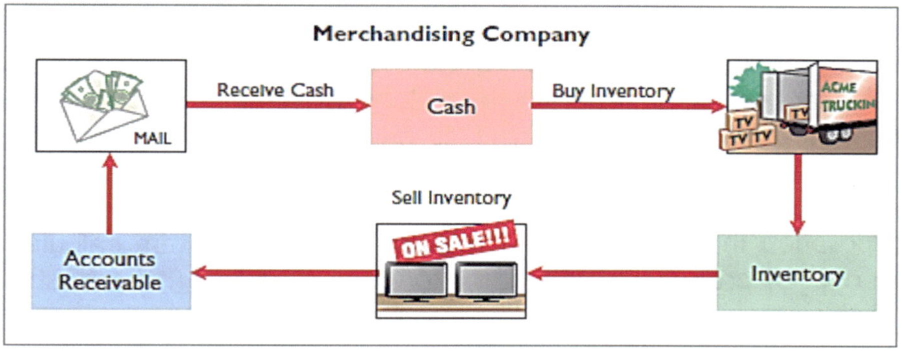

Figure 4.3. Illustration of a merchandising company's operational cycle (Source: Jerry J. Weygandt and Paul D. Kimmel, Creative Commons License).

Remember that the Inventory account is the additional investment account for a retail business. The stock is a current asset on a company's balance sheet (Manyashin, 2021).

4.1.1. Flow of Costs

For a corporation that sells merchandise, costs flow as follows. Adding the cost of the products purchased and the cost of the initial inventory gives the price of the products for sale. As commodities are sold, you can assign the cost of items sold. An ending list refers to things that remain unsold once the accounting period ends. To keep track of their items, businesses utilize a perpetual or periodic inventory system (Ren et al., 2020).

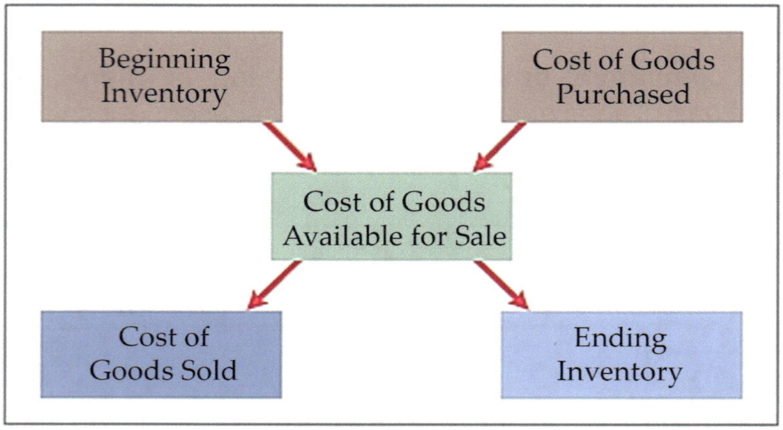

Figure 4.4. Schematic of the flow of costs (Source: Paul D. Kimmel, Creative Commons License).

4.1.2. Perpetual System

Companies that employ a system that allows for perpetual inventory must keep detailed records of the costs connected with the purchase and sale of each item in their list. In these records, the stock that must always be on board for each item is represented in a way that is continuous and ongoing indefinitely. A Ford dealership, for instance, keeps a separate record of inventories for each van, car, and truck on its lot and in its showroom. Similarly, a Kroger grocery shop supports a daily recording of every cereal box and jelly pot it buys and sells using bar codes and optical scanners. A corporation that operates a perpetual inventory system calculates the cost of products sold when a purchase occurs (Khasidashvili, 1994).

4.1.3. Periodic System

Merchandises don't maintain comprehensive inventory records of the products in stock over the period while utilizing a periodic inventory system. Instead, compute the cost of the goods sold periodically or when the accounting period ends. The business then conducts an inventory count to ascertain the cost of the stock of items (Doll, 2001).

The actions below must be taken to calculate the cost of items sold under a periodic inventory system:

- Calculate the inventory cost at the start of the accounting cycle.
- Include the price of the things you bought.

- Consider the inventory value that was on hand after the fiscal year.

The timeliness of the cost of goods sold computations underneath the two inventory systems is contrasted (Pan, 1999).

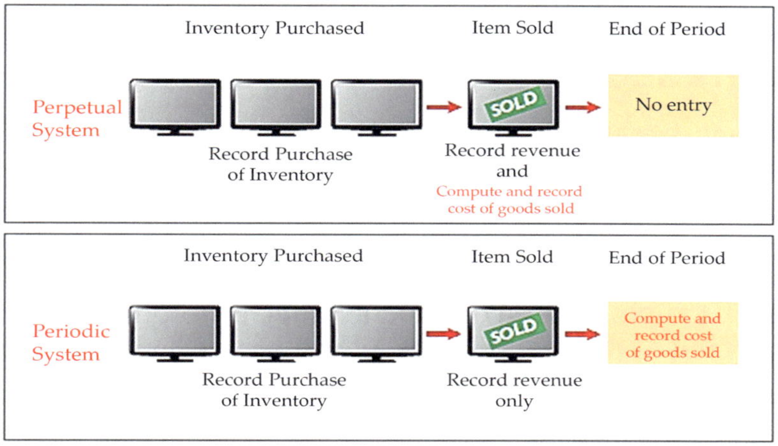

Figure 4.5. Analyzing the differences between perpetual and periodic inventory systems (Source: Donald E. Kieso, Creative Commons License).

Benefits of the Perpetual System: Businesses dealing with elevated products such as furniture, automobiles, and massive home appliances have been the most frequent users of perpetual systems. Many more businesses can now implement endless inventory systems thanks to the proliferation of computers and digital scanners. As the accounting records depict the quantity and the inventory cost that must always be available, the perpetual inventory system gets its name because this information is constantly updated and shown in the records (Swevers et al., 1996).

A perpetual inventory system offers more effective inventory management than a periodic one. The company can check the items at any moment to verify whether the number of items reported in the inventory system and the number of items on board match. The inventory records show the number of goods that should be on sale (Son et al., 2017). If shortages are discovered, the business can look into them right away. A computerized system can reduce this cost, even though a permanent inventory system necessitates additional clerical work and expenditure to maintain the subordinate data. Amazon's efficient inventory system is credited with a significant portion of its success (Wiggins, 2003).

Some companies believe investing in a computerized inventory system like Amazon is unneeded or uneconomical. Many small retailing organizations have discovered that simple automated accounting programs bestow the fundamental applications of a perpetual inventory system. Additionally, several small business managers still find that adopting a periodic inventory system allows them to maintain control over their inventory and oversee day-to-day operations.

4.2. KEEPING TRACK OF MERCHANDISE PURCHASES

Companies can pay for their inventory purchases with either cash or credit. When companies receive products from sellers, they often record assets. Every transaction should be accompanied by official business documentation that records the purchase in writing (Lehdonvirta, 2009). A cash register receipt or canceled check with the items bought and paid amounts should be attached to every cash purchase. Companies report cash acquisitions by increasing their inventory and reducing their cash balance.

A purchase invoice is required to be included with every credit transaction. This invoice lists the total cost of the purchase as well as other essential details. On the other hand, the buyer does not prepare a duplicate receipt. Instead, as the purchase invoice for the transaction, the purchaser uses the sales invoice's duplicate produced by the vendor. Sauk Stereo, the buyer, uses a sales invoice created by PW Audio Supply, Inc (Mokhtarian, 2004). as a sales invoice, although PW Audio Supply, Inc. is the one who successfully sold them the products.

May 4	Inventory	3,800	
	Accounts Payable		3,800
	(To record goods purchased on account from PW Audio Supply)		

A	=	L	+	SE
+3,800				
		+3,800		

Cash Flows
no effect

To appreciate its purchase from PW Audio Supply, Sauk Stereo made the mentioned addition in its journal. The input raises Accounts Payable (credits) and decreases inventory (debits).

Please locate the following elements so that you can better comprehend the substance of this invoice:

- Vendor
- Date of invoice
- Purchaser
- Salesperson

TIPS

To better understand the contents of this invoice, identify these items:

1. Seller
2. Invoice date
3. Purchaser
4. Salesperson
5. Credit terms
6. Freight terms
7. Goods sold: catalog number, description, quantity, price per unit
8. Total invoice amount

- Credit policies
- Freight policies
- Items sold: unit price, summary, quantity, catalog number
- Total invoice cost

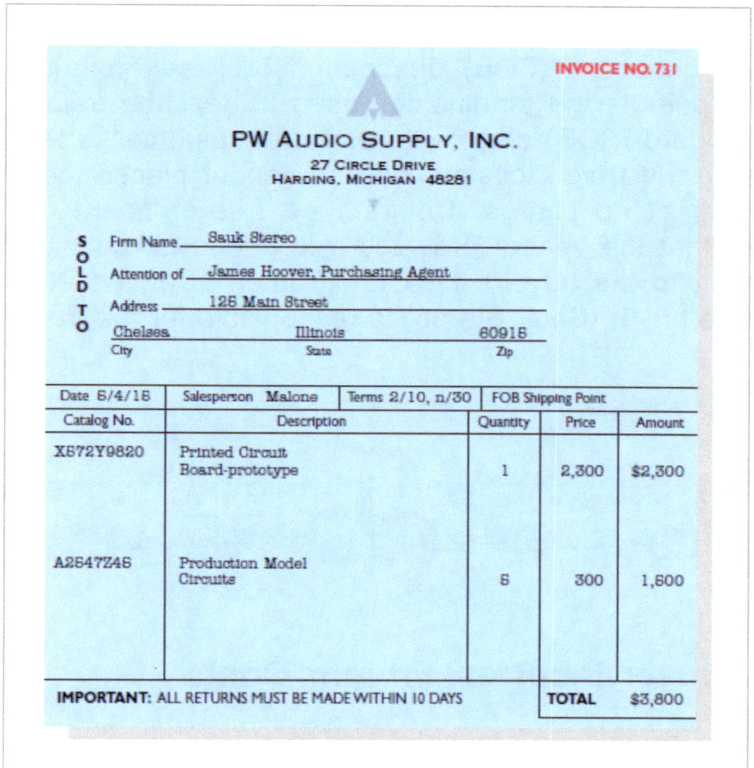
INVOICE NO. 731

PW AUDIO SUPPLY, INC.
27 CIRCLE DRIVE
HARDING, MICHIGAN 48281

SOLD TO
Firm Name: Sauk Stereo
Attention of: James Hoover, Purchasing Agent
Address: 125 Main Street
Chelsea (City) Illinois (State) 60915 (Zip)

Date 5/4/15	Salesperson Malone	Terms 2/10, n/30	FOB Shipping Point		
Catalog No.	Description		Quantity	Price	Amount
X572Y9820	Printed Circuit Board-prototype		1	2,300	$2,300
A2547Z45	Production Model Circuits		5	300	1,500
IMPORTANT: ALL RETURNS MUST BE MADE WITHIN 10 DAYS				TOTAL	$3,800

Figure 4.6. Schematic of Sauk Stereo that used a sales invoice as a purchase invoice (Source: Donald E. Kieso, Creative Commons License).

Companies that use the perpetual inventory system keep an eye on the purchases of merchandise for sale in the Inventory account. As a result, REI would raise inventory for sports gear, clothing, and other items acquired for resale (Kahsay & Zeleke, 2019).

However, not all transactions are deducted from the inventory. Purchases of assets obtained for utilization rather than resale, including equipment, similar goods, and supplies, are recorded as increases to individual asset accounts rather than inventory. REI, for instance, would debit Supplies to document the purchase and sales of items needed to make shelf signage or cash register receipt paper.

4.3. FREIGHT COSTS

It should be mentioned on the agreement whose duty is to transfer the items to the customer's location, the customer, or the seller. The airline creates a freight bill according to the sales agreement if you choose carriers like a railroad, aircraft, or trucking firm for this transportation (Havenga, 2010).

Free on board (FOB) destination or Free on board (FOB) shipping point is the terminology used to describe freight. With a free on board (FOB) shipment point, the customer is responsible for paying the freight costs while the vendor places the items on the carrier at no charge. Contrarily, a free-on-board destination signifies that the vendor provides free goods on board and pays the freight to the buyer's location (Bömer & Meyer, 2022). As a result, the buyer (Sauk Stereo) is responsible for the freight costs.

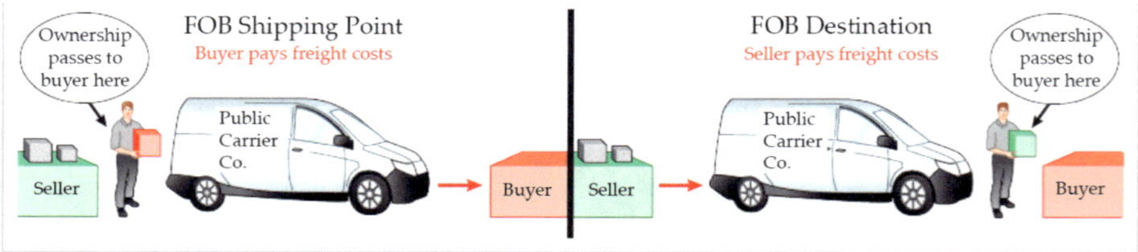

Figure 4.7. Illustration of the Shipping terms (Source: Paul D. Kimmel, Creative Commons License).

4.3.1. Buyer-Incurred Freight Costs

When the purchaser provokes transportation charges, they are included in the inventory cost. Consequently, the purchaser debits the Inventory account. For example, on May 6, if Sauk Stereo pays Public Carrier Co. $150 for freight expenses, the entry on Sauk Stereo's books reads (Chan et al., 2018):

				A = L + SE
May 6	Inventory	150		+150
	Cash		150	−150
	(To record payment of freight on goods purchased)			Cash Flows -150

As a result, all the cargo charges paid by the buyer are included in the price of the goods purchased. This is because inventory expenses should consist of all costs associated with acquiring the inventory and transporting the items to the customer. Once the stock is sold, businesses consider these expenses the price of products sold (Ben-Daya & Hariga 2004).

4.3.2. The Seller's Freight Expenses

On the other hand, the seller's freight expenses for goods being shipped out count as operating expenditures. These expenses raise the Freight-Out expenditure account (Delivery Expense). For instance, if the seller (PW Audio Supply) had been obligated to provide the cargo charges under the freight clauses on the invoice (Chan & Zhang, 2011):

May 4	Freight-Out (or Delivery Expense)	150	
	Cash		150
	(To record payment of freight on goods sold)		

A = L + SE
-150Exp
-150
Cash Flows
-150

When a vendor pays the shipping expenses, the vendor will increase the product's billing price to reflect the shipping expense.

4.4. PURCHASE RETURNS AND ALLOWANCES

Customers may not be pleased with the merchandise they get if it is broken, flawed, of poor quality, or does not fulfill their expectations. In these cases, if the purchase was made on credit or cash, the buyer can return the goods to the vendor for a credit or a cash refund. A purchase return is a legal term for this proceeding. Alternatively, the buyer can keep the products if the seller is ready to offer some reductions on the purchase price. Such a transaction is referred to as a purchase allowance (Seyhun, 1986).

KEYWORD

A purchase allowance is a reduction in the list price offered by a manufacturer or distributor, in exchange for ordering a minimum quantity.

Let's say Sauk Stereo sent $300 worth of merchandise back to PW Audio Supply on May 8. The subsequent Sauk Stereo entry for the returned goods shows a drop (debits). Accounts decrease and are payable (credits) inventory.

A = L + SE
-300
-300
Cash Flows
no effect

May 8	Accounts Payable	300	
	Inventory		300
	(To record return of goods purchased from PW Audio Supply)		

Inventory is decreased when items are returned since Sauk Stereo raised stock when they were received.

Instead, imagine Sauk Stereo choosing to keep the items after being given a $50 stipend. It would conserve $50 on Accounts Payable and $50 on Accounts Receivable (credit) Inventory (Beltratti et al., 2012).

4.5. PURCHASE DISCOUNTS

A bargain on the account's credit terms allows the buyer to receive a monetary concession for a quick transaction. The customer refers to these savings as "a purchasing discount." Both parties benefit from this incentive. By turning accounts receivable into cash, the buyer saves money, and the vendor shortens the operational cycle (Alfares & Ghaithan, 2016).

The amount of the cash discount and the period for which it is proposed are described in the credit terms. They also contain the deadline by which the buyer must pay the invoice. The credit terms on the sales invoice are "two-ten, net thirty," or 2/10, n/30; this implies that if payment is received before ten days of the invoice date, the client may obtain a 2% cash reduction off the invoice amount, less any returns or allowances (Cai et al., 2016). The invoice price is due without a return or allocation within 30 days of the invoice date.

TIPS

The term net in "net 30" means the remaining amount due after subtracting any sales returns and allowances and partial payments.

Additionally, the deal time may be prolonged to a predetermined time after the sale month. For example, 1/10 end of the month (EOM) denotes a 1% discount if the invoice is paid during the first ten days of the following month (Fong & Liu 2011). The credit conditions will only set the maximum available time limit for paying the due amount if the seller opts not to provide a monetary discount. For instance, the period on the invoice could be n/30, n/60, or n/10 EOM; this shows that the client must submit the net sum within 30 days, 60 days, or in the first ten days of the following month.

The discount amount is deducted from inventory when a customer pays an invoice within the discount period (Alfares, 2015). Why? Because corporations record merchandise at cost, the buyer has decreased its price by paying during the discount period. Assume Sauk Stereo pays the amount due of $3,500 on May 14, the last day of the discount period. Sauk Stereo pays $3,430 after the cash discount of $70.

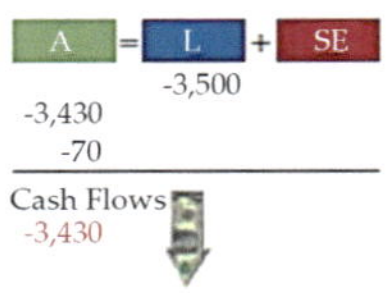

May 14	Acccounts Payable	3,500	
	Cash		3,430
	Inventory		70
	(To record payment within discount period)		

The entry for Sauk Stereo's May 14 payment reduces Accounts, the value of the gross invoice price, which is payable, declines

Inventory drops by the $70 discount Cash less the balance owing. On June 3, if Sauk Stereo paid $3,500 in full rather than taking the discount, Accounts Payable would be debited, and cash would be credited by $3,500 (Belli & Chakraborty, 2022).

June 3	Accounts Payable	3,500	
	Cash		3,500
	(To Record payment with no discount taken)		

A	=	L	+	SE
		-3,500		
-3,500				

Cash Flows
-3,500

Typically, a retail company should accept all reductions provided. Giving up the discount is generally interpreted as paying interest on the money. For example, skipping PW Audio Supply's value would be equivalent to Sauk Stereo paying a 2% interest rate of $3,500 for 20 days; this equates to an annual interest rate of around 36.5%. Borrowing at current bank interest rates of 6% to 10% would be preferable to losing the discount (Munson & Rosenblatt, 1998).

4.6. KEEPING TRACK OF MERCHANDISE TRANSACTIONS AND SALES

Remember

Invoices create legally binding agreements between companies and buyers, especially for larger purchases.

According to the revenue recognition principle, businesses start recording sales income after the required level of performance has been reached. The contractual obligation is often completed when the items are transferred from the vendor to the customer. The purchase has been made, and the buying price has been established.

Credit or cash payments can be accepted by customers when making a purchase. Every business transaction, including a sale, needs to be backed up by a document that verifies the transaction. Cash register records serve as proof of cash sales. Documentation for a sale made on credit can be provided as a sales invoice, such as the one depicted. The vendor will provide the customer with the original copy of the invoice, but they will also keep a copy to precisely document the transaction (Egger & Url, 2006). The date of the sale, the client's name, the total sales price, and any other essential information are all included on the invoice.

The seller typically has two entries for each transaction. The first entry describes the trade: The vendor increases cash and sales revenue. The second entry includes the cost of the sold item: To reflect the cost of those commodities; the seller raises the price of goods sold while lowering inventory. As a result, the Inventory account will display the amount of stock that should always be available (Raman et al., 2001).

To demonstrate a credit purchase transaction, PW Audio Supply, Inc. registered a $3,800 sale to Sauk Stereo on May 4.

A = L + SE	Date	Account	Debit	Credit
A +3,800; SE +3,800 Rev; Cash Flows: no effect	May 4	Accounts Receivable SalesRevenue (To record credit sale to Sauk Stereo per invoice #731)	3,800	3,800
A -2,400; SE -2,400 Exp; Cash Flows: no effect	4	Costs of Goods Sold Inventory (To record cost of merchandise sold on invoice #731 to Sauk Stereo)	2,400	2,400

Did you get it?

Many companies are trying to improve the quality of their financial reporting. For example, General Electric now provides more detail on its revenues and operating profits.

Merchandising firms may employ multiple sales accounts for internal decision-making. For instance, PW Audio Supply might opt to maintain several sales accounts for selling TVs, DVD players, and mobile phones. REI may employ distinct versions for apparel for kids, ski equipment, and camping gear, or it may have even more specialized accounts (Aladejebi & Oladimeji, 2019). By having separate sales accounts for major products rather than a single consolidated sales account, the company's management may more carefully monitor market trends and respond more proactively to changes in sales patterns. For instance, PW Audio Supply could review its pricing and advertising strategies for these products to ensure they are effective if cell phone sales are rising while TV sales are declining.

A merchandising business typically would only include a single sales figure, i.e., the sum of all the separate accounts, on its income statement submitted to outside investors. Two motives drive this action (Fass & Francis, 2004). First, the income statement would become significantly longer if it included information on each of its individual sales accounts. Second, businesses do not want the specifics of their operating performance to be known to their rivals. Microsoft recently increased the number of revenue disclosure types from three to five. The argument: The additional categories made it possible for the customer of financial statements to assess the expansion of the company's consumer and Internet operations more accurately.

4.7. RETURNS AND ALLOWANCES ON RETAIL SALES

This section will examine the "flip side" of allowances and buy returns, which the seller reports as allowances and sales returns (Sullivan, 1997). In these deals, the seller either agrees to the reduction in the price of the items so that the buyer can keep the things or he returns the items. The following are the entries that PW Audio Supply has made to reflect credit for goods that have been produced: (1) an increase in sales returns and allowances, which resulted in a debit. (2) a rise in inventory; and (3) a drop in the Cost of Goods Sold.

KEYWORD

An allowance is an amount of money given or allotted usually at regular intervals for a specific purpose.

May 8	Sales Returns and Allowances Accounts Receivable (To record credit granted to Sauk Stereo for returned goods)	300	 300	A = L + SE -300 (A); -300 Rev (SE) Cash Flows no effect
8	Inventory Cost of Goods Sold (To record cost of goods returned)	140	 140	A = L + SE +140 (A); +140 Exp (SE) Cash Flows no effect

If Sauk Stereo returns items due to damage or a fault, PW Audio Supply should add the item's fair market value rather than their cost in stock and cost of goods sold; this is because Sauk Stereo may return the items because of a fault. For instance, PW Audio Supply would deduct $50 from its inventory if the returned items were defective and had a fair market value of $50; nevertheless, the company would credit its cost of goods sold for the same amount (Thomas et al., 1998).

What would happen if the product wasn't returned, but the seller offered the consumer a price reduction in the form of a discount? In this instance, the seller credits the Account Receivable with the allowance's value and debits Sales Returns and Allowances. The impact of a budget on inventory or the cost of goods sold is zero.

Sales Returns and Allowances are a Contra Revenue Account to Sales Revenue, as was previously stated. It is therefore offset on the income statement against a revenue account (Dzierba et al., 1984). Net sales and allowances typically balance to a debit. Instead of debiting Sales Revenue, businesses use a contra account to keep track of sales returns and allowances in the books and on the income statement. The management needs this information to be disclosed. Frequent returns and allowances often point to issues such as poor goods, inefficiencies in processing orders, billing faults, or flaws with delivery or shipment. A drop attributed straight to the sales revenue hides the proportionate impact of allowances and sales returns as a percentage of total sales. Additionally, it makes it difficult to compare real deals across various accounting periods (Scott & Walker, 2011).

4.8. DISCOUNTS ON PURCHASES

As we discussed in the examination of purchase transactions, the dealer can provide the buyer with a monetary concession, which the seller refers to as a sales discount, in exchange for the timely remission of the outstanding balance. A sales discount is calculated using the invoice price less applicable allowances and returns, similar to a buy discount. For values that are utilized, the seller boosts the Sales Discounts account. For instance, PW Audio Supply records the following transaction to reflect the cash payment from Sauk Stereo on May 14 within the promotional period (Ni Mhurchu et al., 2010).

KEYWORD

Outstanding balance is the amount a borrower is obliged to pay on any debt that incurs interest.

A	=	L	+	SE
+3,430				
				-70 Rev
-3,500				

Cash Flows
+3,430

May 14	Cash	3,430	
	Sales Discounts	70	
	Accounts Receivable		3,500
	(To record collection within 2/10, n/30 discount period from Sauk Stereo		

Sales Discounts are a contra revenue account to Sales Revenue, just like Sales Returns and Allowances. It typically has a debit balance. Rather than debiting Sales Revenue, PW Audio Supply uses this account to show the number of cash discounts that customers have accepted. If Sauk Stereo declines the reduction, PW Audio Supply will debit $3,500 from cash and credit $3,500 from Accounts Receivable at the time of collection (Waterlander et al., 2013).

4.9. STATEMENTS OF FINANCIAL POSITION IN MERCHANDISING

Retailing companies typically use the category balance sheet in addition to one of the two different versions of the income statement. The usage of these financial accounts by merchandisers is described in this section.

Because it demonstrates several phases in calculating net income, the diverse revenue statement gets its name. Two of these processes concern the primary business operations of the corporation. Multiple-step information is considered a method that can be utilized to differentiate between operating and non-operating functions. The statement separates expenses into smaller divisions and highlights intermediate components of revenue (Mulford & Gram, 2007).

4.9.1. Income Statement Presentation of Sales

Sales revenue is presented first in the income statement with many steps. After that, one calculates the net sales by deducting various elements that count against the revenue from the sales revenue, such as sales returns, discounts, and allowances.

KEYWORD

Sales revenue is the income a business generates from the sale of goods or services.

PW AUDIO SUPPLY, INC.
Income Statement (partial)

Sales		
Sales revenue		$ 480,000
Less: Sales returns and allowances	$12,000	
Sales discounts	8,000	20,000
Net sales		$460,000

4.9.2. Gross Profit

Gross profit taught you that to calculate gross profit, a business must first take the revenue from sales and deduct the cost of the goods sold. Merchandises utilize net sales as the measure of sales revenue for this calculation, which includes sales returns, allowances, and discounts. According to sales information and the perpetual inventory system's cost of goods sold, PW Audio Supply's gross profit is $144,000, which is calculated as follows (Goodacre, 2003).

Net sales	$ 460,000
Cost of goods sold	316,000
Gross profit	$144,000

The gross profit rate can show a company's gross profit; this is accomplished by dividing gross profit by net sales. PW Audio Supply's gross profit margin is 31.3%, as calculated below.

Gross Profit	÷	Net Sales	=	Gross Profit Rate
$144,000	÷	$460,000	=	31.3%

KEYWORD

The gross profit margin is calculated by subtracting direct expenses or cost of goods sold (COGS) from net sales (gross revenues minus returns, allowances and discounts).

Analysts believe the gross profit rate is more valuable than the gross profit figure. The rate demonstrates a more significant relationship between total net sales and gross profit. A $1,000,000 gross profit, for example, may appear substantial. However, it is not as spectacular if it is the outcome of a 7% gross profit margin. The gross profit rate expresses, as a percentage, the proportion of each dollar of sales that goes toward the company's profit (Ittner & Larcker, 1998).

The gross profit of a corporation represents its retail profit. Because operational expenses have not yet been removed, it is not an indicator of overall profitability. On the other hand, managers and other relevant individuals keep a close eye on the amount and trajectory of gross profit. They compare gross profit to previous periods' figures. Also, they contrast the business's gross profit margin with its rivals and industry standards. Such competition reveals valuable facts about a company's purchasing function's efficacy and the validity of its pricing criteria.

4.9.3. Operating Expenses and Net Income

Another factor in calculating a company's net income is operating expenses. They are the expenses that are incurred in the process of producing revenue from sales. These costs are similar in retail and service businesses. PW Audio Supply's operating costs were $114,000. They deduct operational expenses from gross profit, which yields net income. As a result, the net income is $30,000, as indicated below (Swinney et al., 2006).

Gross profit	$144,000
Operating expenses	114,000
Net income	$ 30,000

4.9.4. Non-Operating Activities

The company's core line of business is not directly related to the operations that make up its non-operating activities, which comprise a wide range of unrelated revenues, expenses, gains, and losses. When elements that are not operating are included, those aspects are referred to as "Income from operations" (or "Operating income"). The outcomes of the company's typical operations may be easily distinguished using this label (Burt & Sparks, 2003). These results are achieved by subtracting operational expenditures and product-selling expenses from the business's net sales. Payments and receipts from non-core activities are broken down and presented in the following headings: "Other revenues and gains," "Other expenses and losses," and "Other equity changes." (Burt & Sparks, 2003).

ACTIVITY 4.1.

In most industries, sales returns are relatively minor. But returns of consumer electronics can really take a bite out of profits. At one time, the marketing executives at Costco Wholesale Corp. faced a difficult decision. Costco always prided itself on its generous return policy. Most goods had an unlimited grace period for returns. However, a new policy requires that certain electronics must be returned within 90 days of their purchase. The reason? The cost of returned products such as high-definition TVs, computers, and iPods cut an estimated 8¢ per share off Costco's earnings per share, which was $2.30.

If a company expects significant returns, what are the implications for revenue recognition?

SUMMARY

- A company typically has the cost of products sold, revenue, and gross profit due to inventory. Also, a retail firm must choose between a periodic and perpetual inventory system to account for the list. The Inventory account gets debited for the cost of all products and cargo purchases and gets credited for any discounts, refunds, or allowances on those purchases. When a merchandising company sells inventory, the selling price is deducted from Accounts Receivable and credited to Sales Revenue. Simultaneously, it credits stock for the cost of selling product inventories, which is removed from the Cost of Goods Sold account. Allowances, sales returns, and discounts are debited and recorded as contra-revenue accounts. A merchandising firm must fulfill all the processes required for a service company's accounting cycle. Another critical step is to create a worksheet. A perpetual inventory system requires the merchandise to modify the Inventory account to match the physical count. A multiple-step income statement depicts the various steps taken to calculate net income, including non-operating activities sections. A one-step income statement divides all information into two categories: revenues and expenses, and net income is computed in a single step.

REVIEW QUESTIONS

1. "The processes involved in the accounting cycle for a merchandising firm are different from the procedures involved in the accounting cycle for a service organization." Do you agree or disagree? Is the definition of net income for a company that deals in merchandising conceptually equivalent to that of a firm that sells services? Explain
2. Why is it likely that the typical business cycle for a firm that deals in merchandise will be longer than that of a company that sells services?
3. How do organizations focusing on merchandise vs. services differ regarding the revenue and cost components they face? Describe the procedure that is used to calculate income in a merchandising organization.
4. How is income calculated differently for an organization that sells things versus one that provides a service?
5. In a system with perpetual inventories, at what point does the cost of products sold get determined?

MULTIPLE CHOICE QUESTIONS

1. It's possible to increase your gross profit if:

a) Operating costs are lower than net income.

b) Sales revenues exceed operating expenses.

c) Sales revenues exceed the cost of goods sold.

d) Operational expenses exceed product sales costs.

2. In a perpetual inventory system, when a corporation purchases products for resale:

a) Account purchases are deducted from inventory.

b) Account purchases are deducted from Purchases.

c) The amount of the purchase return is removed from the Purchase Returns and Allowances account.

d) Freight expenses are removed from the Freight-Out account.

3. The following are the sales accounts that are expected to have a negative balance::

a) Sales Discounts.

b) Sales Returns and Allowances.

c) Both (a) and (b).

d) Neither (a) nor (b).

4. On June 13, conditions of 2/10 and net/30 are agreed upon for a credit sale of $750. On the 16th of June, a refund of $50 will be given. The sum that was paid in full and accepted as payment on June 23 is as follows:

a) $700.

b) $686.

c) $685.

d) $650.

5. Which of the subsequent accounts is most likely to appear in the ledger of a retail company that uses a perpetual inventory system?

a) Purchases.

b) Freight-In.

c) Cost of Goods Sold.

d) Purchase Discounts.

Answers to Multiple Choice Questions

1. (c) 2. (a) 3. (c) 4. (b) 5. (c)

REFERENCES

1. Aladejebi, O., & Oladimeji, J. A., (2019). The impact of record keeping on the performance of selected small and medium enterprises in Lagos metropolis. *Journal of Small Business and Entrepreneurship Development,* 7(1), 28–40.

2. Alfares, H. K., & Ghaithan, A. M., (2016). Inventory and pricing model with price-dependent demand, time-varying holding cost, and quantity discounts. *Computers & Industrial Engineering, 94*, 170–177.
3. Alfares, H. K., (2015). Maximum-profit inventory model with stock-dependent demand, time-dependent holding cost, and all-units quantity discounts. *Mathematical Modelling and Analysis, 20*(6), 715–736.
4. Belli, S., & Chakraborty, S., (2022). A study consumer perception towards discounts and stockout concerning online Indian designer ethnic wear retailer. *Journal of Positive School Psychology*, 4250–4261.
5. Beltratti, A., Bortolotti, B., & Caccavaio, M., (2012). The stock market reaction to the 2005 split share structure reform in China. *Pacific-Basin Finance Journal, 20*(4), 543–560.
6. Ben-Daya, M., & Hariga, M., (2004). Integrated single vendor single buyer model with stochastic demand and variable lead time. *International Journal of Production Economics, 92*(1), 75–80.
7. Bömer, T., & Meyer, A., (2022). Freight costs versus service level: Optimizing the distribution of a materials trader. In: *International Conference on Computational Logistics* (Vol. 1, pp. 397–411).
8. Burt, S. L., & Sparks, L., (2003). Power and competition in the UK retail grocery market. *British Journal of Management, 14*(3), 237–254.
9. Burt, S., & Sparks, L., (2003). E-commerce and the retail process: A review. *Journal of Retailing and Consumer Services, 10*(5), 275–286.
10. Cai, F., Bagchi, R., & Gauri, D. K., (2016). Boomerang effects of low-price discounts: How typical price discounts affect purchase propensity. *Journal of Consumer Research, 42*(5), 804–816.
11. Chan, C. K., Fang, F., & Langevin, A., (2018). Single-vendor multi-buyer supply chain coordination with stochastic demand. *International Journal of Production Economics, 206*, 110–133.
12. Chan, F. T., & Zhang, T., (2011). The impact of collaborative transportation management on supply chain performance: A simulation approach. *Expert Systems with Applications, 38*(3), 2319–2329.
13. Costin, O., Costin, R. D., & Lebowitz, J. L., (2003). Transition to the continuum of a particle in time-periodic potentials. *Contemporary Mathematics, 327*, 75–86.
14. Doll, K., (2001). Implementation of analytical Hartree–Fock gradients for periodic systems. *Computer Physics Communications, 137*(1), 74–88.
15. Dzierba, S. H., Mirtallo, J. M., Grauer, D. W., Schneider, P. J., Latiolais, C. J., & Fabri, P. J., (1984). Fiscal and clinical evaluation of home parenteral nutrition. *American Journal of Hospital Pharmacy, 41*(2), 285–291.
16. Earl, R., Thomas, O., Kavanaugh, J., & Reed, P., (1999). Teebee's furniture outlet: A case in strategic management of a small business. In: *Allied Academies International*

Conference; International Academy for Case Studies; Proceedings (Vol. 6, No. 1, p. 38).

17. Egger, P., & Url, T., (2006). Public export credit guarantees and foreign trade structure: Evidence from Austria. *World Economy, 29*(4), 399–418.
18. Fass, S. M., & Francis, J., (2004). Where have all the hot goods gone? The role of pawnshops. *Journal of Research in Crime and Delinquency, 41*(2), 156–179.
19. Fong, Y. F., & Liu, Q., (2011). Loyalty rewards facilitate tacit collusion. *Journal of Economics & Management Strategy, 20*(3), 739–775.
20. Golat, M., & Flashner, H., (2002). A new methodology for the analysis of periodic systems. *Nonlinear Dynamics, 28*(1), 29–51.
21. Goodacre, A., (2003). Operating lease finance in the UK retail sector. *The International Review of Retail, Distribution and Consumer Research, 13*(1), 99–125.
22. Havenga, J., (2010). Logistics costs in South Africa–the case for macroeconomic measurement. *South African Journal of Economics, 78*(4), 460–476.
23. Ittner, C. D., & Larcker, D. F., (1998). Are nonfinancial measures leading indicators of financial performance? An analysis of customer satisfaction. *Journal of Accounting Research, 36*, 1–35.
24. Kahsay, G., & Zeleke, G., (2019). Factors affecting use of accounting records on small & micro enterprises (the case of Debre Birhan City, Ethiopia). *Journal of Investment and Management, 8*(1), 1–7.
25. Khasidashvili, Z., (1994). The longest perpetual reductions in orthogonal expression reduction systems. In: *International Symposium on Logical Foundations of Computer Science* (Vol. 1, pp. 191–203).
26. Lebrun, M., (1990). Simulation for developing solid-gas chemical heat pump pilot plants part II. simulation and optimization of discontinuous and pseudo-continuous operating cycles. *Chemical Engineering and Processing: Process Intensification, 28*(2), 67–77.
27. Lehdonvirta, V., (2009). Virtual item sales as a revenue model: Identifying attributes that drive purchase decisions. *Electronic Commerce Research, 9*(1), 97–113.
28. Manyashin, A. V., (2021). Dynamic change of virtual time when modeling vehicle operating cycles in the program 'Stamm.' *International Journal of Transport Development and Integration, 5*(3), 254–263.
29. Mokhtarian, P. L., (2004). A conceptual analysis of the transportation impacts of B2C e-commerce. *Transportation, 31*(3), 257–284.
30. Mulford, C. W., & Gram, M., (2007). The effects of lease capitalization on various financial measures: An retail industry analysis. *Journal of Applied Research in Accounting and Finance, 2*(2), 3–13.
31. Munson, C. L., & Rosenblatt, M. J., (1998). Theories and realities of quantity discounts: An exploratory study. *Production and Operations Management, 7*(4), 352–369.

32. Ni Mhurchu, C., Blakely, T., Jiang, Y., Eyles, H. C., & Rodgers, A., (2010). Effects of price discounts and tailored nutrition education on supermarket purchases: A randomized controlled trial. *The American Journal of Clinical Nutrition, 91*(3), 736–747.
33. Pan, J., (1999). Software reliability. *Dependable Embedded Systems, 1*, 1–14.
34. Raman, A., DeHoratius, N., & Ton, Z., (2001). Execution: The missing link in retail operations. *California Management Review, 43*(3), 136–152.
35. Ren, Z., Yan, J., Yang, X., Yuille, A., & Zha, H., (2020). Unsupervised learning of optical flow with patch consistency and occlusion estimation. *Pattern Recognition, 103*, 107191.
36. Scott, P. M., & Walker, J., (2011). Sales and advertising expenditure for interwar American department stores. *The Journal of Economic History, 71*(1), 40–69.
37. Seyhun, H. N., (1986). Insiders' profits, costs of trading, and market efficiency. *Journal of Financial Economics, 16*(2), 189–212.
38. Son, B., Suh, Y., Kim, S., Jung, H., Kim, J. S., Shin, C., & Ryu, H., (2017). 4.1 A 640× 480 dynamic vision sensor with a 9μm pixel and 300Meps address-event representation. In: *2017 IEEE International Solid-State Circuits Conference* (ISSCC) (Vol. 1, No. 1, pp. 66–67).
39. Sullivan, M. W., (1997). Slotting allowances and the market for new products. *The Journal of Law and Economics, 40*(2), 461–494.
40. Sweeney, D. J., (1973). Improving the profitability of retail merchandising decisions. *Journal of Marketing, 37*(1), 60–68.
41. Swevers, J., Ganseman, C., De Schutter, J., & Van, B. H., (1996). Experimental robot identification using optimized periodic trajectories. *Mechanical Systems and Signal Processing, 10*(5), 561–577.
42. Swinney, J. L., Runyan, R. C., & Huddleston, P., (2006). Differences in reported firm performance by gender: Does industry matter? *Journal of Developmental Entrepreneurship, 11*(02), 99–115.
43. Thomas, R. R., Barr, R. S., Cron, W. L., & Slocum, Jr. J. W., (1998). A process for evaluating retail store efficiency: A restricted DEA approach. *International Journal of Research in Marketing, 15*(5), 487–503.
44. Waterlander, W. E., De Boer, M. R., Schuit, A. J., Seidell, J. C., & Steenhuis, I. H., (2013). Price discounts significantly enhance fruit and vegetable purchases when combined with nutrition education: A randomized controlled supermarket trial. *The American Journal of Clinical Nutrition, 97*(4), 886–895.
45. Wiggins, S., (2003). Periodic orbits. *Introduction to Applied Nonlinear Dynamical Systems and Chaos, 1*, 71–76.

CHAPTER 5

CASH FLOW IN ACCOUNTING

UNIT INTRODUCTION

Cash flow information provides consumers of the income statement with a foundation for assessing an enterprise's capacity to create cash and cash equivalents and its requirements for utilizing those revenues. Users' economic decisions need an appraisal of an enterprise's potential to earn some money and matches, as well as the timeliness and reliability of their creation (Muniroh & Yuliati, 2021).).

The Standard addresses the disclosure of a company's historical variations in cash flows through a financial statement that identifies operating, investment, and financial operations as the sources of cash flows throughout the period. A business must compile and provide cash flow information every time about which income reports are issued.

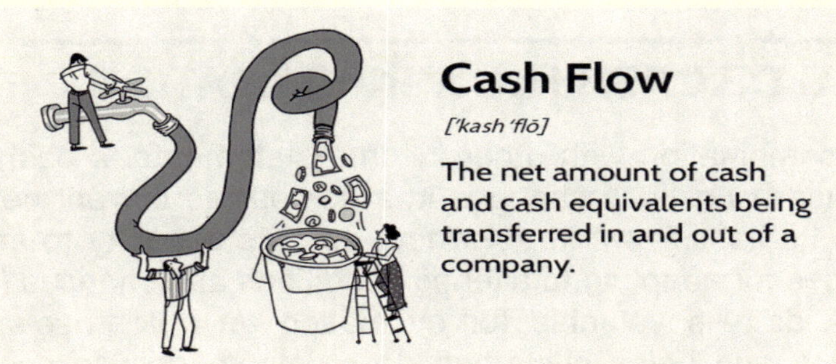

Figure 5.1. Illustration of the Cash Flow (Source: Adam Hayes, Creative Commons License).

Consumers of a business's financial statements are concerned with the enterprise's cash and cash assets generation and utilization (Makar et al., 2013). This is true irrespective of the type of the firm's activity and the extent to which currency can be considered the enterprise's output, as in the instance of a financial enterprise. Regardless of the nature of their primary revenue-generating operations, businesses require cash for the same reasons. They need funds to run their business, meet their responsibilities, and offer dividends to their shareholders.

Learning Objectives

At the end of this chapter, readers will be able to learn:

- Cash flow in accounting
- Benefits of cash flow
- Cash flow in operating and investing activities
- Foreign currency cash flows
- Investment in subsidiaries and associates
- Cash flow for non-financial enterprises

Key Terms

- Cash Flow
- Operating Activities
- Investing Activities
- Taxes
- Interests
- Dividends
- Transactions
- Cash Equivalents

5.1. BENEFITS OF CASH FLOW INFORMATION

When utilized in combination with other income statements, a cash flow statement helps that permits the user to assess changes in a company's current net assets, its economic position (such as its liabilities and solvency), and its capacity to influence the quantities and income changes for adapting to altering conditions and chances (Piotroski & Roulstone, 2005). Cash flow data is valuable for evaluating an enterprise's potential to meet its financial obligations and helps customers to create models to assess and evaluate the current value of the future cash flows of other firms. It also improves the consistency of operational performance reports across businesses by eliminating the disadvantages of utilizing numerous accounting methods for the same activities and incidences.

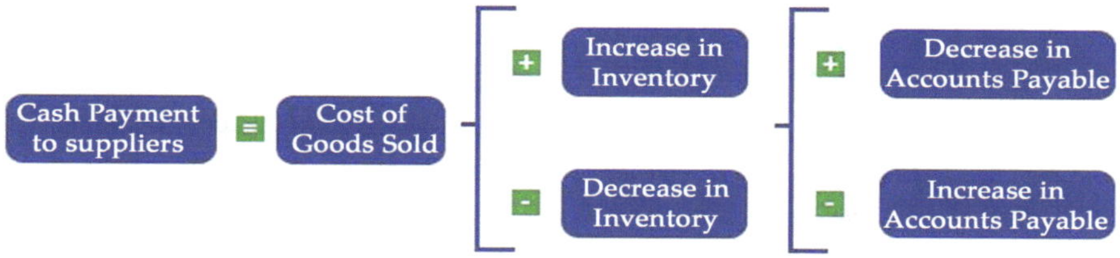

Figure 5.2. Schematic of the cash flow in terms of payment to the supplier (Source: Nirmal Bang, Creative Commons License).

Cash flow information from the past is sometimes used to predict future cash flows' quantity, timing, and predictability (Hales & Orpurt, 2013). It is also beneficial for evaluating the connection between profitability and cash flow, the effect of fluctuating prices, and verifying the correctness of historical projections of future revenues.

TIPS

Investors and analysts should use good judgment when evaluating changes to working capital, as some companies may try to boost up their cash flow before reporting periods.

The following parameters are utilized with the defined definitions in this Standard (Arthur et al., 2010):

1. *Cash* consists of on-hand currency and deposit accounts with banks.
2. *Cash equivalents* are brief, highly liquid investments easily transformed into specified sums of cash whose value fluctuation risk is negligible.
3. *Cash flows* are cash as well as cash equivalent outputs and inflows.
4. *Activities of the company* are the enterprise's primary revenue-generating tasks and all other operations, excluding investing and funding.
5. *Investing operations* involve purchasing and selling lengthy savings and other assets not part of cash equivalents.
6. *Financing operations* are those that lead to modifications to the amount and nature of the enterprise's shareholders' equity (particularly preference shareholding in the instance of a corporation) and its bank loans.

5.2. CASH AND CASH EQUIVALENTS

The goal of holding cash equivalents is to meet short-term monetary obligations instead of for investing or other reasons (Amahalu,

2019). For an asset to serve as a cash amount, it has to be able to be converted to a fixed number of dollars and subjected to low disruption of value fluctuations. Consequently, an investment often only serves as a cash amount if it matures within three months fewer than the acquisition date. Purchases in stocks are omitted from cash equivalents if they are financially stable in fact; for instance, the preferred stock of a firm acquired soon before their stated repayment period (providing there is only a little risk of the company's inability to pay back the cash at maturity) (Brinson et al., 1986). Since cash and cash equivalents are components of a company's cash operations and not its operating, acquiring, or borrowing operations, cash and cash equivalent changes are excluded from cash flows. Cash management involves investing surplus funds in cash and equivalents.

5.3. PRESENTATION OF A CASH FLOW STATEMENT

The cash flow statement should detail investment returns by operational, investment, and finance operations for the period (Donleavy et al., 2018).

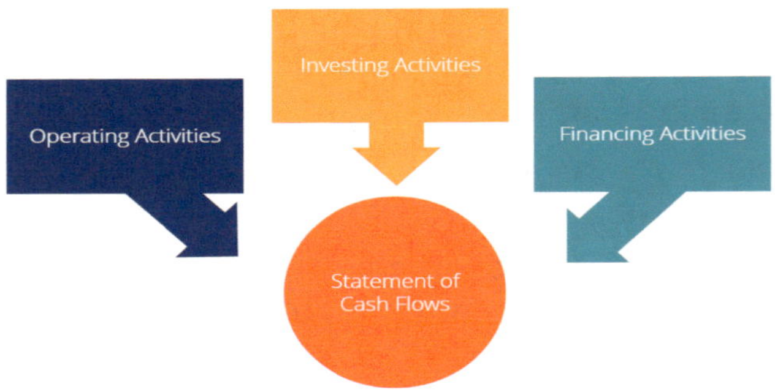

Figure 5.3. Diagram representing the statement of cash flows (Source: CFI Team, Creative Commons License).

Financing activities from operational, investment, and financing operations are most suitable for the organization. Categorization by action gives information that enables users to evaluate the effect of various activities on the enterprise's economic situations, cash reserves, and cash equivalents (Arthur et al., 2010). This data could also be utilized to assess the connections between these operations.

A single transaction may involve cash flows with distinct classifications. For instance, when the instaelment received for a fixed asset purchased based on deferred payments contains both interests and credit, the interest component is classed as cash flows and the loan component as investments.

5.3.1. Operating Activities

The cash flows that arise from continuing operations are an important metric that may be used to determine whether or not the firm's activities have created enough cash flows to continue its operational capacity without depending on external funding, payout dividends, refinance loans, and make fresh investments. In conjunction with other data, data regarding the individual parts of previous cash flows from operations is valuable for estimating future cash flows from operations (Hughes et al., 2010).

TIPS

The dividend payout ratio is the proportion of earnings paid out as dividends to shareholders, typically expressed as a percentage.

Operating activity cash flows are obtained mainly from the enterprise's primary revenue-generating operations. Thus, they typically originate from the events and transactions that contribute to calculating net income or loss. The examples that follow are of operating activity cash flows:

a) Monetary revenues from the purchase of goods and performance of services;

b) Monies received from licenses, royalties, sales, and other sources of revenue;

c) Financial support for products and services to vendors;

d) Cash disbursements to workers and on their part;

e) Cash revenues and payments made by an insurance company for subscriptions, disputes, pensions, and other insurance advantages;

f) Money transfers or returns of taxable income if they can be made electronically.

g) Linked primarily with financial and investing tasks; and

h) Cash revenues and payments associated with futures markets, forward agreements, currency options, and swap agreements are maintained for trading or dealing purposes.

Several activities, like the sale of an asset, may lead to a gain or loss that is factored into the calculation of net income or loss. The cash flows associated with dealings are proceeds from financing activities (Hales & Orpurt, 2013).

Remember

Several activities, like the sale of an asset, may lead to a gain or loss that is factored into the calculation of net income or loss. The cash flows associated with so dealings, though, are proceeds from financing activities.

A business might maintain safety and debts for dealing or trading reasons comparable to goods obtained for the express intention of reselling. Consequently, cash flows resulting from acquiring and selling securities trading are considered continuing operations (Sidhu & Yu, 2021). Likewise, cash advances and loans granted by financial institutions are typically considered continuing operations because they connect to the enterprise's primary revenue-generating activity.

5.3.2. Investing Activities

The different exposure of cash flows subsequent from financing and financing activities is vital since these cash flows show the amount of money that has been paid for resources that will produce future revenue revenues (Sidhu & Yu, 2021). The examples that follow are of cash flows resulting from continuing to invest:

a) Cash payments for the fixed asset purchase (including intangibles). Such charges comprise expenses for the study and development of capitalized and self-constructed capital equipment;
b) Cash revenues from fixed asset sales (containing intangibles);
c) Cash payments to purchase stock, options, or treasury bonds of other firms and interests in strategic partnerships (except purchases for assets deemed to be financially stable as well as those retained for trading or dealing activities);
d) Cash proceeds from the sale of stocks, certificates, or financial products of other firms and stakes in joint ventures (except proceeds from instruments measured to be financially stable and those retained for commercial reasons);
e) Cash transfers and loans issued to 3rd parties (or by a financial institution);
f) Cash receivables resulting from the return of loans or finances given to third parties (apart from advances and borrowings issued by a financial enterprise);
g) Cash disbursements for commodity futures, forward agreements, currency options, and swap agreements, unless the agreements are used for purposes of trading or dealing or the payments are classed as cash flows;

h) Cash revenues from commodity futures, forward contracts, swaps and options, and swap agreements, excluding contracts for trading or dealing or revenues categorized as financing operations.

Whenever a contract is reported as hedging of a location, its cash flows are categorized similarly to the retained earnings of the role being hedged.

5.3.3. Financing Activities

The independent declaration of cash flows resulting from cash flows is crucial because it facilitates the prediction of demands on future revenues by sources of funds to the firm (both capital and bank debt). The examples that follow are of cash flows generated by cash flows (Foster et al., 2012):

a) Cash income from the sale of shares or comparable securities;

b) Funds from the issuance of debt securities, contracts, notes, bonds, as well as other short-term or long-term bank debt; and

c) Cash returns of lent monies.

5.4. CASH FLOWS FROM OPERATING ACTIVITIES

A business must disclose working capital from operating operations utilizing either (Ingram & Lee, 1997):

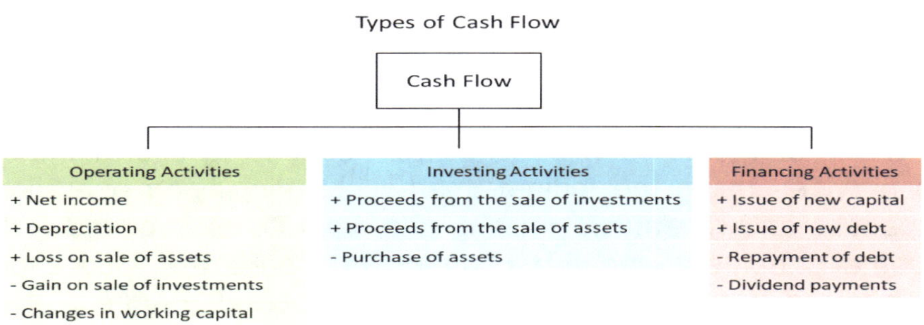

Figure 5.4. Illustration of the types of cash flows (Source: Double Entry Bookkeeping, Creative Commons License).

a) The direct technique, which discloses the key classes of net financial transactions and total cash transactions; or

b) The indirect technique adjusts net revenue or loss for the impact of non-cash operations, any hardship deferment or prepayments of past or future cash flow receipts or repayments, and income or cost items related to trading or financing decisions.

The direct technique gives information that may be relevant in projecting future revenues that is unavailable underneath the method and is therefore deemed more suitable than the technique (Wasley & Wu, 2006). Underneath the method, information about core categories of totally disgusting cash receipts and gross cash transactions can be acquired either:

KEYWORD

A cash receipt is generated when a vendor accepts cash or cash equivalent from an external source, such as a customer, an investor or a bank.

1. from the enterprise's financial accounts
2. by trying to adjust sales, sales costs (involvement and comparable revenue and interest costs and serious charges for a fintech industry), and other objects on the net income for

a) Adjustments in inventories, operational payables, and receivables at the time;

b) Other non-cash goods;

c) Other elements that have cash benefits are investment or finance cash flows.

The indirect technique determines net income from operational operations by modifying profits and losses for the impact of (Burke & Wieland, 2017):

1. Adjustments in inventories, operational receivables, and payments during the time;
2. Non-financial factors such as depletion, allowances, deferred taxation, and unrecognized profits and losses from foreign exchange transactions
3. All other items whose financial consequences are investment or funding cash flows.

Alternately, the cash flow net from continuing operations can be provided using the indirect method by displaying operational expenses and revenues, omitting non-cash items declared in the income statement and the changes in stocks and operational payables and receivables throughout the period (Fairfield et al., 2003).

5.5. CASH FLOWS FROM INVESTING ACTIVITIES

An enterprise must disclose separately significant categories of net cash receipts and net payments made resulting from financing and investing activities unless cash flows are stated on a net basis (Nguyen et al., 2020).

Cash flows reported on a net basis are:

Net amounts may be stated for the main operational, investing, and cash flows from financing

a) Cash inflows and money paid on behalf of clients whenever the cash flows represent the customer's operations and not those of the firm; and
b) Cash collections and repayments for goods with high amounts, short durations, and rapid turnover.

The examples listed below are of payments and cash receipts mentioned in paragraph 22(a):

a) A bank's acceptance and return of deposit accounts;
b) Customer assets held by an equity firm; and
c) Rentals were received in favor of property owners and forwarded to them.

Instances of cash payments and receipts related to paragraph 22(b) include loans for and payback of the following (Gilchrist & Himmelberg, 1995):

a) Principle balances for credit card clientele
b) The acquisition and disposition of savings; and
c) Additional brief borrowings, such as those with maturities of 3 months or less.

Cash flows resulting from all of the following items of a financial institution might well be stated net:

a) Cash received and expenditures related to the receipt and payment of deposit accounts;
b) Deposit and removal of deposits with other financial institutions; and
c) Cash advancements and advances extended to consumers and the return of borrowed money.

Did you get it?

According to Price Waterhouse Cooper, 43% of consumers would pay more for greater convenience, and 42% would pay more for a friendly, welcoming interaction in-store. It pays to test things out for best results.

5.6. FOREIGN CURRENCY CASH FLOWS

Cash flows resulting from operations in foreign exchange must be documented in an enterprise's exchange rate. It can be done by using the exchange rate between the functional currency and the foreign reserves at the time of the cash reserves to the foreign exchange value (Bartram, 2007). A rate close to the actual value could be utilized if the outcome is identical to if the values at the periods of the retained earnings were used. The impact of fluctuations in exchange rates on the cash and cash equivalents kept in foreign exchange must be separately stated in the reconciliation of the variations in money and its equivalents over time.

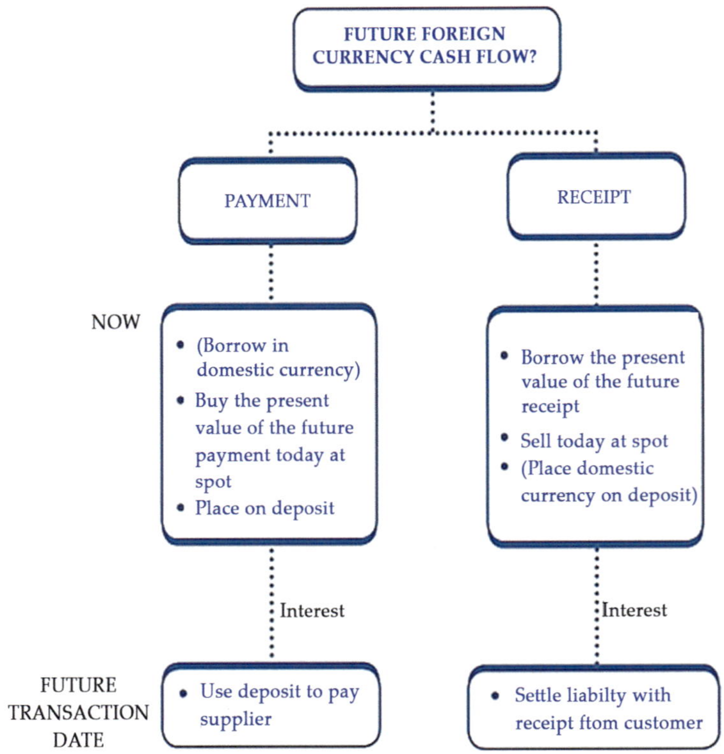

Figure 5.5. Diagram representing foreign currency cash flows (Source: Kaplan Financial Knowledge Bank, Creative Commons License).

The reporting of cash flows in foreign currency denominated conforms to Accounting Standard (AS) 11, The Effects of Changes in Foreign Exchange Rates (Wallace et al., 1997). This enables the utilization of an exchange rate close to the actual value. For instance, a period's weighted stock market can record transactions in foreign currencies.

Movements in currency exchange rates that result in unrealized profits and losses are not free cash flow. To reconcile money and cash equivalents at the start and conclusion of the period, the influence of exchange rate fluctuations on cash and its equivalents owned or payable in foreign exchange is disclosed in the financial statement (Perez et al., 2012). This number is shown independently from retained earnings from operations, investing, and bank loans and reflects the changes, if any, if such earnings had been recorded at period-end exchange rates.

5.6.1. Extraordinary Items

The cash flows linked with unusual things should be categorized as resulting from operational, investing, or financing operations, as applicable, and declared individually.

The cash flows connected with exceptional items are declared individually as deriving from working, spending, or bank loans in the statement of cash flows so that consumers can comprehend their origin and impact on the enterprise's forecasted cash flows (Chen et al., 2015). In addition to the independent declarations of the nature and value of extraordinary things needed by Accounting Standard (AS) 5, Net Income or Loss for the Period, Prior Period Issues, and Changes in Accounting Policies, the following statements are needed.

KEYWORD

A consumer is the one who purchases the product for his/her own need and uses or consumes it.

5.6.2. Interest and Dividends

Cash flows from dividends, and interest payments received and distributed must be individually disclosed. In a financial firm, cash flows resulting from interest charged and income and income earned must be classed as cash flows from continuing operations. In other businesses, cash flows resulting from interest charges must be categorized as cash flows from finance operations. Cash flows resulting from dividends and interest collected should be classified as cash flows from investing and financing activities. The payment of dividends should be categorized as cash flows generated by financing operations (Christensen & Nikolaev 2012).

The total rate of interest received at the time is revealed in the capital account, regardless of whether it was recorded as an expense in the period or capitalized in line with Accounting Standard (AS) 10, Accounting for Fixed Assets.

Interest paid and dividends and interest collected are typically categorized as cash flows from operations for a financial institution

(Chen et al., 2012). Yet, there is no agreement regarding categorizing such financial flows for other businesses. Others contend that interest charged and dividends and interest received may well be categorized as cash flows from operations since they contribute to the computation of net income or loss. Therefore, it is more reasonable to classify interest charged and interest and income earned as finance revenues and participating cash flows, accordingly, since they represent the cost of accessing financial capacity and investment income (Wang et al., 2021).

Some suggest that dividend income should be categorized as a part of free cash flow from operational activities to help users determine a company's current capacity to pay from operating income. Therefore, it is more reasonable to classify dividends as cash flows generated by financing activities, given that they represent a price of accessing monetary capacity.

KEYWORD

Working capital is calculated by taking a company's current assets and deducting current liabilities.

5.6.3. Taxes on Income

The cash flows resulting from income taxes must be stated individually and categorized as working capital from operations management unless they are properly connected with investing and financing operations.

Operations that generate cash flows categorized as operational, investing, or cash flows on a balance sheet are subject to income tax (Desta, 2020). Although tax expense might well be readily identified with investment or finances, it is frequently impractical to recognize the relevant tax revenues, which may come at a different time than the financing costs of the underlying contract. Consequently, tax payments are typically categorized as operating activity cash flows. Suppose it is possible to correlate the tax income stream with a transaction that generates revenues classified as investment or credit lines. The tax income stream is an investment or finance activity, as applicable. Whenever tax cash flows are distributed over many activity classes, the total value of taxes received is revealed.

5.7. INVESTMENTS IN SUBSIDIARIES AND ASSOCIATES

While accounting for an interest in an affiliate, subordinate, or partnership, an investor restricts their balance sheet reporting to financing costs among it and associate/subsidiary/joint ventures, such as income and advances (Reitz, 1991).

5.7.1. Acquisitions and Disposals of Subsidiaries

The free cash flow resulting from purchases and sales of affiliates and other lines of business should be offered individually and classed as investment activities.

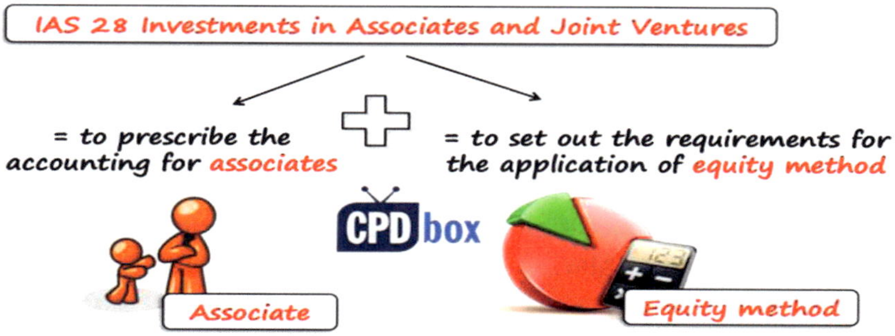

Figure 5.6. Schematic of the investments in associates and joint ventures (Source: Silvia, Creative Commons License).

At the time of the reporting period, a company must declare the following concerning the gaining and sale of subsidiaries or other lines of business:

a) The entire purchase price or sale price; and
b) The acquisition or sale price proportion is settled in cash and cash equivalents.

The depiction of the cash flow impacts of purchases and sales of subsidiaries and other lines of business as discrete line items helps to differentiate such net income from additional financing costs. The effects of disposals on cash inflows are not subtracted from that of purchases (Block et al., 1991).

5.7.2. Non-Cash Transactions

Transactions involving investments and financing that do not call for the usage of cash and cash equivalents cannot be included in a cash flow report. Such transactions ought to be reported in another part of the financial reports, and they ought to be presented in a manner that supplies all pertinent information regarding the investments and financing operations in question (da Silva Rosa, 2004).

However, many investment and financial operations affect a business's assets and capital structure even though they do not directly influence the enterprise's current cash flows. Due to the fact that non-cash activities do not include cash flows during the reporting period in question, it is appropriate to omit such items from a declaration of cash flows. This is in line with the purpose of a statement of cash flows (Woodbury, 1968):

a) The purchase of assets by taking on directly linked obligations is an instance of a transaction that does not involve the exchange of cash;
b) The process of purchasing an existing business through the issuance of new shares
c) The process of transforming debt into equity.

5.7.3. Components of Cash and Cash Equivalents

KEYWORD

Net profit is the amount of money your business earns after deducting all operating, interest, and tax expenses over a given period of time.

An organization is responsible for revealing the elements of cash and cash equivalents. It is also responsible for reconciling the quantities stated in its statement of cash flows with the corresponding items disclosed in its income statement (Pedersen, 2005).

An organization must make public the policy it adheres to when establishing the proportion of cash equivalents in its holdings in light of the cash-handling strategies currently in use.

According to Accounting Standard (AS),

"Net Profit or Loss for the Period, Prior Period Items and Changes in Accounting Policies,"

The impact of any transformation in the strategy for deciding elements of cash and cash equivalents is noted. This is done under the standard's requirements (Zhao et al., 2005).

5.7.4. Other Disclosures

The quantity of significant cash and cash equivalent levels maintained by an enterprise that is unavailable for use by the enterprise should be disclosed together with a commentary provided by management. The enterprise should make this disclosure.

There are a variety of situations in which cash and other currency equivalent balances held by an organization are inaccessible for use by the organization, and each of these situations has its unique set of circumstances. Examples of this include cash and cash equivalent balances held by a branch of the enterprise that operates in a country with exchange controls or other legal restrictions that prevent the balances from being used by the enterprise (Zhao et al., 2015). The enterprise cannot use these balances because the country in which the branch operates is subject to these exchange controls or other legal restrictions. The company will not be able to take advantage of the balances because of the controls and constraints in place.

Users may benefit from access to additional information to better understand an organization's financial situation and liquidity (Welc, 2022). The release of this information, along with a commentary on its significance provided by management, is welcome and encouraged as well as might include the following items:

a) The number of undrawn borrowing facilities that may be available for future operational activities and also to pay capital commitments, noting any limits on the utilization of such capabilities
b) The overall sum of financing costs reflects improvements in continuing operations as opposed to the cash flows necessary to keep operational flexibility at its current level.

It is helpful for the user to identify if the firm is adequately investing in the upkeep of its operating capacity if the cash flows representing growth in continuing operations and net profit needed to keep operational flexibility are disclosed separately (Share, 2009). Suppose an organization does not invest sufficiently in the upkeep of its working capacity. In that case, it risks jeopardizing its potential for future profit to preserve its existing liquidity and continue making dividends to its shareholders.

KEYWORD

A capital commitment is the projected capital expenditure a company commits to spending on long-term assets over a period of time.

5.8. CASH FLOW FOR NON-FINANCIAL ENTERPRISE

This particular term is not included in the accounting standard in any way. The implementation of accounting will be demonstrated as a result of this (Raheman & Rizwan, 2018):

1. The term only depicts amounts for the current period.
2. Data from the statement of profits and losses, as well as the balance sheet, is presented to demonstrate how the accounts of financing costs under both the technique and the indirect approach have been calculated. However, neither report of loss and profit nor the income statement

ACTIVITY 5.1.

If your business is seasonal or cash flow tends to follow a cycle, an annual budget and accurate cash flow statement can shed light on just how much money you'll need each month to pay recurring bills. You'll need to save money from the high-revenue months to cover overhead during lower-revenue months. A monthly cash flow forecast can reveal potential shortfalls and give you time to seek extra cash if needed. Make a cash flow statement for operating activities of your business.

is prepared in a manner that complies with the reporting and presentation requirements mandated by the relevant laws and accounting standards. The working notes provided towards the finish of that kind of example is to make it easier to comprehend the process used to produce the different aspects presented in the cash flow statement. Such working notes are not included in the cash flow statement, and as a result, they are not required to be included.

3. The extra information presented below should also be considered when compiling the cash flow statement (all monetary values are given in thousands of rupees).

a) A total of two hundred and fifty dollars was obtained by issuing new shares of stock, and an additional two hundred and fifty dollars was accepted by taking out long-term loans.

b) The total amount spent on interest was 400, among which 170 were received. In addition, the sum of one hundred dollars owed for interest costs incurred during the past time was paid at the time of the current month.

c) The dividends paid were 1,200.

d) The amount of tax withheld at the source for profits received was forty dollars (this amount was added to the total tax liability of three hundred dollars for the year).

e) During a period, the company invested $350 to purchase fixed assets. The transaction was completed using cash.

f) The plant was sold for twenty dollars, despite having an original cost of eighty dollars and a depreciation expense of sixty.

g) A loss of $40 due to fluctuations in foreign exchange rates reflects a drop in the carrying

h) the value of a brief purchase of foreign-currency specified bonds that have arisen as a result of a shift in currency rate between the date on which the investment was acquired and the time on which the balance sheet was created.

i) Amounts exclusively attributable to credit purchases and purchases are included under "various debtors" and "various creditors," respectively.

SUMMARY

- Transactions in money and cash equivalents, including securities that a company generates or spends during a specified period. Cash on hand influences a business's runway; the greater the cash on hand and the less the capital burn rate, the more maneuverability a firm has and, typically, the higher its value. Profit differs from cash flow. Cash flow is the movement of money into and out of business. However, profit is the amount of money remaining after deducting business expenses from total income. Every corporation that sells or offers public shares must file financial statements and declarations with the Securities and Exchange Commission (SEC).
- The three principal financial statements are the income statement, balance sheets, and cash flow statement. The cash flow statement is a crucial document that lets interested parties obtain insight into a company's transactions.

REVIEW QUESTIONS

1. In the context of accounting, explain and define cash flow.
2. What are some of the advantages of having a positive cash flow in accounting?
3. Explain the flow of cash throughout the business's operational and investing activities.
4. Explain the workings of the cash flow mechanism for foreign currencies.
5. Describe the flow of funds for businesses that are not financial institutions.

MULTIPLE CHOICE QUESTIONS

1. Depreciation Expense

a) Operating
b) Investing
c) Financing
d) Supplemental

2. Proceeds from the sale of equipment used in the business

a) Operating
b) Investing
c) Financing
d) Supplemental

3. Declaration and payment of dividends on the company's stock.

a) Operating
b) Investing

c) Financing
d) Supplemental

4. An increase in the balance in a retailer's Merchandise Inventory.

a) Operating
b) Investing
c) Financing
d) Supplemental

5. A decrease in the balance of Accounts Receivable.

a) Operating
b) Investing
c) Financing
d) Supplemental

Answers to Multiple Choice Questions

1. (a) 2. (b) 3. (c) 4. (a) 5. (a)

REFERENCES

1. Altman, E. I., Sabato, G., & Wilson, N., (2008). The value of qualitative information in SME risk management. *Journal of Financial Services Research, 40*(2), 15–55.
2. Amahalu, N., (2019). Determinants of cash holdings: Evidence from agricultural firms listed on Nigeria stock exchange. *International Journal of Academic Research in Accounting, Finance and Management Sciences, 9*(2), 211–223.
3. Arthur, N., Cheng, M., & Czernkowski, R., (2010). Cash flow disaggregation and the prediction of future earnings. *Accounting & Finance, 50*(1), 1–30.
4. Bartram, S. M., (2007). Corporate cash flow and stock price exposures to foreign exchange rate risk. *Journal of Corporate Finance, 13*(5), 981–994.
5. Block, D. J., Warren, I. H., & Meierhofer, Jr. G. F., (1991). Model rule of professional conduct 5.7: Its origin and interpretation. *Geo. J. Legal Ethics, 5*, 739.
6. Brinson, G. P., Hood, L. R., & Beebower, G. L., (1986). Determinants of portfolio performance. *Financial Analysts Journal, 42*(4), 39–44.
7. Burke, Q. L., & Wieland, M. M., (2017). Value relevance of banks' cash flows from operations. *Advances in Accounting, 39*, 60–78.
8. Chen, L., Da, Z., & Priestley, R., (2012). Dividend smoothing and predictability. *Management Science, 58*(10), 1834–1853.

9. Chen, S., Miao, B., & Shevlin, T., (2015). A new measure of disclosure quality: The level of disaggregation of accounting data in annual reports. *Journal of Accounting Research, 53*(5), 1017–1054.
10. Christensen, H. B., & Nikolaev, V. V., (2012). Capital versus performance covenants in debt contracts. *Journal of Accounting Research, 50*(1), 75–116.
11. Da Silva, R. R., Lee, P., Skott, M., & Walter, T., (2004). Competition in the market for takeover advisers. *Australian Journal of Management, 29*, 61–92.
12. Desta, T. T., (2020). Challenges of business income tax administration with special emphasis on the collection process in Ethiopia: The case of Hadiya zone, Hossana town case. *Journal of Accounting and Taxation, 12*(3), 85–98.
13. Dixit, P., & Sharif, R. J. M., (2020). Standard taxation gaps & reforms: A critical review of revenue policies of Kurdistan Region of Iraq. *Sriwijaya International Journal of Dynamic Economics and Business, 3*(4), 341–354.
14. Donleavy, G. D., Poli, P. M., Conover, T. L., Albu, C. N., Dahawy, K., Iatridis, G., & Zuelch, H., (2018). How numeracy mediates cash flow format preferences: A worldwide study. *The International Journal of Management Education, 16*(2), 180–192.
15. Fairfield, P. M., Whisenant, S., & Yohn, T. L., (2003). The differential persistence of accruals and cash flows for future operating income versus future profitability. *Review of Accounting Studies, 8*(2), 221–243.
16. Foster, III. T. W., McNelis, L. K., & Smith, W. L., (2012). The statement of cash flows: An indirect to direct conversion tool to enhance user understanding and analysis. *Journal of Accounting and Finance, 12*(2), 94–119.
17. Gilchrist, S., & Himmelberg, C. P., (1995). Evidence on the role of cash flow for investment. *Journal of Monetary Economics, 36*(3), 541–572.
18. Hales, J., & Orpurt, S. F., (2013). A review of academic research on the reporting of cash flows from operations. *Accounting Horizons, 27*(3), 539–578.
19. Hughes, M., Hoy, S., & Andrew, B., (2010). Cash flows the gap between reported and estimated operating cash flow elements. *Australasian Accounting, Business and Finance Journal, 4*(1), 96–114.
20. Ingram, R. W., & Lee, T. A., (1997). Information provided by accrual and cash-flow measures of operating activities. *Abacus, 33*(2), 168–185.
21. Kallunki, J. P., Laitinen, E. K., & Silvola, H., (2011). Impact of enterprise resource planning systems on management control systems and firm performance. *International Journal of Accounting Information Systems, 12*(1), 20–39.
22. Kotane, I., (2015). Use financial and non-financial indicators to evaluate a company's performance. In: *CBU International Conference Proceedings* (Vol. 3, pp. 224–233).
23. Makar, S., Wang, L., & Alam, P., (2013). The mixed attribute model in SFAS 133 cash flow hedge accounting: Implications for market pricing. *Review of Accounting Studies, 18*(1), 66–94.

24. Makino, S., Beamish, P. W., & Zhao, N. B., (2004). The characteristics and performance of Japanese FDI in less developed and developed countries. *Journal of World Business, 39*(4), 377–392.
25. Mirza, H. H., & Azfa, T., (2010). Ownership structure and cash flows as determinants of corporate dividend policy in Pakistan. *International Business Research, 3*(3), 210–221.
26. Muniroh, I., & Yuliati, A., (2021). Do cash flow and accounting profit information affect stock prices? *Journal of Accounting and Strategic Finance, 4*(1), 108–121.
27. Nguyen, D. V., Dang, D. Q., Pham, G. H., & Do, D. K., (2020). Influence of overconfidence and cash flow on investment in Vietnam. *The Journal of Asian Finance, Economics, and Business, 7*(2), 99–106.
28. Pedersen, J., (2005). How is culture rendered in subtitles? In: *MuTra 2005–Challenges of Multidimensional Translation: Conference Proceedings* (Vol. 1, pp. 1–18).
29. Perez, M. F., Brada, J. C., & Drabek, Z., (2012). Illicit money flows as motives for FDI. *Journal of Comparative Economics, 40*(1), 108–126.
30. Piotroski, J. D., & Roulstone, D. T., (2005). Do insider trades reflect contrarian beliefs and superior knowledge about future cash flow realizations? *Journal of Accounting and Economics, 39*(1), 55–81.
31. Raheman, A., & Rizwan, F., (2018). Working capital management and corporate cash holdings: A comparative analysis of large and small scale non-financial Pakistani firms. *Abasyn University Journal of Social Sciences*, 1–12.
32. Rees, W., & Sutcliffe, C., (1994). Quantitative non-financial information and income measures: The case of long-term contracts. *Journal of Business Finance & Accounting, 21*(3), 331–347.
33. Reitz, H. D., (1991). Model rule 5.7: A well-intentioned but misdirected reform. *Geo. J. Legal Ethics, 5*, 975.
34. Share, E. P., (2009). Profit and loss account. *Institutions, 11*, 2–218.
35. Sidhu, B. K., & Yu, C., (2021). Direct method operating cash flow disclosures: Determinants and incremental usefulness. *Abacus, 57*(3), 421–467.
36. Tugas, F. C., (2012). A comparative analysis of the financial ratios of listed firms belonging to the education subsector in the Philippines for 2009–2011. *International Journal of Business and Social Science, 3*(21), 1–10.
37. Wallace, R. O., Choudhury, M. S., & Pendlebury, M., (1997). Cash flow statements: An international comparison of regulatory positions. *The International Journal of Accounting, 32*(1), 1–22.
38. Wang, Z., Yin, Q. E., & Yu, L., (2021). Real effects of share repurchases legalization on corporate behaviors. *Journal of Financial Economics, 140*(1), 197–219.
39. Wasley, C. E., & Wu, J. S., (2006). Why do managers voluntarily issue cash flow forecasts? *Journal of Accounting Research, 44*(2), 389–429.

40. Waterlander, W. E., De Boer, M. R., Schuit, A. J., Seidell, J. C., & Steenhuis, I. H., (2013). Price discounts significantly enhance fruit and vegetable purchases when combined with nutrition education: A randomized controlled supermarket trial. *The American Journal of Clinical Nutrition, 97*(4), 886–895.
41. Welc, J., (2022). Real-life case study: A flight to a bankruptcy of Norwegian air shuttle. In: *Evaluating Corporate Financial Performance* (Vol. 1, pp. 257–309).
42. Woodbury, C., (1968). Allocation of the costs of urban renewal among the three levels of government and private enterprise. *U. Toronto LJ, 18*, 259.
43. Zhao, L., Zhang, X., Xu, J., Ou, X., Chang, S., & Wu, M., (2015). Techno-economic analysis of bioethanol production from lignocellulosic biomass in China: Dilute-acid pretreatment and enzymatic hydrolysis of corn stover. *Energies, 8*(5), 4096–4117.

CHAPTER 6

ESSENTIALS OF COST AND MANAGEMENT ACCOUNTING

UNIT INTRODUCTION

One of the three strategic dimensions to accomplish competitive benefit in an industry, together with differentiation strategy and emphasis or niche, according to Michael E. Porter's concept of generic competitive approaches, is Cost Leadership. Cost leadership refers to delivering services or producing items at the lowest possible cost while retaining quality for more competitive pricing (Keller, 2015). An item must fit into one of the three competitive strategy dimensions in a corporate environment where every entity strives to obtain the top position not just in the domestic but also in the global market for competition.

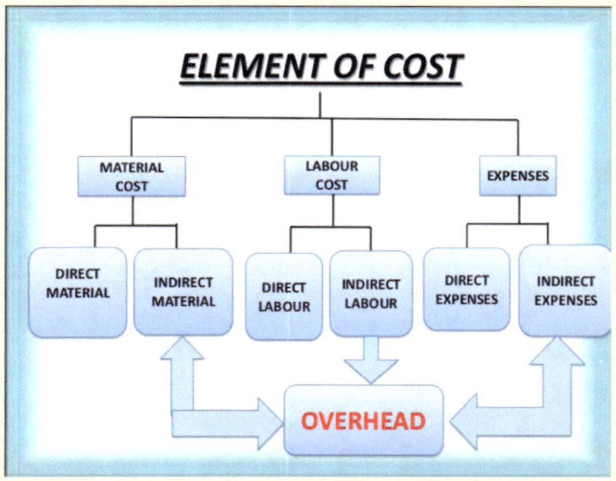

Figure 6.1. Schematic showing different components of Cost (Source: School of Development and Academic Information, Creative Commons License).

Suppose a company or organization has a solid price and management accounting system. In that case, it will be better equipped to attain cost leadership, which is also in line with cost and management accounting. This chapter will explore many facets of management and cost accounting and its applications in various services and manufacturing settings (Corbett, 1998).

Learning Objectives

At the end of this chapter, readers will be able to learn:

- Meaning and definitions of cost and management accounting
- Aims and purpose of cost accounting.
- Scope of cost accounting.
- Relationship of cost accounting with other types of accounting.
- Role and function of cost and management accounting.
- Users of cost and management accounting.
- Limitations of cost accounting.

Key Terms

- Cost Accounting
- Management Accounting
- Financial Accounting
- Financial Management
- Cost Drivers
- Information Technology
- Cost Units

6.1. MEANING AND DEFINITION

There are multiple definitions of cost and management accounting:

- Cost as a noun: The amount of money (actual or fictitious) spent on or related to a particular item, product, or activity (Crespi & Yanega, 1995).
- As a verb: To determine the price of a specific item or activity.
- Costing is defined as the method and procedure of determining costs.
- CIMA states that a firm's costing system is the core of its internal financial database for managers. It gives the knowledge necessary for management to manage and regulate the organization's actions and make future choices.
- Cost Accounting: It is described as the procedure of price accounting that starts with recording revenue and expenses or the grounds on which they are computed and culminates with the creation of periodic statements and documents for cost ascertainment and control.
- Cost Accountancy: It has been described as the science, art, and practice of price control and the determination of profitability through pricing and cost accounting concepts, methodologies, and procedures. It also comprises the dissemination of data obtained from it for management decisions (Baader, 1996).
- Management Accounting: According to CIMA, it is the practice of financial and accounting management concepts to establish, defend, maintain, and increase value for investors of for-profit and not-for-profit organizations in the private and public sectors.
- Accounting for management purposes is an essential component of management. It provides management with the information to effectively plan, organize, and control many aspects of the business and make decisions.
- Cost Management: It implements management accounting ideas and techniques for gathering, analyzing, and presenting data to deliver the necessary data for price planning, monitoring, and control (Smith & Reilly, 2007).

KEYWORD

Cost ascertainment is the process of determining costs on the basis of actual data.

6.2. AIMS OF COST ACCOUNTING

The key aims of price and management accounting are described below.

6.2.1. Determination of Cost

The critical aim of price accounting is collecting and determining costs. Costs are gathered, assigned, and selected for every price object.

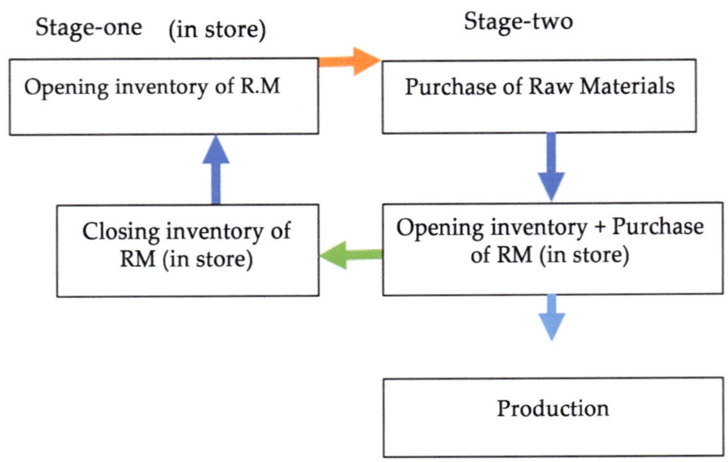

Figure 6.2. Schematic of the diagrammatic method in determining material price (Source: Geoffrey Mbuva, Creative Commons License).

6.2.2. Assessing Sales Price and Profitability

A cost object's sale price, and consequently its profitability, can be more accurately estimated with the assistance of a costing system. A cost accounting system is a foundation for cost fixing and rate bargaining, even though in a fiercely competitive business environment, sales prices are decided by factors external to the company (Cots et al., 2011).

6.2.3. Cost Control

A solid costing system should have as one of its key goals the maintenance of spending restraint. It guarantees that expenses align with previously established criteria and that any deviation from these norms is noticed and documented regularly.

6.2.4. Setting Pre-Determined Standards or Outcomes

Before beginning the manufacturing or service activity, typical cost or efficiency objectives for a product cost or cost center are established. These are the intended costs or outcomes that must be met.

6.2.5. Measurement of True Performance

The actual expenditure or outcome of the product cost or cost center is determined. To have a consistent foundation for reference, performance must be evaluated in the same way as the objectives, i.e., if the goals are set operation-wise, the actual costs must likewise be gathered and assessed operation-wise (Tan et al., 2011).

KEYWORD

Disparity is the condition of being unequal, and a disparity is a noticeable difference.

6.2.6. Comparing Actual Performance with the Pre-Determined Standard

The overall performance that has been measured in this way is then compared to the standard that has been established and the objective that is sought. Any disparity (variation) between the two is recorded and sent to the relevant individual or authority as soon as possible.

6.2.7. Examination of Discrepancy and Action

The differences in results that have been identified are then subjected to additional analysis to determine the factors that led to the differences, after which suitable measures are made to assure consistency in the future. If it turns out to be essential, the guidelines are modified even more to account for the developments (Keel et al., 2011).

6.2.8. Cost Reduction

It can be described as an actual and permanent decrease in the unit cost of the products created or services supplied without compromising their fitness for the desired application or a reduction in the product quality. It is a management strategy where the price of an item is thought to be further decreased. No fee is seen to be the lowest, and every avenue for cost containment is investigated.

The following actions are performed to reduce costs:

Every activity inside an entity is divided to analyze and distinguish between non-value-added and value-added operations. All non-value-added functions are removed without impacting the product's or procedures' fundamental qualities. Michael Porter's Value Chain Analysis, a competitive tool, is one approach for performing value management (Yalcin, 2012).

Remember

All non-value added activities are eliminated without affecting the essential characteristics of the product or process. Value chain Analysis, a strategic tool, developed by Michael Porter, is one of the method to do value analysis.

Constant study and investigation to learn better ways to perform everything:

- The three suppositions behind the concept of cost reduction are summed up as follows:
- The unit cost is reduced.
- These savings are permanent.
- The effectiveness and caliber of the products and services are untouched, if not enhanced.

6.2.9. Helping Management Make Decisions

Price and management accounting help management strategy, execute, measure, regulate, and evaluate various activities by giving essential information. A solid price and management accounting system provide the industry with internal and external data.

6.3. PURPOSE OF COST ACCOUNTING

The following tasks fall under the cost accounting's scope of application (Christ & Burritt, 2015):

Costing is the method and procedure of determining the cost of goods or services. Some cost accounting concepts and guidelines control the cost determination technique. Typically, the price is determined through some arithmetic technique.

6.3.1. Cost Accounting

This is the procedure of cost accounting that starts with documenting expenditures and concludes with creating periodic statements and documents for cost determination and control. It is a formalized method of cost determination.

6.3.2. Cost Analysis

It entails determining the variables responsible for the discrepancy in actual costs compared to the planned expenditures and then assigning tasks for cost variances based on the findings of that process. This also assists in bettering the management of costs and making strategic decisions (Schreyögg et al., 2006).

6.3.3. Cost Comparisons

It also covers costs from different courses of action, including the usage of various production technologies, the price of producing various goods and services, and the price of the same interest or service over time.

Cost Comparison	Text Here	Text Here
Text Here	$100	$1593
Text Here	$140	$1458
Text Here	$120	$1560
Text Here	$160	$1639
Text Here	$160	$1780
Text Here	$180	$1592
Text Here	$130	$2025

Figure 6.3. Data showing price comparison (Source: Slide Geeks, Creative Commons License).

6.3.4. Cost Control

It entails a thorough analysis of each expense in the context of the benefit realized due to the price incurrence. So, it can be said that cost analysis is done to see whether costs are within budget and whether additional cost reduction is feasible.

6.3.5. Cost Reports

This is cost accounting's fundamental function. These documents are mainly designed to be utilized by management at various levels. These aid in budgeting and management, performance evaluation, and managerial decisions (Wijewardena & De Zoysa,1999).

6.3.6. Statutory Compliances

We are preserving cost records associated with the usage of materials, labor, and other cost items about the manufacturing of items or provision of services following the statute and these guidelines.

6.4. ASSOCIATION WITH OTHER DISCIPLINES

Cost and Management Accounting is interdependent and connected with other accounting fields (Couture et al., 2005).

6.4.1. Cost Accounting with Management Accounting

As it is already known, although the terms Cost Accounting and Management Accounting are sometimes used interchangeably, there are several key differences between them. Management accounting discipline is broad and allows managers to make educated decisions. The inputs into management accounting include cost accounts, financial holdings, statistics and operation management systems, and so on (Pickering & King, 1995).

6.4.2. Cost Accounting with Financial Accounting

Cost accounting compiles and determines expenses for stocks and commodities sold. It offers inputs for the financial accounting system's cost recording.

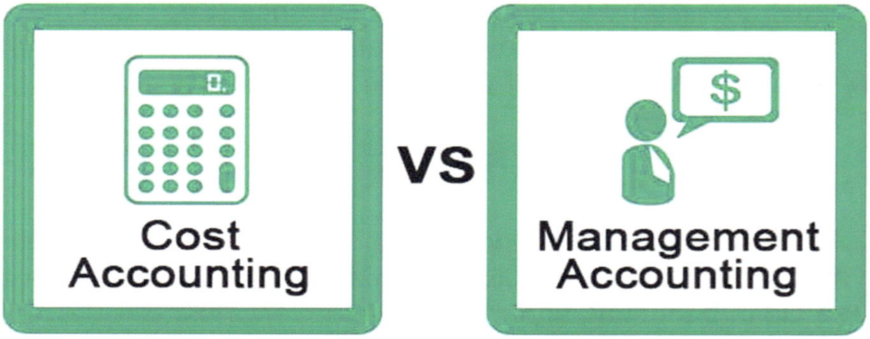

Figure 6.4. Illustration of the Cost Accounting versus Financial Accounting (Source: Ashish Kumar Srivastav, Creative Commons License).

	Basis	Financial Accounting	Cost Accounting
(i)	**Aim**	It gives details on a company's financial performance.	Cost estimation for the aim of cost management and the making of a decision
(ii)	**Nature**	It categorizes financial documents and evaluates financial transactions.	It categorizes, costs records, presents, and evaluates the data meaningfully.
(iii)	**Recording of information**	It records *Historical data*.	It employs historical and pre-determined expenses.
(iv)	**Users of information**	Investors, lenders, financial experts, as well as the government and its organizations, among others, utilize financial accounting statements.	Internal management typically uses cost accounting data. But occasionally, governmental agencies as well.
(v)	**Examination of price and profit**	It demonstrates whether the company in its entirety or individual departments made a profit or loss.	It gives the cost data for every cost unit, such as an item, procedure, job, or contract, among other things.
(vi)	**Period**	Financial Statements are typically prepared for one year.	Documents and statements are generated when necessary.
(vii)	**Demonstration of information**	For the presentation of financial data, a standard format is employed.	In most cases, the cost information is not presented in any pre-determined format.

Table 6.1. The Dissimilarity Between Cost Accounting and Financial Accounting (Source: Ashish Kumar Srivastav, Creative Commons License)

6.4.3. Cost and Management Accounting with Financial Management

It is a financial management application. Making decisions involves financial management strategies (Khan et al., 2012).

The picture below can be used to understand the association between cost accounting, management accounting, financial accounting, and financial management.

6.5. ROLE OF MANAGEMENT AND COST ACCOUNTING

A management and cost accounting system's purpose is to:

i. Give appropriate information to the administration for the making of a decision,
ii. Help management with business activity planning, assessment, evaluation, and control.
iii. Facilitate the cost allocation of items and stocks for internal and external users (Geiger & Ittner, 1996).

Although multiple writers use the terms management accounting and cost accounting interchangeably, the focus of cost accounting is on the absorption of costs and their distribution to a wide range of different cost items. On the other hand, management accounting is more involved with controlling costs. On the other hand, management accounting focuses on providing information to employees inside an organization to make better decisions (Haldma & Lääts, 2002).

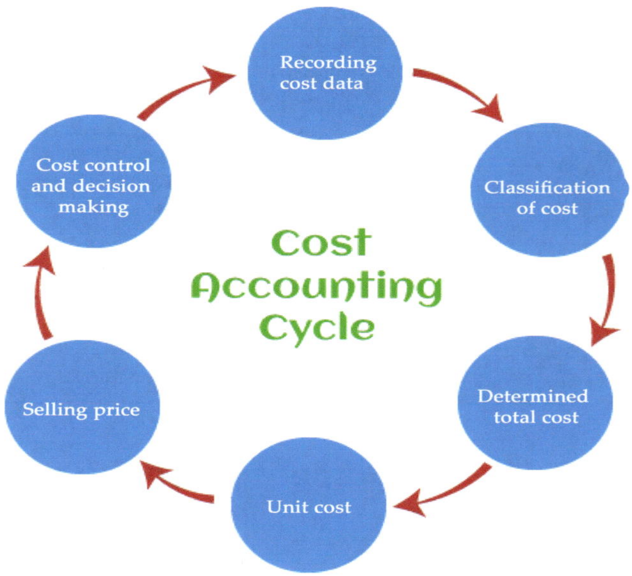

Figure 6.5. Diagram showing a cost accounting cycle (Source: Java Point, Creative Commons License).

The following are some of the functions that cost accounting and management accounting perform:

i. Cost gathering and aggregation for every cost component.
ii. Attributing prices to expensive goods to determine the price.

iii. The management and cost accounting division (whatever vocabulary is chosen to indicate the division) prepares a budget and guidelines for a specific period or action, which are then compared to the allocated and determined cost. Any violation of the established criteria is investigated and documented. These mechanisms are in place to keep costs under control (Christ & Burritt, 2015).

iv. The primary objective of management and cost accounting is to provide management with pertinent data for making decisions. A system environment commonly known as MIS (management information system) is established. The MIS delivers internal and external data that is pertinent and timely, allowing managers at all levels to make informed decisions. Decisions include cost optimization, price setting, and the execution of any item, procedure, or marketing-related plan.

v. The effectiveness of a responsibility center is assessed by comparison to the guidelines that have been established. The purpose of management and cost accounting is to collect data such as the amount of time something takes, the amount of waste produced, the amount of time a procedure is idle, etc., analyze the data, make reports, and then take the appropriate steps (Kremere et al., 2019).

TIPS

Cost units are usually the units of physical measurement like number, weight, area, volume, length, time and value.

6.6. USERS OF MANAGEMENT AND COST ACCOUNTING

Various stakeholders use the management and cost accounting data generated or gathered. Users of the data can be roughly divided into those who are inside and outside of the entity.

The following are some examples of internal consumers who might use knowledge from management and cost accounting.

6.6.1. Managers

The individuals utilize the knowledge

a. to know an object's and a center's price.
b. To determine the cost of the good or service.
c. to gauge and assess the effectiveness of responsibility centers.

d. to understand profitability—from an item, division, or customer perspective.

e. evaluating the available alternatives strategically and making judgments.

6.6.2. Operational Level Staff

The individuals, such as controllers, supervisors, and group leaders, need the information

a. to know their aims and performance targets.

b. to understand service and product requirements such as quantity, quality, and procedure.

c. To be aware of the performance characteristics against which their managers evaluate the performance.

d. To be mindful of departmental profitability etc.

KEYWORD

Profitability and profit are metrics that are used to analyze the financial success of a company.

6.6.3. Employees

Employees are interested in factors like time and attendance, job benefits, performance requirements, and so on (Breen et al., 2004).

External users of management and cost accounting information might consist of the following individuals.

6.6.4. Regulatory Authorities

These are concerns with price accounting data and knowledge for various purposes, such as determining tariffs, giving subsidies, and setting rates, among other things. To accomplish this goal, regulatory agencies demand information organized according to specific criteria and in a particular manner.

6.6.5. Auditors

Information concerning costing and documents that have been examined by management, among other things, is required by the auditors to conduct a review of financial accounts or a specific purpose investigation such as a cost audit, etc. (Zhang, 2009).

6.6.6. Shareholders

These people are worried about information affecting their stake in the organization. The management updates the investors on new orders acquired, product enhancement, market dominance for goods, etc., through frequent communications, yearly reports, etc.

6.6.7. Creditors and Lenders

These are associated with information and data that impact how well a company can look after its creditors or borrowers. For instance, continuous monitoring of net external debt and equity balances is more important to financial organizations that lend money to a business against financial liabilities and stocks.

KEYWORD

A borrower is an individual or entity that is using money, assets, or services on credit.

6.7. COST ACCOUNTING WITH THE UTILIZATION OF IT

In today's corporate world, a commercial organization's information technology (IT) has become indispensable (Emmett & Forget, 2005). With the growth of e-commerce and the growing competition in the corporate setting, information technology is integrating into every aspect of an organization, mainly cost and management accounting. With the emergence of the ERP (Enterprise Resource Planning) system, the management and cost accounting functions have been drastically altered by the advancements in information technology. The procedure for price accounting and management reporting was automated and enhanced. Industry 4.0, the emerging technological renaissance in digital innovation, focuses more on digitizing and automating corporate processes to retain cost management and market competitiveness. The Costing system has resulted in significant time, monetary, and labor savings. Among the potential effects of IT on cost accounting are the following:

i. Various functional tasks have been combined after the implementation of ERPs. As a result, a single entry into the accounting information system produces tailored reports for each function and spares an organization from generating various sets of papers. Comparing cost outcomes versus financial accounting systems has become less complex and more straightforward (Azoulay et al., 2007).
ii. Documents such as Bills of Material, Purchase Request Notes, Goods Receipt Notes, Labor Utilization reports, and

so on are no longer necessary to be generated in extra copies; instead, the linked division can obtain an e-copy from the network.

iii. The use of IT, with the assistance of the internet (including intranets and extranets), is to assist in acquiring and mobilizing resources. For instance, the production team doesn't have to physically issue a material request letter to obtain items from the retailers. Similarly, order forms can be sent to the suppliers via the extranet to commence the process (Tu & Huang, 2019); this makes it possible for an organization to switch to a Just-in-Time (JIT) method of managing inventories and producing goods.

iv. Accurate and timely cost data for a cost center or unit is gathered. Every cost center and the team is given a code, and all costs that go with it are put on the cost center or cost unit using the code; this makes adding up and figuring out costs automatic. The information about fees can be changed to fit the needs. For instance, when a company makes something or gives a service, it can know about each job, batch, procedure, cost center, etc.

v. IT can help promote consistency in developing reports, budgets, and regulations. ERP software is critical in achieving consistency regardless of location, currency, language, or standards.

vi. Cost and profit variation data are produced on a factual foundation, allowing management to take quick corrective action.

vii. Information technology helps an organization monitor and analyze each production or service procedure to reduce non-value-added operations.

viii. Those mentioned above are only a few instances of how IT is used in cost accounting (Carmona et al., 1997).

Did you get it?

CIMA Official terminology defines cost driver as "Factor influencing the level of cost. Often used in the context of ABC to denote the factor which links activity resource consumption to product outputs, for example the number of purchase orders would be a cost driver for procurement cost."

6.7.1. Cost Objects

A cost object is something that requires a particular cost measurement. A cost object could be an item, service, program, client, brand segment, activity, division, or program.

6.7.2. Cost Driver

It is a variable or factor that influences the expense level. Costs are typically incurred as a result of a particular action. Activity levels or total production is an instance of a cost driver. A move might be an occurrence, a task, a labor item, etc.

Cost drivers include the number of machines set up, the number of purchase requisitions, the amount of time spent on the inspection process, the number of tests conducted, etc. (Macdonald & Reuter, 1973).

6.8. LIMITATIONS OF COST ACCOUNTING

Cost accounting has some restrictions, just like other accounting specialties. The following are some drawbacks of cost accounting:

Figure 6.6. Diagram representing limitations of Cost Accounting (Source: Anjali J, Creative Commons License).

6.8.1. Costly

It is expensive because assessment, distribution, and assimilation of overheads necessitate significant additional work and extra funds.

6.8.2. Requirement of Settlement

The outcomes indicated by cost accounts and financial accounts are distinct. Consequently, reconciliation reports are required to confirm their veracity.

ACTIVITY 6.1.

Keeping in view the contents of this chapter, enlist some potential users of cost and management accounting. Moreover, also enlist some uses of cost accounting along with its use in Information Technology.

6.8.3. Repetition of Work

The company needs to keep track of two different kinds of accounts—the financial and the cost accounts—which means more work for everyone involved.

6.8.4. Ineffectiveness

Costs are not controlled by the costing method but by its application (Perez et al., 1993).

SUMMARY

- Cost accounting involves calculating and evaluating expenditures and costs associated with the acquisition or production of an item. It pertains to calculating unit costs using various costing methods. Its primary function is to aid managers in making decisions.
- Management accounting provides relevant selection, planning, cost control, and performance evaluation data. Management accounting transforms data into knowledge, knowledge, and wisdom on the activities of a company entity; this goes one step beyond cost accounting. Management accounting investigates the causes of loss or profit and the elements that affect efficiency to aid decision-making. Consequently, cause and effect is an essential component of management accounting.

REVIEW QUESTIONS

1. What are the objectives of cost accounting?
2. Define and explain the scope of cost accounting.
3. Describe the relationship of cost accounting with other types of accounting.
4. What is the role and function of cost and management accounting?
5. Who are the users of cost and management accounting?
6. What are the limitations of cost accounting?

MULTIPLE CHOICE QUESTIONS

1. Which statements measure the entity's financial position at a particular time?

a) Income Statement
b) Balance Sheet
c) Cash Flow Statement
d) Statement of Retained Earning

2. Which of the following is a characteristic of a process cost accounting system?

a) Material, Labor, and Overheads are accumulated through orders
b) Companies use this system if they process custom orders
c) Opening and Closing stock of work in process are related in terms of completed units
d) Only the Closing stock of work in process is restated in terms of completed units

3. Fixed cost per unit decreases when _______________.

a) Production volume increases.

b) Production volume decreases.

c) Variable cost per unit decreases.

d) Variable cost per unit increases.

4. The cost of production report is a ______________.

a) Financial statement

b) Production Process report

c) Order Sheet

d) None of above

5. The difference between total revenues and total variable costs is known as ______________

a) Contribution margin

b) Gross margin

c) Operating income

d) Fixed costs

Answers to Multiple Choice Questions

1. (b) 2. (c) 3. (a) 4. (b) 5. (a)

REFERENCES

1. Azoulay, A., Doris, N. M., Filion, K. B., Caron, J., Pilote, L., & Eisenberg, M. J., (2007). The use of the transition cost accounting system in health services research. *Cost Effectiveness and Resource Allocation, 5*(1), 1–9.
2. Baader, F., (1996). A formal definition for the expressive power of terminological knowledge representation languages. *Journal of Logic and Computation, 6*(1), 33–54.
3. Brandl, R., Bichler, M., & Ströbel, M., (2007). Cost accounting for shared IT infrastructures. *Wirtschaftsinformatik, 49*(2), 83–94.
4. Breen, J., Sciulli, N., & Calvert, C., (2004). The role of the external accountant in small firms. *Small Enterprise Research, 12*(1), 5–14.
5. Carmona, S., Ezzamel, M., & Gutiérrez, F., (1997). Control and cost accounting practices in the Spanish royal tobacco factory. *Accounting, Organizations and Society, 22*(5), 411–446.
6. Christ, K. L., & Burritt, R. L., (2015). Material flow cost accounting: A review and agenda for future research. *Journal of Cleaner Production, 108*, 1378–1389.
7. Corbett, T., (1998). *Throughput Accounting: TOC's Management Accounting System, 1*, 41–80.

8. Cots, F., Chiarello, P., Salvador, X., Castells, X., & Quentin, W., (2011). DRG-based hospital payment: Intended and unintended consequences. *Diagnosis-Related Groups in Europe: Moving Towards Transparency, Efficiency, and Quality in Hospitals* (Vol. 1, pp. 75–92).
9. Couture, M., Lizotte, M., Dussault, G., Mokhtari, M., Bernier, F., Lam, S., & Lalancette, C., (2005). 6.4. 2 capability engineering process within Canadian defense: Some engineering issues. In: *INCOSE International Symposium* (Vol. 15, No. 1, pp. 953–962).
10. Crespi, B. J., & Yanega, D., (1995). The definition of eusociality. *Behavioral Ecology, 6*(1), 109–115.
11. Emmett, D., & Forget, R., (2005). The utilization of activity-based cost accounting in hospitals. *Journal of Hospital Marketing & Public Relations, 15*(2), 79–89.
12. Geiger, D. R., & Ittner, C. D., (1996). The influence of funding source and legislative requirements on government cost accounting practices. *Accounting, Organizations and Society, 21*(6), 549–567.
13. Haldma, T., & Lääts, K., (2002). Contingencies influencing the management accounting practices of Estonian manufacturing companies. *Management Accounting Research, 13*(4), 379–400.
14. Keel, G., Savage, C., Rafiq, M., & Mazzocato, P., (2017). Time-driven activity-based costing in health care: A systematic review of the literature. *Health Policy, 121*(7), 755–763.
15. Keller, W. D., (2015). *Cost and Managerial Accounting II Essentials, 2*, 2–10.
16. Khan, K., Wasserman, G. A., Liu, X., Ahmed, E., Parvez, F., Slavkovich, V., & Factor-Litvak, P., (2012). Manganese exposure from drinking water and children's academic achievement. *Neurotoxicology, 33*(1), 91–97.
17. Kremere, E., Morgan, E., & Obani, P., (2019). Goals 6.3, 6.4, and 6.5: Water quality, water efficiency, and integrated water resource management. In: *SDG6–Clean Water and Sanitation: Balancing the Water Cycle for Sustainable Life on Earth* (Vol. 1, pp. 25–45).
18. Macdonald, L. K., & Reuter, IV. L. F., (1973). A patient-specific approach to hospital cost accounting. *Health Services Research, 8*(2), 102.
19. Noseworthy, T. W., Konopad, E., Shustack, A., Johnston, R., & Grace, M. P. E., (1996). Cost accounting of adult intensive care: Methods and human and capital inputs. *Critical Care Medicine, 24*(7), 1168–1172.
20. Perez, C. A., Kobeissi, B., Smith, B. D., Fox, S., Grigsby, P. W., Purdy, J. A., & Wasserman, T. H., (1993). Cost accounting in radiation oncology: A computer-based model for reimbursement. *International Journal of Radiation Oncology Biology Physics, 25*(5), 895–906.
21. Pickering, J. M., & King, J. L., (1995). Hardwiring Weak Ties: Interorganizational Computer-Mediated Communication, occupational communities, and organizational change. *Organization Science*, 6(4), 479-486.

22. Schreyögg, J., Tiemann, O., & Busse, R., (2006). Cost accounting to determine prices: How well do prices reflect costs in the German DRG system? *Health Care Management Science, 9*(3), 269–279.
23. Smith, C., & Reilly, L., (2007). What work does the artwork do? A question for art. *Journal of Visual Art Practice, 6*(1), 5–12.
24. Tan, S. S., Serdén, L., Geissler, A., Van, I. M., Redekop, K., Heurgren, M., & Hakkaart-Van, R. L., (2011). DRGs and cost accounting: Which is driving which. In: Busse., R., Geissler, A., Quentin, W., & Wily, M., (eds.), *Diagnosis-Related Groups in Europe: Moving Towards Transparency, Efficiency, and Quality in Hospitals* (Vol. 1, pp. 59–74). Buckingham, Open University Press and WHO Regional Office for Europe.
25. Tu, J. C., & Huang, H. S., (2019). Relationship between green design and material flow cost accounting in the context of effective resource utilization. *Sustainability, 11*(7), 1974.
26. Wijewardena, H., & De Zoysa, A., (1999). A comparative analysis of management accounting practices in Australia and Japan: An empirical investigation. *The International Journal of Accounting, 34*(1), 49–70.
27. Yalcin, S., (2012). Adoption and benefits of management accounting practices: An inter-country comparison. *Accounting in Europe, 9*(1), 95–110.
28. Zhang, H., (2009). Effect of derivative accounting rules on corporate risk-management behavior. *Journal of Accounting and Economics, 47*(3), 244–264.

CHAPTER 7

FRAUD AND INTERNAL CONTROL IN ACCOUNTING

UNIT INTRODUCTION

Fraud and Internal Control in Accounting are two essential topics in accounting. Fraud is any intentional deception that results in financial gain for an individual or entity. Fraudulent activities may involve using false information, concealing relevant information, or manipulating accounts or other records. Internal control in accounting is establishing and maintaining a system of checks and balances to ensure the accuracy and integrity of financial information. It also ensures that assets are safeguarded, liabilities are correctly reported, and financial reporting is reliable and complies with laws, regulations, and organizational policies. Internal control in accounting is a crucial element of a company's financial management system and is essential to preventing and detecting fraud (Fernandhytia & Muslichah, 2020).

Figure 7.1. Illustration of the accounting fraud notice (Source: Amanda Cutshall, Creative Commons).

According to a 2014 Association of Certified Fraud Examiners survey, the average business will lose 5% of annual sales to fraud, with a median loss of $145,000. The study quantified this decline as a global amount of $3,7 trillion. Internal Controls are guidelines that businesses must implement to prevent such losses. (Kurniawan & Azmi, 2019). The chapter will conclude by examining banking operations as an instrument for business owners to regulate cash flow and a review of bank statements.

Learning Objectives

At the end of this chapter, readers will be able to learn:

- Concept of fraud and petty cash in accounting
- Concept of internal control
- Principles of internal control
- Role of internal control in accounting
- Technological impact on fraud and internal control

Key Terms

- Petty Cash
- Fraud
- Internal Control
- Entries
- Record Keeping
- Processing Error
- Assets
- Technological Impact

7.1. ACCOUNTING FRAUD

In a broad sense, according to the Association of Certified Fraud Examiners, fraud is "any violent act for profit that utilizes dishonesty as its primary modus operandi [mode of operating condition."

Therefore, any deliberate or intentional action intended to deny another of their assets or money through trickery, deceitfulness, or other adverse outcomes is considered fraud (Bao et al., 2021).

Cash is one of the most challenging resources for any institution to manage. An organization can manage its cash flow by mandating that all payouts be managed to make by verification. Even so, there are some circumstances where using a check is not feasible. Think about the Galaxy's Best Yogurt, for instance, running out of milk one night after work. Operating without milk is impossible, and the supplier's expected shipment will not arrive for 48 hours. This becomes sufficient to visit the supermarket throughout the road and buy three milk gallons to keep things running. Companies establish cash on hand, a predefined amount of money held on the side that can be used to pay cash for simple daily sales because it is not period or cost-effective to compose a check for this little transaction (Bao et al., 2020). A petty cash fund is a payable and receivable account, meaning it has a fixed sum of money in it that is removed as it is used to keep a certain balance.

ACTIVITY 7.1.

The retired mayor of Enid, Oklahoma, Ernst Currier, had a job as a loan officer and then as a senior vice president at Security National Bank. In his bank job, he allegedly opened 61 fraudulent loans. He used the identities of at least nine real people as well as eight fictitious people and stole about $6.2 million.1 He was sentenced to 13 years in prison on 33 felony counts.

Currier was able to circumvent one of the most important internal controls: segregation of duties. The American Institute of Certified Public Accountants (AICPA) states that segregation of duties "is based on shared responsibilities of a key process that disperses the critical functions of that process to more than one person or department. Without this separation in key processes, fraud and error risks are far less manageable."2 Currier used local residents' identities and created false documents to open loans for millions of dollars and then collect the funds himself, without any oversight by any other employee. Creating these loans allowed him to walk up to the bank vault and take cash out of the bank without anyone questioning him. There was no segregation of duties for opening loans, or if there was, he was able to easily override those internal controls.

How could internal controls have helped prevent Currier's bank fraud in Enid, Oklahoma?

A little cash reserve gets used up as it is refilled with receipts. The amount of cash in the box plus any receipts for purchases should always equal the balance in the petty cash box.

Galaxy's Best Yogurt, for instance, consistently maintains a petty cash box with a balance of $75. The balance is ascertained once the box has been examined as follows.

Cash in box	$50
Receipt showing purchase of stamps from Postal Service	15
Receipt from Quick Market for the purchase of milk and bananas	10
Total balance in petty cash box	75

A petty cash account enables staff to purchase little and essentials buying to assist the operation of a business if it is not feasible to follow the formal expense procedure (Caskey & Hanlon, 2013). This is because it might not be a supervisor with verification signing perks obtainable to join an inspection for unexpected costs. The cost of the purchase made with pocket money would always be regarded as not material. Remember that "materiality" refers to the degree to which the dollar figure in the inquiry would materially affect quarterly earnings or investor choices.

Remember

A truly unexpected expense is something that you can't predict, such as a natural disaster or a medical emergency.

7.2. DEMONSTRATION OF TYPICAL PETTY CASH

A sequence of journal entries is used to maintain petty cash accounts. Entries are required to

a) create the fund,

b) raise or reduce the fund's amount (reduce the fund as money is used),

c) account for cash extra fees and shortfalls.

Take the following scenario (Sarker, 2016). On July 1, The Galaxy's Best Yogurt creates a cash balance by writing a check for $75 out of its savings account and depositing money in the little money box. The personal money box currently contains $75, which can be utilized for minimal expenditures with the approval of the supervisor or manager. The following is the journal entry to generate the fund for petty cash (Nyangarika & Bundala, 2020).

JOURNAL			
Date	**Account**	**Debit**	**Credit**
July 1	Petty cash Cash *To record establishment of petty cash fund*	75	 75

The profile titled "Petty Cash" is formed as this small cash is established; this is an attribute on the financial statements of several smaller firms. The account balance, which also contains current accounts, is reduced in this scenario, and the funds are shifted to the petty check account. Within the same account, one investment increases while another asset decreases. Because the petty cash profile is an impressive record, the balance can never change. Therefore, it will stay at $75 on the income statement unless details of the proposed modification of the petty cash position (de Bont et al., 2019).

A few payments are drawn from Galaxy's Best Yogurt's petty cash account throughout the period. Consider the following scenarios.

Date	Transaction	Amount
Jul. 10	Postage stamps are purchased	$30
Jul. 15	Milk purchased	10
Jul. 25	Window cleaner purchased from Dollar Store	5

At the end of July, there ought to be a certificate for the postal stamp sale, a ticket for the milk, a refund for the cleaning lady, and any leftover cash in the little money box. The worker in the little money box must sign every invoice whenever a purchase is made. The total of the receipt purchases ($45) and the surviving cash inside the box must equal $75. The box should be refilled with items spent during the month as the receipts are reviewed (Shanmugam et al., 2012). The following is the record of refilling the personal money account.

JOURNAL			
Date	**Account**	**Debit**	**Credit**
Jul. 31	Postage Expense Inventory Miscellaneous Expense Cash *To record replenishment of petty cash fund*	30 10 5	 45

Petty cash transactions are typically repaid after a set period. Numerous smaller companies would perform this monthly to ensure

KEYWORD

A receipt is a document acknowledging that a person has received money or property in payment following a sale or other transfer of goods or provision of a service.

that costs are identified during the appropriate accounting period. If all of the funds in the account are spent well before the end of the specified timeframe, it may be refilled similarly whenever more money is required (Béné et al., 2009). If the petty cash account frequently needs to be resupplied well before the financial year's end, management might decide to boost the account's cash position. For instance, if managers at Galaxy's Best Yogurt choose to raise the petty cash position from $75 to $100 on August 1, the journal entry would look like it continues to follow.

JOURNAL			
Date	**Account**	**Debit**	**Credit**
Aug. 1	Petty Cash Cash *To increase balance of petty cash fund to $100*	25	25

If management decides to lower the balancing act in the petty cash account afterward, the prior entry will be overturned, with cash subtracted and petty cash credited (Jahnke & Weisser, 2019).

KEYWORD

A cash surplus is the cash that exceeds the cash required for day-to-day operations.

Errors may be made occasionally, affecting the balancing act of the petty cash account. This could be due to a worker not receiving a receipt or receiving an inaccurate transformation from the shop in which the buy was made. In this particular instance, expenditure is incurred, resulting in a cash surplus or scarcity.

Consider Galaxy's July expenditures. Expenses totaled $45 during the month. If the petty cash checking account is $75, the little cash box must comprise $45 in signature invoices and $30 in cash. After counting the box, assume there are $45 in revenues and $25 in money. In this scenario, the petty cash is $70 instead of $75. This results in a $5 shortfall that must be replenished from the bank account. The following is the entry that indicates a cash shortfall (Escobal, 2001).

JOURNAL			
Date	**Account**	**Debit**	**Credit**
Jul. 30	Cash Over and Short Cash *To replenish petty cash balance for cash shortage during period*	5	5

Whenever there is a cash deficit, it is reported as a "debit," which has a similar effect as a cost. If someone has a money overpayment, he or she reports it as a credit, which has a similar effect as if they were reporting income. If there is a cash overpayment, the petty cash will be debited, while the money over the short account is paid. The expense balance drops in this instance, while the year-end version is the total net of all overage charges and shortfalls throughout the year (Miller, 2012).

In certain firms, a petty cash system might be substituted by using an on-site preloaded credit or debit card (or debit card). Which are the advantages and disadvantages of keeping cash on hand for the petty cash system vs. a recharged debit card that workers can utilize for little money? If someone was a small company manager, what would they choose for a petty chequing account?

7.3. INTERNAL CONTROL SYSTEM

Internal controls are employed to assess risk and reduce the possibility of fraud within an organization. The accounting software, the management plan, and the processes referred to as checks and balances make up the internal control scheme (Altamuro & Beatty, 2010). The issue of internal control weaknesses in organizational processes and account books was addressed by the Committee of Sponsoring Organizations (COSO), a unique, private entity for which five helping to fund organizations regularly identify and address financial reporting purposes troubles or projects. Following that, they released a document known as COSO's Internal Control-Integrated Framework. The internal management triangle in Figure 7.2 contains the five elements they decided were essential to efficient internal control (Ge & McVay, 2005).

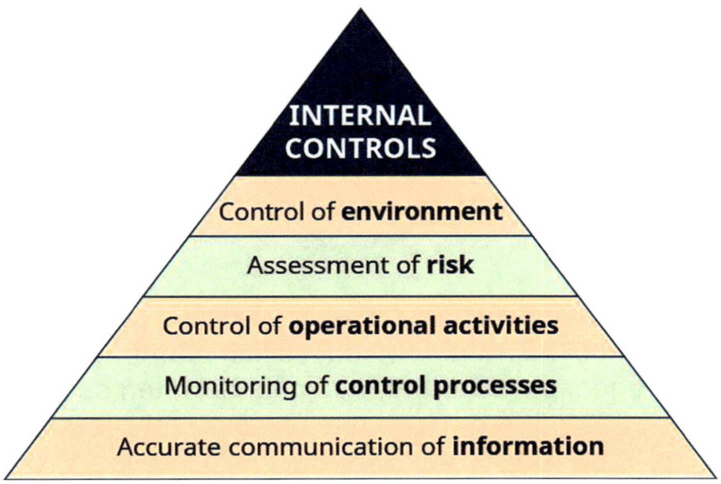

Figure 7.2. Schematic of the Internal Control (Source: Penn State, Creative Commons License).

The official procedures and guidelines that accomplish the following are part of the internal control scheme (Yasui, 2009).

- Necessary to cover assets are used appropriately.
- Verify the efficiency of the accounting information system.
- keep an eye on organization operations so that maximum effectiveness.
- Make sure that valuables are protected.
- Verify that staff members are adhering to corporate policies.

Financial statements accurately reflect a company's financial activities, while internal control safeguards profits and prevents legal violations. Accurate accounting records are used to create the accounting records that investors use to assess a company's operations, including all corporate and employee acts. Internal controls involve evaluating how events are documented in the financial records and comparing accounting information to the company's activities (Smeets et al., 2006).

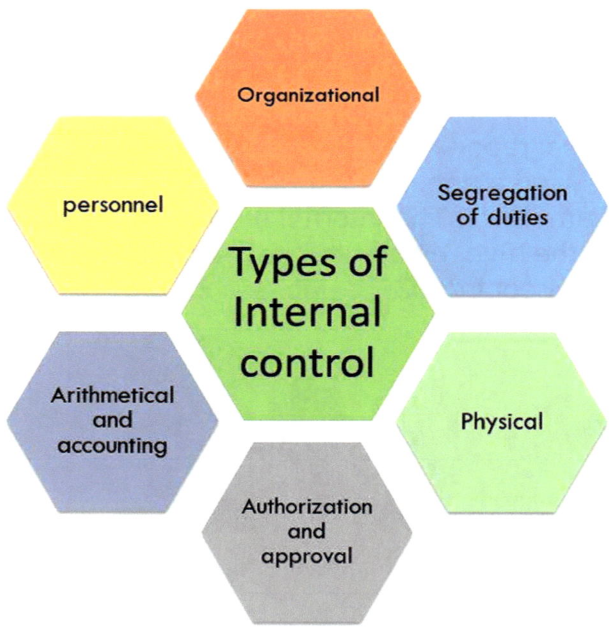

Figure 7.3. Schematic of the types of Internal Control (Source: Anjali J, Creative Commons License).

For instance, a movie theater receives most of its income from selling soda and popcorn at the concession stand. Even if popcorn and drinks are inexpensive, the food counter often sells expensive items (Mayr, 2001). The owners may use internal control measures to guarantee that staff is not wasting the company's revenue by selling Coke and popcorn.

7.4. ROLE OF INTERNAL CONTROLS

If a business is an income or not, cost accounting is its foundation. It is the management's responsibility to establish interaction between workers, supervisors, clients, vendors, and any other external and internal financial information users, as well as to connect the chart of accounts with other functions within the company (Ge & McVay, 2005). With complete knowledge of internal control systems, management can devise an internal management system that promotes a productive workplace where customers are best served.

For instance, a consumer walks into a store to buy a set of pants. The following core actions take place as the cashier joins the denim into the point-of-sale scheme (Altamuro & Beatty, 2010):

1. The company's journal records sales, raising profits on the financial statements. When a purchase is made with a bank card, the bank usually promptly deposits the money into the retailer's account.
2. The jeans are taken out of stock at the merchant where the transaction was made.
3. A fresh pair is purchased from the store's stock to repair the jeans purchased from the distribution warehouse.
4. To replenish its stock, the fulfillment center buys a fresh pair of pants from the manufacturer.
5. Marketing experts can track the volume and pattern of pants bought in a specific size over the years. The store inventory level could be changed if a change in overall sales to a certain extent is seen.
6. The business has proper access to the precise sales volumes of every product in every location, ensuring the best possible customer availability of products.

Remember

If a petty cash account is frequently low, it could be a signal that the account is not being properly controlled, and managers might wish to explore adding extra procedures to monitor and analyze petty cash.

As a result of the interconnectedness of numerous systems via technology, which influences the choices made by a large number of stakeholders both within and outside the organization, internal controls are required to protect the integrity of data and maintain its flow (Engelke et al., 1980). A system of internal controls supports consumers in better understanding a business and ensures that all resources are used properly and correctly.

Effectively conceived and executed internal control systems will decrease, but not eliminate, the risk of loss.

Organizations confront various risks; however, when internal control procedures are slack, fraud, asset theft, and employee or workplace misconduct are at risk. Accounting is responsible for understanding an organization's internal controls and aiding in their upkeep (Jensen, 1993).

Under SOX, managers, and auditors of publicly traded companies are required to establish and evaluate their internal control systems. Additional requirements include (Ahmad & Norhashim, 2008):

a) Directors on boards and managers must implement efficient internal controls.
b) Auditors must evaluate control activities.
c) Penalties for infractions are severe, involving imprisonment and hefty fines.
d) The Public Company Accounting Oversight Board is in charge of monitoring the work of auditors (PCAOB).

7.5. PRINCIPLES OF INTERNAL CONTROLS

Internal controls will vary from organization to organization based on the size and type of business being conducted. The following are essential ideas (Hammersley et al., 2012).

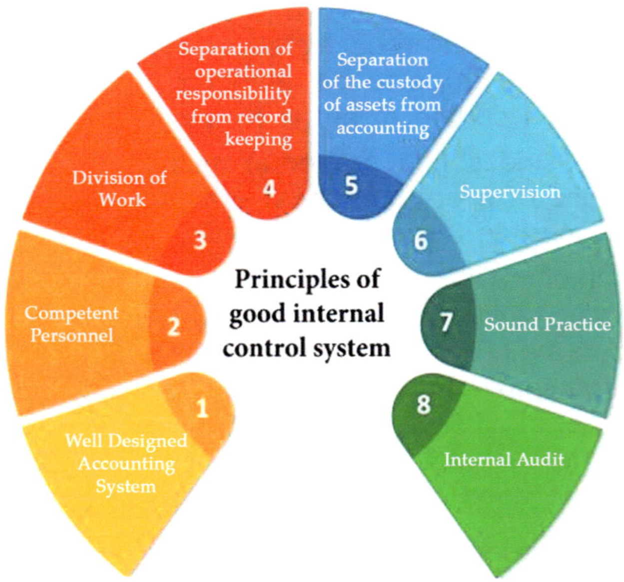

Figure 7.4. Illustration of internal control concepts (Source: Brain Kart, Creative Commons License).

7.5.1. Define Responsibilities

If a problem arises, it is easy to determine who is to blame since each duty is allocated to a specific person. For instance, it might be challenging to determine who was responsible for missing cash if two cashiers utilized the same amount.

7.5.2. Maintain Proper Records

Keeping correct, detailed records assists firms in monitoring their assets and preventing theft. A chart of accounts makes it simpler to ensure that transactions are recorded in the proper arrangements. For example, an up-to-date asset register (a list of all assets identified by asset number) makes it simpler to maintain and assemble asset-related information such as book values, purchase dates, and cumulative depreciation (Cheng et al., 2018).

Did you get it?

The Sarbanes-Oxley Act (SOX) of 2002 is a law created by the United States Congress in response to significant accounting scandals at large US firms, which caused billions of dollars in shareholder losses and a loss of confidence in accounting data.

7.5.3. Provide Surety Bonds for Key Personnel

All assets should be adequately insured. Bonding workers is equivalent to purchasing an insurance policy against losses caused by employee theft; bonding is especially advantageous if employees handle high-value assets. For example, a company owner who employs management to deposit cash needs requires a surety bond if the manager leaves with the cash.

7.5.4. Separate Asset Custody and Recordkeeping

A person with access to or control over an item is not authorized to examine the accounting records for that asset. For example, an employee who uses a work vehicle will not use it for personal reasons if the firm requires mileage reporting.

7.5.5. Separate Duties for Related Transactions

A procedure's responsibilities should be distributed among two or more individuals or departments so that one may serve as a check on the other. This is referred to as the separation of roles. If supplies are necessary, for instance, separate employees should make the order, collect the items, and pay the vendor (Khanna & Arora, 2009).

7.6. TECHNOLOGICAL IMPACT ON FRAUD AND INTERNAL CONTROL

While firms are increasingly using technology in their operations, data processing, and reporting tools, it is essential to consider the consequences of such technology on internal control and fraud (Klamm & Watson, 2009).

7.6.1. Reduced Processing Errors

Modern systems reduce but do not eliminate processing errors.

7.6.2. Comprehensive Testing of Records

More data samples may be examined when records are in electronic rather than manual form.

7.6.3. Limited Evidence of Processing

Modern systems may provide additional information (beyond the data itself), such as an electronic log of who made an entry, when it was made, where it originated, etc.

ACTIVITY 7.2.

By keeping in mind the concept of accounting fraud and internal control. Identify any accounting fraud in any small business and try to rectify the fraud using principles of internal control.

7.6.4. Separation of Duties

Those responsible for programs and files should not also handle payments and other financial operations.

7.6.5. Expanding E-commerce

As e-commerce grows, so do the additional technical risks that firms must be prepared to manage:

a) Computer infections
b) Identity theft
c) Credit card number theft

SUMMARY

- Accounting fraud is the blatant deception of financial statements to provide a misleading impression of a company's financial health. In addition, it entails an employee, an accountant, or the corporation deceiving shareholders and investors. A firm can fake its financial information by inflating its revenues, omitting its expenses, and misrepresenting its assets and liabilities.
- When setting your firm's risk security and management strategies, creating internal controls is essential. Implementing internal control measures can mitigate financial, strategic, and reputational risks. Controls are a type of audit to guarantee that your organization's operations are practical and efficient.
- Internal cash control mechanisms may incorporate your organization's management, all organizational policies, and the separation of roles. Other controls essential for financial security include demanding purchase approvals, signature authority, and reconciliation of all transactions and bank account activity.

REVIEW QUESTIONS

1. What is the concept of fraud and petty cash in accounting?
2. Define and explain the concept of internal control.
3. What are the principles of internal control in accounting?
4. Describe the role of internal control in accounting.
5. What are the impacts of technology on fraud and internal control?

MULTIPLE CHOICE QUESTIONS

1. Internal control is used in a business to enhance the accuracy and reliability of its accounting records and to:

a) safeguard its assets

b) prevent fraud

c) produce correct financial statements

d) deter employee dishonesty

2. The principles of internal control do not include the following:

a) establishment of responsibility

b) documentation procedures

c) management responsibilities

d) independent internal verification

3. **Permitting only designated personnel such as cashiers to handle cash receipts is an application of the principle of:**
   a) segregation of duties
   b) establishment of responsibility
   c) independent internal verification
   d) human resource controls
4. **Which of the following is an example of a fraudulent activity?**
   a) Conducting internal audits
   b) Implementing segregation of duties
   c) Manipulating financial statements
   d) Enforcing ethical policies
5. **Internal controls are designed to:**
   a) Prevent all types of fraud
   b) Detect all types of fraud
   c) Eliminate all risks in a company
   d) Provide reasonable assurance over achieving objectives

Answers to Multiple Choice Questions

1. (a) 2. c) 3. (b) 4. (c) 5. (d)

REFERENCES

1. Ahmad, Z., & Norhashim, M., (2008). An empirical analysis of the control environment, employee fraud, and counterproductive workplace behavior. *Communications of the IBIMA, 3*, 145–155.
2. Altamuro, J., & Beatty, A., (2010). How does internal control regulation affect financial reporting? *Journal of Accounting and Economics, 49*(1, 2), 58–74.
3. Bao, Y., Ke, B., Li, B., Yu, Y. J., & Zhang, J., (2020). Detecting accounting fraud in publicly traded US firms using a machine learning approach. *Journal of Accounting Research, 58*(1), 199–235.
4. Bao, Y., Ke, B., Li, B., Yu, Y. J., & Zhang, J., (2021). A response to" critique of an article on machine learning in the detection of accounting fraud." *Econ Journal Watch, 18*(1), 71–78.
5. Béné, C., Steel, E., Luadia, B. K., & Gordon, A., (2009). Fish as the "bank in the water"–evidence from chronic-poor communities in Congo. *Food Policy, 34*(1), 108–118.

6. Caskey, J., & Hanlon, M., (2013). Dividend policy at firms accused of accounting fraud. *Contemporary Accounting Research, 30*(2), 818–850.
7. Cheng, Q., Goh, B. W., & Kim, J. B., (2018). Internal control and operational efficiency. *Contemporary Accounting Research, 35*(2), 1102–1139.
8. De Bont, C., Komakech, H. C., & Veldwisch, G. J., (2019). Neither modern nor traditional: Farmer-led irrigation development in Kilimanjaro Region, Tanzania. *World Development, 116*, 15–27.
9. Engelke, D. R., Ng, S. Y., Shastry, B. S., & Roeder, R. G., (1980). Specific interaction of a purified transcription factor with an internal control region of 5S RNA genes. *Cell, 19*(3), 717–728.
10. Escobal, J., (2001). The determinants of nonfarm income diversification in rural Peru. *World Development, 29*(3), 497–508.
11. Fernandhytia, F., & Muslichah, M., (2020). The effect of internal control, individual morality, and ethical value on accounting fraud tendency. *Media Ekonomi Dan Manajemen, 35*(1), 112–127.
12. Ge, W., & McVay, S., (2005). The disclosure of material weaknesses in internal control after the Sarbanes-Oxley Act. *Accounting Horizons, 19*(3), 137–158.
13. Hammersley, J. S., Myers, L. A., & Zhou, J., (2012). The failure to remediate previously disclosed material weaknesses in internal controls. *Auditing: A Journal of Practice & Theory, 31*(2), 73–111.
14. Jahnke, B., & Weisser, R. A., (2019). How does petty corruption affect tax morale in Sub-Saharan Africa? *European Journal of Political Economy, 60*, 101751.
15. Jensen, M. C., (1993). The modern industrial revolution, exit, and the failure of internal control systems. *The Journal of Finance, 48*(3), 831–880.
16. Khanna, A., & Arora, B., (2009). A study to investigate the reasons for bank fraud and the implementation of preventive security controls in the Indian banking industry. *International Journal of Business Science & Applied Management (IJBSAM), 4*(3), 1–21.
17. Klamm, B. K., & Watson, M. W., (2009). SOX 404 reported internal control weaknesses: A test of COSO framework components and information technology. *Journal of Information Systems, 23*(2), 1–23.
18. Kurniawan, P. C., & Azmi, F., (2019). The effect of management morality on accounting fraud with internal control as a moderating variable (study in pemalang regency). *Riset Akuntansi dan Keuangan Indonesia, 4*(2), 177–185.
19. Mayr, U., (2001). Age differences in the selection of mental sets: The role of inhibition, stimulus ambiguity, and response-set overlap. *Psychology and Aging, 16*(1), 96.
20. Miller, L. J., (2012). Visitor reaction to pacing behavior: Influence on the perception of animal care and interest in supporting zoological institutions. *Zoo Biology, 31*(2), 242–248.

21. Nyangarika, A., & Bundala, F. S., (2020). Socio-economic factors affecting deposits growth in Sacco's development case of Geita Tanzania. *International Journal of Advance Research and Innovative Ideas in Education, 6*(2), 1273–1288.
22. Sarker, R., (2016). Migration and employment: A study of Bangladeshi male migrant workers in Malaysia. In: *International Migration in Southeast Asia* (Vol. 1, pp. 125–148).
23. Setiawan, S., (2018). The effect of internal control and individual morality on the tendency of accounting fraud. *Asia Pacific Fraud Journal, 3*(1), 33–41.
24. Shanmugam, J. K., Haat, M. H. C., & Ali, A., (2012). The impact of internal control on the performance of small and medium enterprise: Malaysian evidence. *Small, 100*, 18–2.
25. Smeets, R. J., Vlaeyen, J. W., Kester, A. D., & Knottnerus, J. A., (2006). Reducing pain catastrophizing mediates the outcome of both physical and cognitive-behavioral treatment in chronic low back pain. *The Journal of Pain, 7*(4), 261–271.
26. Yasui, T., (2009). 7.3. 3 claim-payment failures of Japan's insurance companies and designing better payment architecture: Finding a standard solution to socio-critical systems by applying the system engineering vee model approach (first report). In: *INCOSE International Symposium*, (Vol. 19, No. 1, pp. 1167–1177).

CHAPTER 8

PROSPECTS OF ACCOUNTING

UNIT INTRODUCTION

The goal of accounting is to provide users with financial information. For users to be capable of making the right decisions, they must trust the data in those accounting records (Tyuleneva, 2017).

There are frequently many different approaches to valuing items decided to enter into the bookkeeping system, as well as various approaches for figuring what portion of an object should appear on the financial statements and what percentage of the financial position statement. a few of these methods are entirely subjective, depend on opinion and judgment.

Figure 8.1. Diagram representing the goal of accounting (Source: IEduNote, Creative Commons License).

Accountants require direction in the process of creating financial statements. This chapter examines a few of the strategies used by accountants to decide on the accounting and evaluation practices for various items. The function of auditors, who verify that financial regulations have been observed, is also covered in this chapter (Bampton & Cowton, 2002).

Learning Objectives

At the end of this chapter, readers will be able to learn:

- Conventions used in accounting
- Accounting policies and estimation techniques
- Regulations in accounting
- International accounting standards
- The IASB network
- The role of the auditor in an accounting
- The part of management in accounting

Key Terms

- Conventions
- Estimation Techniques
- Regulations
- International Standards
- IASB Network
- Auditor
- Management

8.1. ACCOUNTING CONVENTIONS

A list of accepted accounting standards does not exist. The relative weight that different authors give per each conceivable convention that may be determined varies. However, there is broad agreement that the norms covered below are particularly significant (Ball et al., 1991).

Conventions are also called "concepts," "rules," "practices," "assumptions," etc. One should focus on comprehending the terms' meanings rather than worrying about how they should be defined. They are listed. However, they are not given in priority order. However studies, you'll discover that some conventions are valued more highly than others, but for now, focus on understanding what each one implies.

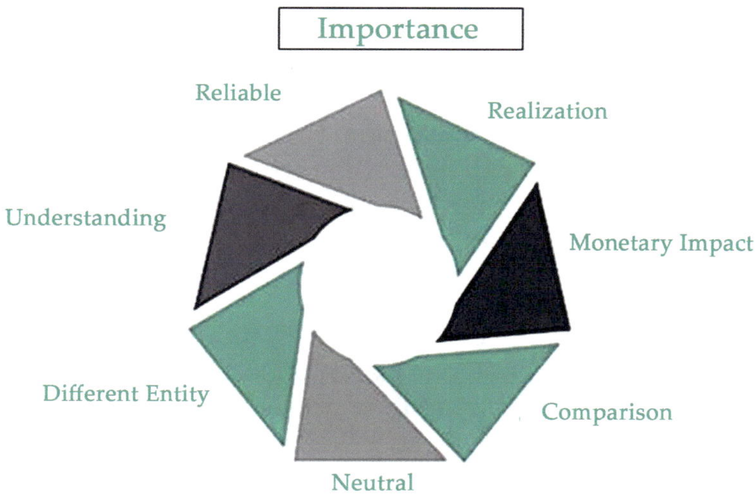

Figure 8.2. Illustrating accounting conventions (Source: Ashish Kumar Srivastav, Creative Commons License).

The conventions may also be connected to the qualitative traits outlined in this chapter. Nevertheless, they are currently being offered as different individual conventions (Semieniuk & Weber, 2020).

The conventions listed below are all essential terminology.

8.1.1. The Standard for Commercial Entities

This practice only records activities in the accounts that impact the company, separating the person or persons running a business from the firm itself. There are two approaches to interpreting this convention (Robb, 1987):

1. When a business is a sole proprietorship or partner, the corporation is seen as a means by which the owner(s) participate in profitable economic activity.
2. When a firm is involved, the entity is seen as having a distinct personality and its own goals, with the shareholders serving as merely other parties with interests even against an entity.

8.1.2. The Convention for Measuring Things in Money

This only allows accounting events that may be stated in monetary terms to be recognized. Because of this norm, several other economic issues discussed under socially responsible accounting are not recorded. For instance, significant people within the organization are not given any value. Financial measurements are utilized so that the cost of each element included in an accounting sheet can be viewed, and their total cost can be calculated. As a result, financial statements have a consistent meaning that facilitates understanding and acts as a basis for economic research (Murphy, 1976).

Did you get it?

Keeping up with technology and regulatory changes are significant concerns of 51% and 24%, respectively, of CPA and accounting firm survey participants, according to Accounting Today's survey.

The historical cost section stipulates that an asset's financial information is the original purchase price. The cost accounting is objective, which is a benefit of this convention. Non-current items are reported at actual cost, less cumulative depreciation. The accounting information might be less trustworthy for users if another value—for instance, the price at which the asset might be sold—was utilized.

The convention of objectivity states that the individual producing financial information should not have any personal biases (Copeland, 1949). As a result, the data utilized in financial statements needs to be impartial. This should imply that every two accountants would arrive at a similar effect, such as the profit amount. Whenever producing financial accounts, judgment is always necessary. Still, the accountant ought to be objective and stop getting to make a larger or smaller profit, for example, to further their objectives. Trustworthy financial statements ought to be accurate.

The dual aspect principle, which forms the cornerstone of double-entry bookkeeping, stipulates that each transaction impacts the entity's status and representation in the ledger accounts at the moment of the action (Kaplan & Roll, 1972).

8.2. ACCOUNTING POLICIES AND ESTIMATION TECHNIQUES

It follows certain principles, conventions, norms, and norms whenever a corporation calculates the financial assets, expenses, and revenues shown in the economic situation statement and operating income—this revenue recognition. The management ought to implement the procedures that it thinks will benefit some who depend on the income statement much more. Some of these users might be stockholders and lenders. By considering the traits of relevant information, the management can determine which policies are most beneficial. Examples of these are dependability and usefulness (Hagerman & Zmijewski, 1979).

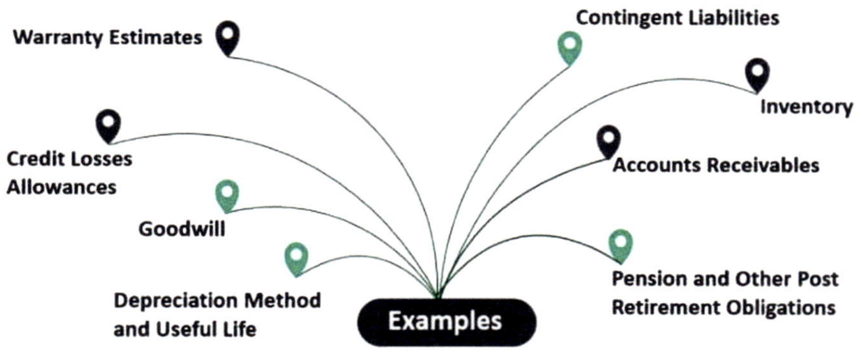

Figure 8.3. Illustrate the accounting estimates (Source: Sayantan Mukhopadhyay, Creative Commons License).

The application of accounting policies necessitates the estimation of some elements. Not all numbers can be deemed "correct," and the production of financial accounts depends on judgment. Accountants have devised many methods to get at numbers that must be guessed. As an illustration, it can be seen that businesses figure out tolerance for debts, but this is a guess as to what receivables won't pay. This limit might well be determined as a percentage of the total amount still owing or as an allocation for specific clients. In either case, those are two methods for estimating bad debts. Another illustration is depreciation, wherein two methods are utilized to calculate how much a non-current asset will be consumed over a given time: the straight-line approach and the reducing-balance approach (Joyce et al., 1982).

8.3. REGULATIONS IN ACCOUNTING

Except for assuring the tax office of the money gained during every accounting cycle, there are few regulations governing the creation of accounting records for single proprietors and corporations. Furthermore, many forms of law and guidelines aid the accountant in generating similar financial information for limited corporations, charities, and other organizations (Holthausen, 2009). Most of the ideas they cover can and must be fairly applied to other organizations.

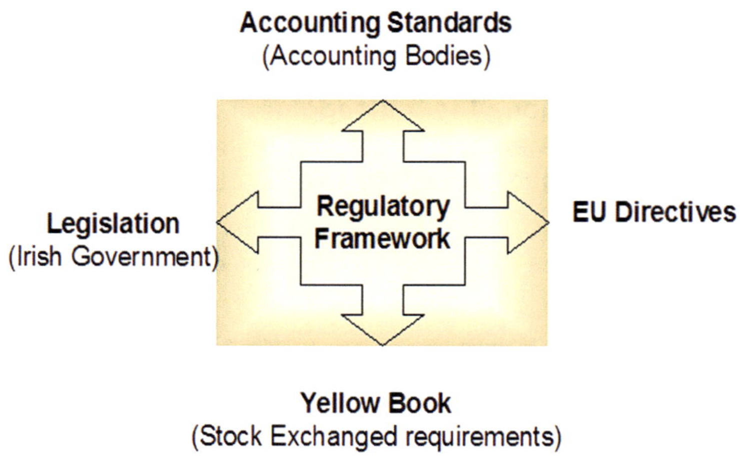

Figure 8.4. Schematic of the regulations in Accounting (Source: Black Hall Publishing, Creative Commons License).

8.3.1. Company Law

"Company law" refers to the laws that apply to businesses in most nations. The level of specificity in company law would differ by country, but generally, they handle broad issues instead of specific accounting details. Company law frequently specifies which businesses must have a certified auditor review their income reports.

8.3.2. The Profession of Accounting

Each nation has its professional accounting qualification. For instance, they are called Certified Public Accountants in the USA (CPA). When a country lacks its accounting profession certification, trainee accountants must accept the level of education of another nation (Moyer, 1990). This also applies to pupils who think a foreign country's accountant degree is more renowned than their local degree. As a result, many professional accounting organizations that were only domestic in the past now offer international credentials. In the UK, two instances are:

1. Chartered Institute of Management Accountants (CIMA),
2. Chartered Certified Accountants Association (ACCA).

Such organizations demand that their members meet particular qualifications, including passing exams, gaining the necessary practical experience for helping to ensure their skills and abilities, and upholding ethical norms (Pandey et al., 2022).

8.4. INTERNATIONAL ACCOUNTING STANDARDS

According to the Fundamentals of Financial Accounting syllabus, it is unnecessary to be familiar with any particular accounting treatment found in the international financial reporting standards (IFRSs). Thus, such IFRSs have not been mentioned in this learning system, even though this content is predicated on IFRSs. Three primary effects of IFRSs on the range are as follows (Barth et al., 2008):

Remember

Accounting can be divided into several fields including financial accounting, management accounting, tax accounting and cost accounting.

8.4.1. Vocabulary

This article uses IFRS-specific terminology, definitions, and so on.

8.4.2. Presentation

The balance sheet is shown following IFRS forms, particularly for the company's balance sheet and the cash flow statement. According to the syllabus, such financial statements must be prepared using the IAS 1 Presentation of Financial Statements (Revised) forms and the IAS 7 Statement of Cash Flows.

8.4.3. Professional

For instance, in the explanation above, the technical criteria of the IFRS were adhered to when accounting for the property.

The way these IFRSs are created is briefly described here. They are pretty significant.

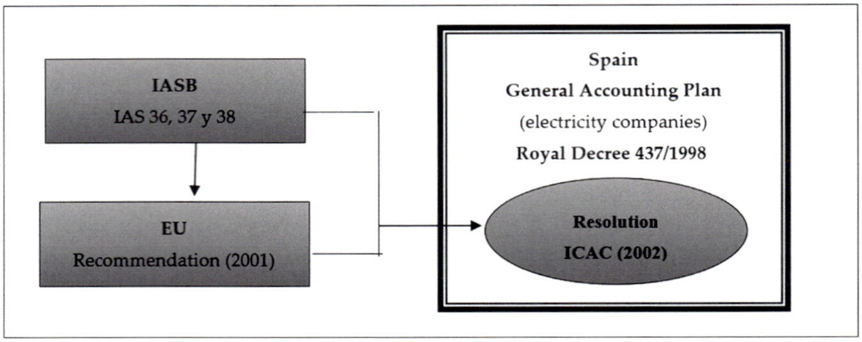

Figure 8.5. Schematic of the Legislation, Regulations, and Reflections on Environmental Accounting (Source: Maripaz Muñoz Prieto, Creative Commons License).

Four different but connected authorities govern the setting of (IFRS)s. They are set up in the following diagram (Schipper, 2005).

8.5. THE INTERNATIONAL ACCOUNTING STANDARDS BOARD (IASB) FRAMEWORK

Like chemistry and physics, accounting is a social science rather than a natural one. Unlike physics and chemistry, which follow natural principles, accounting must create its own “rules” or the conventions mentioned above. The financial statements and the IFRSs that the IASB produces must be compatible with one another and with the norms.

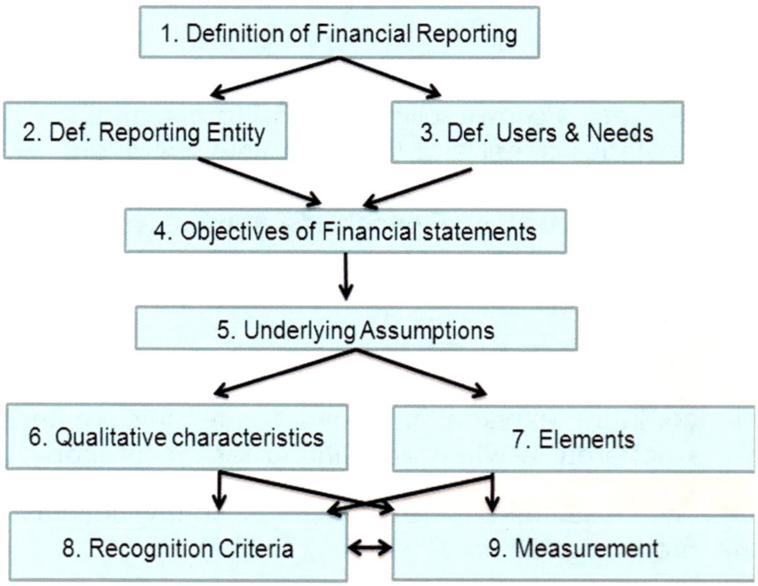

Figure 8.6. Illustration of the IASB Framework (Source: Audra Knight, Creative Commons License).

The IASC created a document that offers a structure into which all norms are defined to ensure this happens. All accounting principles are supported by this document, which also serves as the foundation for the development of all upcoming standards. This document is known as the "Framework." Below is a summary of the Framework's principles, which engage with the fundamental problems in financial statements (Ashbaugh & Pincus, 2001).

1. The goal of financial reports is to give users crucial data, like financial statements and an analysis of income status.
2. The norms mentioned above, such as accruals, continuing concern, materiality, prudence, and identification, are examples of presumptions and are accurate.
3. The five main parts of financial statements and financial position reports are the following: income and expenditure, investments, equity, and obligations.
4. The idea of capital maintenance utilizing various asset valuation techniques, such as worth in usage and cost of repairs, and the assessment of income and capital management using multiple methods of profit measurement, such as CPP and CCA.

TIPS

Company management can select accounting policies that are advantageous to their own financial reporting, such as selecting a particular inventory valuation method.

8.6. THE ROLE OF THE AUDITOR

Financial statements are generated to teach a range of various user groups. The assertions must be trustworthy and reasonably accurate to be beneficial (Whittington, 2008). Thus, financial activities should be created to guarantee enough precision. Financial statements are referred to as presenting a fair portrayal or being accurate and equitable in financial reporting. The auditor's job is to ensure that the accounting records are prepared correctly and conform to accounting rules and corporate law.

Nevertheless, the manager's obligation, not the auditor's, is to create income statements (the directors in a limited company) (Beck, 1973). In other instances, the auditors are hired to develop the financial statements in addition to their core responsibilities, though management remains in charge of these tasks. Some organizations must legally employ an independent, licensed accountant to review their banking statements. Others want to voluntarily have their financial accounts audited since they may benefit from having an independent audit.

Fair representation, also known as "true and fair," refers to the idea that financial statements made for outside publishing should accurately reflect the organization's financial situation. They must be freed of severe mistakes brought on by carelessness or exploitation (Flint, 1971). The fair presentation assumes that the accounting information does not include some material inaccuracies that could substantially impact the decisions of individuals reading them. However, it may be financially viable to verify every activity or to guarantee 100% accuracy. This is dependent on the norm of physicality that is covered below. The certified auditor's responsibility is to check the financial accounts of severe misstatements and to produce a report on their fair presentation.

8.6.1. The Auditor and the Responsiveness Conference

Remember

A balance sheet or statement of financial position, reports on a company's assets, liabilities, and owners equity at a given point in time.

The goal of an audit is to allow the auditor to decide if the accounting information correctly represents the company and to reflect on that determination (Franco, 1999).

To accomplish this, the auditor will run several tests using the accounting records and additional data from board meeting notes and conversations with the members. The auditor won't be able to review anything if they do this thoroughly. Instead, the implications of any potential inaccuracies will be considered; if they do not significantly or materially impair the general faithful representation of the reports, they are unnecessary (Khan, 1985). Without the materiality principle, accounting information will always need to be 100% correct, which would be exceedingly expensive and impossible. Additionally, the additional correctness would only provide a small additional value to the reported financial' consumers.

The auditor may decide to conduct one of two primary kinds of tests. The first is called acceptance tests, which entail evaluating the dependability of accounting systems, practices, and procedures (Taylor, 1996). The auditors can rely on these to a certain extent if they seem to perform correctly, implying they are not required to test such areas thoroughly. The auditors can decide to conduct substantive procedures, which is a more thorough audit if there are any areas of uncertainty, high risk, or significant items.

The objective of the independent audit is to arrive at an opinion regarding the company's financial accounts. This is the job of the audit firm (Hoque & Thiagarajah, 2015). The independent auditors' job will change depending on the organization's size and the fact that the organization does not have a separate internal auditing division. The research could be analyzed using two different classification systems:

1. Verify the dependability of the methods and systems that are being utilized (compliance testing);
2. Testing particular transactions guarantee they have appropriately paid for (substantive testing).

A judgment will be made that will be represented in audit findings, on the foundation of the information above, in addition to their conclusions and testing conducted by the audit function (where necessary) (Rahayu, 2002).

The entries in the accounting records are not scrutinized in depth by the auditors. They create their annual audit with the primary goal of determining whether or not the organization has adequate control processes and systems in place to make an independent verification of its financial status. They may undertake further, more extensive tests in certain areas, like tracking individual transactions thru the system, based on how they evaluate the procedures and practices that are currently in place. In addition to that, they will carry out checks on the controllers, like consolidations, the separation of duties, authorization procedures, and paperwork, as well as investigate whether or not non-current assets are there. They also focus on ensuring that items are appropriately evaluated in line with established financial accounting, which was the issue in this chapter (Hartle, 1975). Following the completion of the audit, a report will be compiled that will summarize the auditors' findings.

KEYWORD

An audit is the examination of the financial report of an organisation - as presented in the annual report - by someone independent of that organisation.

8.6.2. Fraud and the Auditor

It is neither the auditor's responsibility to identify fraudulent activity. Auditors should design their audit procedures so that it is probable that fraud cases will be called to their attention. However, auditors should not place any greater significance on detecting fraud than they might put on finding mistakes and omissions.

8.6.3. The Function of Internal Auditing

A significant proportion of the more substantial businesses run their internal review departments. The tasks associated with internal auditing can be classified into two parts (Scanlan, 1998):

1. Providing advice on various accounting methods;
2. Conduct audits on the financial records and the reports provided by the internal operations.

The auditing of an organization does not need to be limited solely to complying with regulatory obligations to be considered a value-for-money audit. Audits can be conducted on various other topics, including management effectiveness, the planning and execution of computerized systems, and various other topics. One variety of audits is known as a value-for-money audit. Its purpose is to investigate an organization's expenditures to determine whether or not they provide the greatest possible return on investment. The term "expense" can refer to money spent on non-current resources, current assets, or costs (Johnston et al., 1980).

Audits of this kind might be conducted either by internal audit function or by auditors from the outside.

KEYWORD

Consolidation refers to the aggregation of financial statements of a group company as consolidated financial statements.

8.7. THE ROLE OF MANAGEMENT

When a person engages in the company as a sole proprietor, it is entirely up to the sole owner to operate the business in whichever way they see fit. If they don't do a great job of it, they will only have themselves to blame, and they will only have themselves to account for. If they don't do excellent work of it, they will pay the consequences.

Even so, in a body corporate (as well as in other kinds of organizations, like charity organizations, clubs, and communities), the people in charge of planning are not inevitably the similar people who contribute to the organization's capital, and they are not the primary recipients of the organization's ongoing success (Papadakis et al., 1998). In a limited corporation, the owners are the ones who give the capital, and the investors expect that the capital will be used appropriately and intelligently, either to create a profit or to make it possible for them to purchase additional shares in the future. Beneficiaries are individuals of a foundation, club, or organization who receive the advantages of being a part of the organization, whether in the form of membership privileges or other benefits.

On the other hand, shareholders, employees, and beneficiaries frequently do not participate in the organization's management; instead, they designate (or elect) someone else to handle these responsibilities on their behalf (Simons, 2019). In a corporation, these individuals serve as directors; in a charitable organization, club, or club, they serve as trustees or committee members.

It is the duty of management, regardless of who occupies those positions, to see to it that the organization's resources are protected in any circumstances. This may include making specific considerations, such as (Van Helden, 2005):

a) All assets have been correctly recorded, can be located, are maintained in good condition, and have adequate insurance coverage;
b) There are protocols in place to avoid the wrongful usage of assets or their misappropriation;
c) Ensuring that the accounting is both functional and effective
d) No expense is spent, nor is any obligation accepted, unless appropriate procedures for their authorization and control have been followed;
e) The financials have been produced in a manner that complies with the applicable laws and accounting rules currently in effect.

ACTIVITY 8.1.

Organizations and businesses make their own policies accounting to gain maximum output from the given resources. Keeping in mind the international standards, accounting policies and roles of auditor and management, devise an accounting framework for starting a small business.

SUMMARY

In this chapter, we examined the following:

1. The primary accounting principles that underlie the creation of accounting records;
2. The limits of the historical price convention and some solutions for addressing them.
3. The regulatory regime comprises the corporate governance system and accounting rules, a description of the objective of external and internal audits, company's guardianship duty.

REVIEW QUESTIONS

1. Describe some conventions used in accounting.
2. Explain accounting policies and estimation techniques.
3. What are the regulations in accounting?
4. Describe some International Accounting Standards.
5. What is the IASB network? Explain its application in accounting.
6. Explain the role of the auditor in accounting.
7. Explain the role of management in accounting.

MULTIPLE CHOICE QUESTIONS

1. The global critical professional accounting body is __________.

a) The International Accounting Standards Committee
b) The Institute of Chartered Accountants of India
c) The International Accounting Standards Board
d) The Financial Accounting Standards Board

2. Which of the following is not a tax haven?

a) Bermuda Islands
b) Mauritius
c) Cayman Islands
d) England

3. The International Accounting Standards Committee was set up in __________.

a) 1982
b) 1967
c) 1976
d) 2009

4. The accounting process in which the financial statements of a parent company and its subsidiaries are added together to yield a unified set of financial statements is called __________.

a) consolidation

b) amortization

c) translation

d) amalgamation

5. What is the role of technology in the future of accounting?

a) Technology will replace the need for accountants.

b) Technology will automate routine tasks, allowing accountants to focus on higher-level analysis.

c) Technology will decrease the demand for accounting professionals.

d) Technology will have no impact on the accounting field.

Answers to Multiple Choice Questions

1. (c) 2. (d) 3. (c) 4. (a) 5. (b)

REFERENCES

1. Ashbaugh, H., & Pincus, M., (2001). Domestic accounting standards, international accounting standards, and the predictability of earnings. *Journal of Accounting Research, 39*(3), 417–434.
2. Ball, R., Thomas, R. E., & McGrath, J., (1991). Influence of R&D accounting conventions on internal decision-making of companies. *R&D Management, 21*(4), 261–270.
3. Bampton, R., & Cowton, C. J., (2002). The teaching of ethics in management accounting: Progress and prospects. *Business Ethics: A European Review, 11*(1), 52–61.
4. Barker, R., Lennard, A., Nobes, C., Trombetta, M., & Walton, P., (2014). Response of the EAA financial reporting standards committee to the IASB discussion paper A review of the conceptual framework for financial reporting. *Accounting in Europe, 11*(2), 149–184.
5. Barth, M. E., Landsman, W. R., & Lang, M. H., (2008). International accounting standards and accounting quality. *Journal of Accounting Research, 46*(3), 467–498.
6. Beck, G. W., (1973). The role of the auditor in modern society: An empirical appraisal. *Accounting and Business Research, 3*(10), 117–122.
7. Cenar, I., (2012). Accounting policies and estimates in municipalities between norms and reality. Annals of the university of Petroşani. *Economics, 12,* 49–60.

8. Copeland, M. A., (1949). Suitable accounting conventions to determine business income. *Journal of Accountancy (pre-1986), 87*(000002), 107.
9. Flint, D., (1971). The role of the auditor in modern society: An exploratory essay. *Accounting and Business Research, 1*(4), 287–293.
10. Florin-Constantin, D., (2012). Controversy and convergences in defining the concepts of accounting policies and options. *Ovidius University Annals Economic Sciences Series, 1*, 1059.
11. Franco, J. R., (1999). The role of the auditor in the prevention and detection of business fraud: SAS No. 82. *Western Criminology Review, 2*(1), 3–10.
12. Hagerman, R. L., & Zmijewski, M. E., (1979). Some economic determinants of accounting policy choice. *Journal of Accounting and Economics, 1*(2), 141–161.
13. Hartle, D. G., (1975). The role of the auditor general of Canada. *Can. Tax J., 23*, 193.
14. Holthausen, R. W., (2009). Accounting standards, financial reporting outcomes, and enforcement. *Journal of Accounting Research, 47*(2), 447–458.
15. Hoque, Z., & Thiagarajah, T., (2015). Public accountability: The role of the auditor-general in legislative oversight. *Making Governments Accountable, 4*, 3–23.
16. Johnston, D. J., Lemon, W. M., Neumann, F. L., Warren, Gorham and Lamont, Inc, & United States of America, (1980). The Canadian study of the role of the auditor. *Journal of Accounting, Auditing & Finance, 1*, 251–263.
17. Joyce, E. J., Libby, R., & Sunder, S., (1982). Using the FASB's qualitative characteristics in accounting policy choices. *Journal of Accounting Research*, 654–675.
18. Kabir, H., & Rahman, A., (2018). How does the IASB Use the conceptual framework in developing IFRSs? An examination of the development of IFRS 16 leases. *Journal of Financial Reporting, 3*(1), 93–116.
19. Kaplan, R. S., & Roll, R., (1972). Investor evaluation of accounting information: Some empirical evidence. *The Journal of Business, 45*(2), 225–257.
20. Khan, M. A., (1985). Role of the auditor in an Islamic economy. *Journal of King Abdulaziz University: Islamic Economics, 3*(1), 5–15.
21. McGregor, W., & Street, D. L., (2007). IASB and FASB face challenges in pursuit of a joint conceptual framework. *Journal of International Financial Management & Accounting, 18*(1), 39–51.
22. Moyer, S. E., (1990). Capital adequacy ratio regulations and accounting choices in commercial banks. *Journal of Accounting and Economics, 13*(2), 123–154.
23. Murphy, G. J., (1976). A numerical representation of some accounting conventions. *The Accounting Review, 51*(2), 277–286.
24. Pandey, A., Tripathi, A., & Guhathakurta, K., (2022). The impact of banking regulations and accounting standards on estimating discretionary loan loss provisions. *Finance Research Letters, 44*, 102068.

25. Papadakis, V. M., Lioukas, S., & Chambers, D., (1998). Strategic decision-making processes: The role of management and context. *Strategic Management Journal, 19*(2), 115–147.
26. Peasnell, K., Dean, G., & Gebhardt, G., (2009). Reflections on the revision of the IASB framework by EAA academics. *Abacus, 45*(4), 518–527.
27. Rahayu, D. S., (2002). Anteseden dan konsekuensi tekanan peran (role stress) pada auditor independen. *The Indonesian Journal of Accounting Research, 5*(2). 5–45.
28. Robb, F. F., (1987). Accounting conventions. A cause of economic instability and company failure? *European Management Journal, 5*(2), 94–100.
29. Scanlan, L., (1998). The role of the auditor-general in the accountability framework and recent developments in Queensland. *Accountability and Performance, 4*(1), 53–73.
30. Schipper, K., (2005). The introduction of international accounting standards in Europe: Implications for international convergence. *European Accounting Review, 14*(1), 101–126.
31. Semieniuk, G., & Weber, I. M., (2020). Inequality in energy consumption: Statistical equilibrium or a question of accounting conventions? *The European Physical Journal Special Topics, 229*(9), 1705–1714.
32. Simons, R., (2019). The role of management control systems in creating competitive advantage: New perspectives. In: *Management Control Theory* (Vol. 2, pp. 173–194).
33. Whittington, G., (2008). Harmonization or discord? The critical role of the IASB conceptual framework review. *Journal of Accounting and Public Policy, 27*(6), 495–502.

INDEX

N

O

P

R

S

T

V

W